GRASS

its production and
utilization

GRASS

its production and
utilization

Edited by W. Holmes

PUBLISHED FOR

THE BRITISH GRASSLAND SOCIETY BY
BLACKWELL SCIENTIFIC PUBLICATIONS

OXFORD LONDON EDINBURGH

BOSTON MELBOURNE

© 1980 by
Blackwell Scientific Publications
Editorial offices:
Osney Mead, Oxford, OX2 OEL
8 John Street, London, WC1N 2ES
9 Forrest Road, Edinburgh, EH1 2QH
52 Beacon Street, Boston,
    Massachusetts 02108, USA
99 Barry Street, Carlton
    Victoria 3053, Australia

First published 1980
Reprinted 1982

Set by Santype Ltd, Salisbury
and printed and bound in
Great Britain by
Billing & Sons Ltd, Worcester

DISTRIBUTORS

USA
  Blackwell Mosby Book Distributors
  11830 Westline Industrial Drive
  St Louis, Missouri 63141

Canada
  Blackwell Mosby Book Distributors
  120 Melford Drive, Scarborough
  Ontario, M1B 2X4

Australia
  Blackwell Scientific Book
  Distributors
  214 Berkeley Street, Carlton
  Victoria 3053

British Library
Cataloguing in Publication Data

Grass
  1. Grasses—Great Britain
  I. Holmes, W   II. British Grassland
  633'.2'00941   Society   SB202.G7

ISBN 0-632-00618-8

Contents

List of Contributors

JOHN CRAVEN BSc, PhD (Newcastle upon Tyne)
Head of Farm Management Services, Milk Marketing Board from 1979; Previously Consulting Officer and then Head of Consultancy Services with Milk Marketing Board (1963–1979).

WILLIAM HOLMES BSc, PhD (Glasgow), DSc (London), FI Biol, NDA (Hons), NDD.
Professor of Agriculture and Head of Department of Agriculture, Wye College, University of London from 1955; member of staff and then in charge of the Grass and Dairy Husbandry Department, the Hannah Dairy Research Institute, Ayr, Scotland (1944–1955); President British Grassland Society, 1969–1970; President British Society of Animal Production, 1970; first recipient of the British Grassland Society Award, 1979.

JAMES BRIAN KILKENNY BSc (Leeds), Dip Stat
Head of Livestock Records and Consultancy Unit, Meat and Livestock Commission from 1968; previously statistician with the Beef Recording Association from 1966.

JOHN C. MURDOCH BSc (Glasgow), PhD (Edinburgh)
Professor of Crop and Animal Production, Queen's University, Belfast and Director of the Agriculture Research Institute for Northern Ireland, Hillsborough, Co. Down from 1966; previously in Department of Dairy Husbandry, National Institute for Research in Dairying, Shinfield, Reading from 1951 to 1965; President British Grassland Society, 1978–1979.

JOHN NIX BSc (Econ), MA (Cantab), FBIM.
National Westminster Professor of Farm Business Management at Wye College from 1982. Previously, Reader in Farm Management and Head, Farm Business Unit, School of Rural Economics, Wye College, University of London, from 1975; Agricultural Economist and Senior Agricultural Economist/Senior Research Officer in Farm Economics Branch, School of Agriculture, University of Cambridge, 1951–1961; Farm Management Liaison Officer and Lecturer/Senior Lecturer in Farm Management, Wye College, University of London from 1961; Chairman, Centre for Farm Management (B.I.M.) 1979–1981.

DENNIS F. OSBOURN BSc (Hons), Dip Agric (Cantab) Dip Trop. Agric. (Trinidad), Ph.D. (Reading), F.I. Biol.

Head of the Division of Animal Nutrition and Production and Assistant Director of the Grassland Research Institute from 1978. Previously Agricultural Officer, Her Majesty's Overseas Civil Service (Tanganyika) 1959–1961. Lecturer in Animal Production, University of West Indies, 1961–1964. Member of staff and head of various departments, Grassland Research Institute from 1964.

T. E. WILLIAMS BSc (Hons) Wales (Retired 1976)

Research assistant Welsh Plant Breeding Station 1938–1940. Agronomist, Ministry of Agriculture and Fisheries, Drayton, Stratford-on-Avon (Grassland Improvement Station) 1940–1949. Agronomist and Head of Agronomy Department, Grassland Research Institute, 1949–1976. Deputy Director 1955–1968.

Foreword

by A. S. CHRISTENSEN
President of the
British Grassland Society
1980–1981

In 1979 the Council of the British Grassland Society considered that the time had come for a textbook covering recent developments in grassland science and husbandry to be prepared. It commissioned Professor Holmes to edit the book and he wisely called on several outstanding grassland specialists to contribute.

Never has the need been greater for grassland to play its full part in the nation's economy. The present day value of grassland to British agriculture exceeds £2500 million and if it were fully developed and utilized it could make an even greater contribution to the nation and to the hard pressed British livestock industry.

In the more distant future when oil has disappeared and even the reserves of coal are dwindling, grass and clover with recycled nutrients will remain to clothe our land and harness the natural resources of soil, sun and rain for food production.

It is only recently that grassland has received the attention it deserves from research workers, and because its final return depends on soil, plant and animal, progress to improved utilization on every farm will inevitably be slow, especially when economic resources are restricted.

To be a successful farmer you need to have confidence in the crops which you grow. That is probably why at present only a relatively small band of enthusiastic farmers take full advantage of the potential which grass has to offer. This book should extend that confidence and increase the number of progressive, forward-looking farmers, advisory staff and students who believe in the value of grass.

Editor's Preface

The preparation of this book was initiated by the Council of the British Grassland Society. The editor was invited to organize its preparation and enlisted several authors, each expert in his field to contribute chapters within a general plan. Although the original intention was to prepare a concise book, such is the breadth of the subject that despite editing and condensation, the present volume is fairly substantial. Nevertheless no book can be fully comprehensive in such a wide-ranging and developing scientific subject. We have therefore listed other publications of particular interest under the heading of 'further reading' and give a full list of references at the end of the book. To the many workers whose efforts whether referred to or not, have increased our knowledge of the subject, we offer our thanks.

The book has adhered to metric units but we have at times preferred percentages where the insistence on $g\ kg^{-1}$ would have appeared pedantic and we have retained weight (W) and liveweight gain in preference to mass when dealing with animals.

The work is the responsibility of the authors and editor but we are grateful to many colleagues and assistants who have willingly given of their time and advice, in particular to Dr R. C. Campling of Wye College who read the whole text in draft and made many helpful suggestions. We also thank the publishers for their work in producing the final copy.

The first edition has now been revised to include minor corrections and to update some factual information.

Finally we express our gratitude to our wives for their assistance, or at least their tolerance, even if they did not always share our enthusiasm for grass.

Glossary and conversion table

ADF	acid detergent fibre	kf	efficiency for growth
ADL	acid detergent lignin	kg^{-1}	per kilogram
CC	cell contents	kl	efficiency for lactation
CF	crude fibre	km	efficiency for maintenance
CP	crude protein	L	degree of lignification
CW	cell walls	LAI	leaf area index
CWD	cell wall digestibility	LW	live weight
d^{-1}	per day	MADF	modified acid detergent fibre
DCC	digested cell contents	ME	metabolizable energy
DCW	digestible cell wall	MJ	megajoules
DE	digestible energy	MLC	Meat and Livestock Commission
dg	degradability		
DM	dry matter	MMB	Milk Marketing Board
DMD	dry matter digestibility	MP	microbial protein
DOMD	digestible organic matter in dry matter	NFE	nitrogen-free extractives
		NPN	non-protein nitrogen
DOMI	digestible organic matter intake	OMD	organic matter digestibility
		PN	protein nitrogen
D-value	DOMD	RDP	ruminally degraded protein
EE	ether extract	RO	retention time of organic matter in the rumen
EV	energy value		
FCM	fat corrected milk	RSD	residual standard deviation
GE	gross energy	t	tonne
GM	gross margin	UDP	undegraded dietary protein
HI	heat increment	VEF	ingestibility of forage
ha^{-1}	per hectare	VFA	volatile fatty acids
IP	protein entering the small intestine	W	live weight
		WSC	water-soluble carbohydrates

1 litre	= 0.22 gal
1 kg	= 2.205 lb
1 tonne	= 2205 lb
1 metre	= 3.28 ft

1 hectare	= 2.471 acres
1 kg per ha	= 0.89 lb per acre
	= 0.8 'units' of fertilizer per acre
0.1 kg per litre	= 1 lb per gal

Chapter 1

Introduction

1.1 OBJECTIVES

The term grassland refers to a plant community in which grasses are dominant, shrubs are rare and trees absent. Grassland is a major agricultural resource of the United Kingdom and is of considerable importance in many other temperate and tropical regions. Its study can be traced over 150 years but only in the last 50 years has grass received sustained scientific attention. Indeed the major advances in our knowledge of grassland and in their application to practical farming have been made in the last 25 years. It is the aim of this book to provide a concise outline of the current state of knowledge on the production, feeding value and utilization of grassland in a temperate climate. The authors have endeavoured to assemble and outline current knowledge on the main factors affecting the production and utilization of grass and forage crops with full reference to other important sources of information and research data. The book is intended to give guidance to students and farmers and to give a broad outline of the subject for more specialist scientists.

1.2 THE DEVELOPMENT OF GRASSLANDS

There are few natural grasslands in Britain. The major grasslands of the country are not areas of natural climax vegetation but are the result of man's past activities. The clearing of forest, its cultivation for arable crops, the subsequent development of grassland and the discouragement of the regeneration of forest by herding cattle or sheep on the pastures or by cutting or burning; these practices, or the deliberate sowing of leys, have formed the majority of our pastures. But the sequence of regeneration to the woodland climax can still be seen wherever land is enclosed and protected from fire, or from grazing by domestic or wild animals.

TABLE 1.1 Changes in land use in Great Britain.

Land use	1875	1938	1944	1975
		(million hectares)		
Total crops	5·57	3·36	5·55	4·74
Temporary grass	1·76	1·44	1·71	1·84
Permanent grass	5·39	7·01	4·37	4·60
Rough grazing	not recorded	6·50	6·69	6·32

1938 and 1944 were the years of minimal and maximal tillage in the last 50 years

These influences have resulted in large areas of the United Kingdom being under grassland. Table 1.1 shows the areas in Great Britain designated as temporary grass, permanent grass and rough grazing between 1875 and 1975. Changes in the total agricultural area, because of urbanization, and changes in the precise definition of the categories prevent precise comparisons, but throughout the period, temporary and permanent grassland on the lowlands have considerably exceeded the total arable area while the area of rough grazings, generally above 300 metres, has usually exceeded that of permanent pasture. If, as is conventional, six hectares of rough grazing are regarded as equivalent to one hectare of lowland pasture, grassland has accounted for 55 to 75% of the effective agricultural area of Great Britain during the past 100 years.

Grass is not uniformly distributed over Britain. In the South and East, on land over sedimentary rocks, much of which is suitable for arable cultivation, grassland occupies a small proportion while in the West and North where rainfall is higher and topography less suited to arable crop production, it is the dominant crop. An indication of the proportions of grass and arable crops in different regions in England and Wales is given in Figure 1.1. The suitability of soils for grassland is treated in detail by Harrod (1979).

1.3   LEYS AND PERMANENT PASTURES

Much of the impetus for improved grassland farming in Britain followed the publication of *Ley farming* by Stapledon & Davies (1942) which coincided with the ploughing up campaign of the 1939–1945 war, when increased home food production was vital.

The essentials of ley farming were the alternation of crops with grass in a regular sequence, with the temporary grass or ley

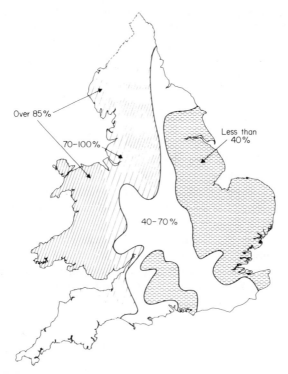

FIGURE 1.1. Proportion of agricultural land in grass (including rough grazing with sole rights) in England and Wales. From June 1971 census. (By courtesy of the Grassland Research Institute.)

normally lasting from two to five years. This provided a 'balanced' system of farming with many technical and managerial advantages. The particular rotation was chosen to fit the conditions of the farm, while retaining the principles of balanced exploitation of soil fertility with control of weeds, pests and diseases. However, chemicals have reduced the need for crop rotations and there are several disadvantages in ley farming. The financial returns from all but the most intensive use of grass are less than from cash crops. The cost of fencing and water supplies is high and the capital investment is higher per ha. Establishing grass leys is costly and failures can occur. Moreover grass leys do not suppress all weeds, e.g. couch grass (*Agropyron repens*) thrives under conditions of high fertility and infrequent utilization.

These factors and a growing realization that leys could never occupy a major proportion of the land of Britain have led to a growing interest in the permanent pastures of the country. The merits and attributes of the various pasture types are referred to later.

1.4 GRASSLAND POTENTIAL

Grass has great potential as a crop receiving and transforming the sun's radiant energy into the products of photosynthesis. It covers the ground almost completely, so that the leaf area index (LAI), the total area of leaf in relation to the area of ground covered, is typically from 2 to 6 and light energy is fully received throughout the year. In these conditions provided temperatures are not below 5°C and soil moisture is not limiting, grass can grow throughout the year. Maximal yields of some 25 t dry matter (DM) per ha could be produced in the normal British growing season of 5 to 7 months (Cooper 1970). Moreover, unlike the arable crops, such as cereals, potatoes or sugar beet, the useful economic yield is the whole crop, compared with some 52% of the total dry matter from a cereal crop, 85% from potatoes or 45% from sugar beet (Monteith 1977).

1.5 GRASS UTILIZATION

The grass crop requires to be harvested by an animal or machine and utilized by an animal, directly or after storage, before it is converted into useful products. There are losses in harvesting and in conservation and the animal converts a relatively small proportion of the food into edible nutrients (and conversion efficiency to wool is also low). As a result, even the maximal yield of 25 t of dry matter per ha which would provide 360 GJ* of gross energy and about 215 GJ of metabolizable energy (ME) per ha would yield, in animal products, about 41 GJ edible energy and 486 kg of protein if converted through dairy cattle, and only 11 GJ and 110 kg protein if converted by a suckler herd or sheep flock (Holmes 1980). It is in this area, the definition and quantification of the many steps in the process of grass utilization, that much new information has been accumulated in recent years.

* GJ, gigajoules, 1 000 000 000 joules or 1000 megajoules

1.6 GRASS AS A SOURCE OF FEED

Wright (1940) estimated that grass contributed about 67% of the total annual feed supply for farm animals in the United Kingdom in the late 1930s. The most recent figures indicate that about 71% of the metabolizable energy and 67% of the crude protein consumed by British ruminant livestock are derived from grazing and conserved grass. On average dairy cows derive 60%, beef cattle 79% and sheep 97% of their feed energy from grass (Jollans 1981).

1.7 CHANGES IN GRASSLAND PRODUCTIVITY

The measurement of grassland productivity is difficult, but comparison of the data of Wright (1940) with NEDO (1974) suggests that the average utilized ME from grassland has almost doubled from 1938 to about 40 GJ per ha in 1972/73. This increase is probably related to a greater realization of the potential of grassland, an increase in fertilizer use and an increase in the proportion of silage which now accounts for about 40% in terms of dry matter of all grass conserved in the United Kingdom. But since a crop of 10.5 t DM per ha could provide 115 GJ and a 25 t crop some 215 GJ of metabolizable energy per ha, there is still a vast gap between potential and performance. Many factors contribute to this discrepancy. Production may be impaired by unsuitable soil conditions such as excess or deficiency of moisture, acidity, mineral deficiencies and the presence of unproductive grass species and of weeds. There is usually incomplete harvesting by machine or animal and there are losses in conservation and in utilization by the animal. These have been the subject of research and development in recent years and are considered in some detail in later chapters.

FURTHER READING

DAVIES W. (1960) *The Grass Crop.* Spon, London
JOLLANS J. L. (1981) (ed) *Grassland in the British Economy.* CAS Paper No. 10. Centre for Agricultural Strategy, Reading.
NEDO (1974) *Grass and Grass Products.* National Economic Development Office, London
STAPLEDON R. G. & DAVIES W. (1942) *Ley farming.* Penguin Books, Harmondsworth, Middlesex

Chapter 2

Herbage production: grasses and leguminous forage crops

2.1 THE GRASSES AND LEGUMES

Grasses and grassland legumes maintain a cover of vegetation under conditions of repeated defoliations because of their morphological characters. The growing points of grasses are near the soil surface and are rarely damaged by defoliation. Grassland legumes, similarly, survive by having the greater proportion of their growing points as axillary buds near ground level. These are stimulated into growth if the apical growing point is removed. Herbage legumes perennate, or become perennial, by means of crown buds from a perennial tap root or, in white clover, by rooted stolons. An understanding of some of the salient features of their morphology and the physiology of growth is an aid to their rational management in practice. The following sections consider first the individual plant and then the sward.

2.1.1 *The grass plant*

The vegetative grass plant consists of a collection of shoots or tillers, each composed of a tubular structure made up of the leaf sheaths surmounted by the leaf blades or laminae. The leaf sheaths at this stage form a pseudo stem; the true stem, in the vegetative condition, is very short. The leaves arise from the nodes which are tightly packed on the stem. Removal of the leaf blades and their sheaths reveals a bud in the axil of each leaf which, under suitable conditions, will develop into a tiller (Figs 2.1 and 2.2). Other features of the leaf, not always present, are the ligule and auricles. The former is a membraneous structure varying in size and outline at the junction of the leaf lamina and sheath while the auricles are extensions of the margin of the lamina that clasp around the enclosed leaf sheath. The ligules and auricles, from their presence or absence, size and form

6

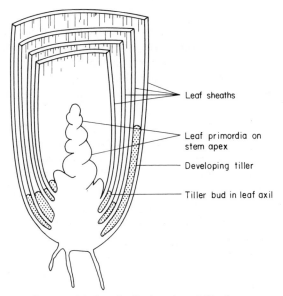

FIGURE 2.1. Longitudinal section of tiller base.

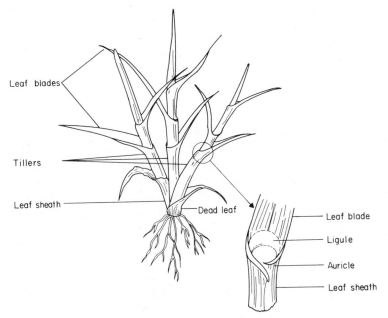

FIGURE 2.2. The grass plant.

are morphological characters that assist in the recognition of many grasses in their vegetative state (Hubbard 1968). Roots arise from the basal nodes of the tiller stem. These are known as adventitious or secondary roots to distinguish them from the seminal roots that arise from the embryo of the germinating seed.

The onset of flowering in grasses is first shown by lengthening of the stem by elongation of the upper three to five internodes followed by the emergence of the inflorescence. The characteristic unit of the inflorescence is the spikelet consisting of one or more florets arranged on a central axis, the rachilla, and subtended by a pair of glumes. In different grass species spikelets vary in number of florets, sexuality of florets and in the shape, size and form of the glumes. The form of the inflorescence varies greatly between species depending on the degree of branching of the main stem or rachis. When there is no branching and the spikelet rests directly on the rachis (e.g. perennial ryegrass, couch grass) the inflorescence is known as a spike, when the spikelet is borne on a stalk directly on the main stem the inflorescence is a raceme (e.g. *Brachypodium*), further branching on the stalks arising from the main axis produces an inflorescence known as a panicle. The branches may be long (meadow or tall fescue, cocksfoot, *Agrostis*) or short with the florets arranged close to the main axis giving rise to spikelike panicles, (timothy, meadow foxtail, crested dogstail).

2.1.2 *The leguminous forage crops*

In contrast to grasses, leguminous forage crops do not exhibit the same uniformity of morphology that renders them suitable for periodic defoliation. As a seedling plant, white clover has a short primary stem, carrying a rosette of trifoliate leaves, and a tap root. The initial stolons arise in the axils of the leaves on the primary stem and remain close to the soil surface. The internodes on the stolons may be from a few millimetres to a few centimetres in length. At each node, a leaf and an adventitious root arise, while the bud in the leaf axil is capable of developing into a stolon branch. The primary stem and tap root is relatively short-lived, rarely surviving for more than 18 months. White clover perennates by means of the continuous development of stolons which are normally out of reach of the grazing animal or mower.

The other forage legumes, red clover, lucerne and sainfoin have a perennating tap root with a well marked crown of stem buds and short shoots. In the spring with increasing temperatures and day length the internodes of the buds and shoots lengthen and stem branches may be produced at the lower nodes. In red clover the stem and its branches terminate in the ovoid or globular inflorescence. After defoliation of red clover, lucerne or sainfoin regrowth occurs by the development of crown buds and of the axillary buds and young shoots from the remaining basal stem nodes. Such regeneration takes place throughout the growing season until in the autumn with lower temperature and shorter days the plants enter the over-wintering rosette condition.

These erect legumes cannot spread and death of individual plants results in thinning crops although surviving plants will within limits, increase in size to compensate for the loss.

An important feature of leguminous crops is their ability to use atmospheric nitrogen and thus be independent of N supplied by soil or fertilizer. Nitrogen fixation can take place only if there is symbiosis with effective root-nodule bacteria of the genus *Rhizobium*. These nodule bacteria show host preference in that a strain may produce nodules on one group of leguminous crops, but not in others. Thus white clover, red clover and most other *Trifolium* species are successfully inoculated by one group of rhizobia but lucerne requires a rhizobium of another group. Within strains that successfully inoculate and produce nodules on a particular crop species, there may be considerable variation in their ability to fix atmospheric nitrogen. Strains of low effectiveness produce numerous small nodules on the root system and the host plant is small, yellow and stunted, showing signs of N starvation unless there is adequate N in the soil. Effective strains produce nodules that are large, relatively few in number and reddish in colour and the host plant is of dark green colour and grows vigorously.

Most agricultural soils in Britain contain sufficient numbers of effective rhizobia for red and white clover, although on poor, acid soils with typical hill and moorland vegetation, the proportion of effective to ineffective strains may be low. Improvement in the fertility and reduction in acidity of soils increase the proportion of effective strains. In Britain, except in newly reclaimed hill soils, it is unlikely that there is a deficiency in the effectiveness of symbiosis in red and white clover. In contrast, most soils are deficient in the appropriate lucerne rhizobia and it is advisable always to inoculate the seed.

2.2   DEVELOPMENTAL GROWTH IN GRASS

2.2.1   *Origin and growth of leaves*

While grass tillers are in the vegetative stage, the stem is only a few millimetres in length, and lies within the leaf sheaths at the base of the tiller. The stem apex or growing point is a dome-like structure of meristematic tissue. The leaf primordia are microscopic protuberances on alternate sides of the meristematic dome, increasing in age and size away from the apex. By lateral cell division, the leaf primordium assumes firstly a crescent-like structure, but eventually encircles the stem to form the juvenile leaf sheath. At this early stage, a protuberance appears by cell division on the stem axis in the axil of the leaf primordium which will eventually develop into a tiller bud.

In the development of the leaf primordium, the meristematic tissue remains at its base with the enlarging cells at its tip. At an early stage, the zone of meristematic tissue itself divides horizontally by a band of tissue from which at a later stage of development the ligule becomes differentiated. Thus the growing leaf has two meristematic zones, one at the base of the leaf sheath and the other at the base of the leaf blade, each producing their parts of the leaf. By continued division and elongation of cells, the leaf sheath and blade are carried up within the sheaths of older leaves and themselves enclose younger leaf initials. As the tip of the leaf blade emerges from the sheaths of the older leaves into the light it begins to photosynthesize and simultaneously cell expansion ceases in the exposed parts. Meristematic activity ceases in the leaf blade when the ligule is differentiated and that in the sheath when the ligule is exposed. This also marks the end of leaf growth.

2.2.2   *The rate of leaf appearance*

The quantity of leaf per unit area of a sward is of importance: it influences the photosynthetic efficiency of the crop and the nutritive value since the leaf is the most digestible part of the plant. The ability of a sward, repeatedly defoliated, to replace its leafy canopy is dependent on the rate of leaf appearance which varies with the season. In winter, the time taken for successive new leaves to appear may be as much as three weeks, but in summer, less than a week. The rate of leaf appearance is positively related to the temperature and light energy, to which the grass plant is exposed. The optimum is between 18 and 28°C for grasses of the cool temperate regions such as Britain, and higher for tropical grasses.

Differences in the rate of leaf appearance are not large between the grasses commonly used in Britain, but may occur in decreasing rate order of timothy, cocksfoot, ryegrass, meadow fescue and tall fescue (Patel & Cooper 1961, Ryle 1964). Typically, on each tiller, only about one leaf is actively elongating at any one time, slightly more with higher temperatures and high N nutrition.

2.2.3   Leaf size

Successive leaves produced on a tiller increase in size under constant environmental conditions. With rising temperature individual leaves increase in length and area, but are reduced in width. The optimum is from 20 to 25°C. Except when severely limiting, reduced light intensity has the same effect. The increase in leaf area at low light intensity may partly compensate for the reduced net photosynthesis. Increasing temperature and reduced light also cause leaves to be thinner. Improved mineral and particularly nitrogen nutrition increase leaf size.

2.2.4   Longevity of leaves

The number of leaf laminae on a tiller under sward conditions is typically from three to four although tillers on single plants may possess about one more leaf and elongating flowering stems will have more. Assuming average rates of leaf appearance and the relatively constant number of leaves on a tiller, the life-span of an individual leaf is from four to five weeks in summer and about twice as long in winter. Senescence begins at the leaf tip, the oldest part; concurrently photosynthesis declines and there is transfer of cell constituents from the dying leaf to other parts of the plant. Death and decay of leaves occur under the shade-producing conditions of a long-standing heavy crop.

2.2.5   Tiller development

The tillers arising on the main stem of the seedling, are known as primary tillers; these produce the secondary tillers and so on. The rate of tillering is positively influenced by an increase of temperature but the optimum temperature is lower than that for leaf appearance. However, the rate of tillering is most markedly affected by light energy which determines the supply of plant assimilates. Numerous studies (see Langer 1963) have shown that shading reduces the rate of tillering. Lower night-time than daytime temperatures, by reducing respiration losses, cause increased tillering. Plants removed from shaded conditions to full light immediately increase the rate of tillering to equal that of unshaded plants. However, tiller buds inhibited in their development by shading are not easily stimulated to growth by the return to improved conditions. Presumably the immediate response is by the younger tiller buds.

At the time of stem elongation, preparatory to flowering, the production of tillers declines and may cease and may not be resumed until after ear emergence or later, depending on the grass species and variety. Change in the rate of tillering with the onset of flowering is considered to be influenced by hormonal changes within the plant and/or changes in the partitioning of assimilates between the various parts of the grass plant, but the course of events remains to be fully investigated.

Deficiencies of the major nutrients N, P or K reduce tillering in proportion to the deficit and show interactive effects. Increasing N supply increases tiller numbers when adequate P and K are present but not when they are in short supply. The effect of mineral nutrition also interacts with other environmental conditions and is increased by high light intensity and optimum temperature.

2.2.6   Genetic control of tillering

Species and varieties differ in their rate of tiller production. At equal leaf development of the main shoot, the number of visible tillers on the species investigated were in descending order, perennial ryegrass S24, meadow fescue S215, tall fescue S170, cocksfoot S37 and timothy S48 (Ryle 1964). Differences in tiller production of varieties within species are widely recognized.

2.3 TILLER POPULATIONS AND TILLER PRODUCTION IN SWARD CONDITIONS

Tiller production proceeds continuously subject to the environmental conditions, while the grass plant is in the vegetative condition and is only seriously retarded at the onset of stem elongation prior to flowering. Under sward conditions, it is therefore not surprising that the numbers of tillers per unit area are at their maximum at the end of the vegetative period. Such annual fluctuations are evident irrespective of frequency of cutting or grazing or harvesting for seed, but in any year differences in detail will occur as a result of differences in weather and growing conditions. Greater fluctuation in tiller numbers per unit area have been observed in perennial ryegrass than in cocksfoot or timothy (Garwood 1969). In these species tiller numbers were at their peak in early spring and declined through summer to autumn. Irrigation had no significant influence on seasonal variation, but had the effect of slightly reducing the total numbers of tillers present during the summer. It was only in a dry summer that irrigation brought about an earlier resumption of new tiller production.

Changes in tiller numbers in a sward depend on changes in the rate of production of new tillers, on their longevity and on the death rate of tillers. Normally new tillers arise and old tillers die in each month. With monthly cutting tillering rate was least before and after flowering, it then increased through the summer into autumn, declined in winter and then increased rapidly in spring. Tiller deaths were maximal following ear emergence and then declined in summer and autumn (Garwood 1969).

The longevity of tillers is greatly influenced by the time of the year at which they first appear. Tillers appearing immediately after flowering tend to survive in a vegetative condition through the following winter and form the bulk of the inflorescences the following year, after which they die. Tillers arising at a later time are subject to competition from previously established tillers (Jewiss 1966) and a proportion of the tillers established in late autumn and early spring may succumb to the competitive effects of shading before flowering. Thus the length of life of individual tillers may vary from a few weeks for those initiated in the spring to upwards of a year for those initiated in the summer immediately after flowering.

Although tillers have a finite life, their continued production confers perenniality on grasses whether as single plants or as swards. The maintenance of conditions conducive to the regular tillering propensities of a grass species is essential for swards of long duration.

2.4   FLOWERING AND SEED FORMATION IN GRASSES

The vegetative shoot or tiller develops under suitable environmental conditions into the reproductive shoot which by elongation of internodes carries the inflorescence upwards to escape from the leaf sheath.

2.4.1   *The reproductive phase*

The first evidence of the transition from the vegetative to the reproductive condition appears at the apical meristem of the shoot but can be observed only after careful dissection of the stem apex and examination under a low power microscope. The meristematic apex produces leaf primordia at an accelerated rate but these do not themselves develop beyond forming ridges along the stem apex. However, the buds in the axils of the leaf primordia begin to develop and continue to grow while the growth of the leaf primordia ceases, giving rise to a double structure of a leaf and bud primordium. The formation of these double ridge structures on the stem apex is taken as a definite indication that the reproductive phase has begun in the grass tiller. The axillary buds grow and branch in those grasses that form panicles, each branch terminating in a spikelet. In grasses where the inflorescence is a spike, the axillary bud develops directly into a spikelet. The spikelet primordium differentiates further to form the florets. Following the conversion of the shoot apex from the vegetative to the reproductive stage and the formation of the juvenile inflorescence the next morphological change is the elongation of a number of the internodes immediately below the inflorescence beginning with the lowermost of these and proceeding upwards. This process carries the inflorescence upwards through the leaf sheaths until it emerges from the sheath of the uppermost leaf, known as the flag leaf.

Some weeks after inflorescence emergence, the anthers emerge (anthesis) from the opening florets to release pollen and expose the stigmata. The grasses are wind pollinated. Most British herbage grasses are self sterile but some small degree of self fertilization may occur in some species. Florets within an inflorescence flower over a period of time while anthesis shows a regular daily periodicity, although affected by the weather, as the florets remain closed on wet dull days. The majority of grass species flower early in the morning, between sunrise and 9.00h, a few at midday, others in the evening and some in the morning and evening. Environmental conditions of weather and mineral nutrition affect the size of inflorescence in respect of spikelet and floret numbers in some species and the proportion of the florets that set seed.

2.4.2   Environmental conditions for reproduction

Before the apex of a grass shoot can proceed to the production of an inflorescence, it must experience certain conditions of temperature and light in a correct sequence. Most grasses of the temperate regions have a prior requirement of exposure to winter conditions, that is low temperature and/or short day-lengths. The exceptions are annual grasses, e.g. annual meadow grasses (*P. annua*), Westerwolds ryegrass and some strains of Italian ryegrass (*L. multiflorum*) and exceptionally amongst the perennial grasses, timothy (*P. pratense*) and tall oat grass (*A. elatius*). The satisfying of these conditions of low temperature between 0 and 10°C, is known as vernalization since it brings the plants to the condition it normally reaches in the spring. Differences occur between species and even between varieties within a species in the amount of low temperature needed for vernalization. Thus the requirement for low temperature is greater in the persistent varieties like Kent and S23 and less in Irish and New Zealand varieties of perennial ryegrass. Species also vary in the stage of development at which they are capable of being vernalized. In some, moistened seed may be vernalized if subjected to an appropriate low temperature, while others require a minimum degree of vegetative growth and in some species a period of short days normally above 10°C can replace low-temperature vernalization (see Cooper 1960).

Once conditions for vernalization if necessary have been met, inflorescence initiation occurs in response to photoperiodic stimulus. Most perennial grasses of temperate regions require a day-length longer than a critical minimum and are known as long-day plants. The intensity of the light and temperature may have a modifying effect. Other species native of different latitudes and climatic

CHAPTER 2

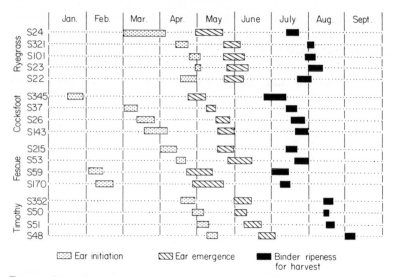

FIGURE 2.3. Inflorescence development in some grass species and varieties. (From Spedding & Diekmahns (eds) 1972.)

regions do not flower unless the day-length is shorter than a critical period and these are known as short-day plants. In addition, a number of grass species are indifferent to day-length in respect to flowering needs. Annual meadow grass which flowers at all seasons of the year is an example.

After flower initiation temperature and day-length continue to play their part. For timothy, the warmer the conditions and longer the photoperiod the shorter is the period from initiation to ear emergence (Ryle & Langer 1963). Field investigations with perennial ryegrass also have shown how season and locality affect ear emergence (Cooper 1952). In early-flowering perennial ryegrass, the date of ear emergence was dependent on March and April temperatures while that of the later flowering S23 was dependent on those of April and May. Approximate dates of flower initiation, emergence and seed ripeness for a selection of species and varieties are given in Figure 2.3.

2.4.3 *The development of the inflorescence*

The ultimate size of the inflorescence is much influenced by the age and size of tillers. In long-day plants, to which nearly all British agricultural grasses belong, the number of spikelets, when the inflorescence is a spike, or of primary branches if a panicle, is greatest in tillers formed early in autumn which have a long period of vegetative growth before the appropriate photoperiod initiates inflorescence differentiation. These older and larger tillers have larger stem apices and more double ridge sites to give rise to larger inflorescences. Tillers formed later initiate inflorescence at the same time and are therefore smaller. Thus in a crop of cocksfoot, tillers originating before September contributed about three-quarters of the ears in the final crop, while tillers formed in each subsequent month contributed only a small fraction of the total (Lambert 1963). Mineral and nitrogen nutrition, have a marked effect on tiller and hence inflorescence size, but excessive tillering caused by high nitrogen may reduce tiller fertility. Many small tillers may suffer from competition for light within the crop. Competition for light energy has been shown to differ between species. Thus shading of cocksfoot plants reduced the percentage fertility of main tillers more than for meadow fescue, while light intensity had to be very markedly reduced for ryegrass plants before fertility was affected (Ryle 1967). Such differential behaviour of species is reflected in practice. Row culture is advocated for seed crops of cocksfoot and timothy while broadcast or sward culture of ryegrass is the preferred practice. Seed production is dealt with by MAFF (1979a & b) and WPBS (1978).

2.5   GROWTH OF GRASS

The behaviour of the grass plant is most readily understood by accepting the tiller as the basic plant unit from which the development and growth of the plant and the sward may be investigated and described. Light provides the energy for growth through photosynthesis. The distribution of the products of photosynthesis under the influence of environmental conditions produces the growth and development described in preceding sections. In summary, within the grass tiller, assimilates are preferentially deployed to maintain the production of leaves, variation in light intensity has little influence on the rate at which leaves are formed, but temperature has a greater effect. The development of tillers from the axillary buds is much increased by increasing light intensity, but the optimum temperature for tiller development is less than that for leaf production. Finally, the change from the vegetative to the reproductive is under the control of temperature and/or day-length.

2.6   DEVELOPMENTAL GROWTH IN FORAGE LEGUMES

Information on the effects of the individual components of environmental conditions on the development of stem, leaves, roots and inflorescence in the forage legumes is not as extensive as in the grasses. Much of the information has been obtained under natural conditions where light intensity and temperature conditions are correlated. However, it would appear that optimum temperature for growth in legumes is in the range of 20 to 25°C and does not greatly differ from that for grasses. In relation to utilization of light energy, red clover and white clover reach light saturation and maximum photosynthesis at about 20 000 to 30 000 lux, values similar to perennial ryegrass, but lucerne can utilize much higher intensities before light saturation.

2.6.1   *Environmental control of flowering*

Initiation and development of the inflorescence in legumes are dependent on suitable photoperiods and temperature. The forage legumes discussed here are basically long-day plants. Winter requirements vary between and within the species. In white clover, varietal differences in winter requirement are related to persistency (Cooper 1960). There is an obligatory winter requirement in S100 and S184 white clovers, but not in the less persistent Ladino clover while New Zealand and Dutch white clovers contained plants of each category. The critical day-length below which flowering will not occur in white clover ranges from 13.5 h to more than 15 h according to variety. Red clover has no clearly defined winter requirement but is a long-day plant with a critical day-length of 13 to 15 h depending on the latitude of origin of the varieties. Lucerne has no winter requirement and a critical day-length of about 13 h.

2.6.2   *Pollination and seed setting*

The legumes considered are cross-pollinated and highly self-sterile. Pollination is by insects, visiting the flowers for nectar or pollen.

The anthers shed pollen within the staminal column while the flowers are in bud but self-pollination is prevented in the clovers and sainfoin because the style projects beyond the anthers. In lucerne, the style is protected by a membrane. Bees alighting on the open flowers in search of nectar or pollen cause the flowers to 'trip' exposing the stigma, and pollen from other flowers is then deposited on the stigma by the visiting bee. White clover and sainfoin are normally fertilized by honey bees or bumble bees. Only the long-tongued bumble bees can gather nectar from the base of the sta-minal tubes of red clover and they are the preferred pollinators, although honey bees gathering pollen are effective. In lucerne, as in red clover, bumble bees are the preferred pollinators. The abun-dance and activity of efficient pollinators can affect seed yields of legumes. Delaying the flowering period in red and white clover and lucerne by grazing or cutting in May or June ensures that flowering in the seed crops takes place later in the year when bumble and other solitary bees are more abundant than earlier in the season.

2.7   GROWTH IN THE GRASS SWARD

The preceding sections have largely dealt with the morphological development of the plant and the environmental conditions of temperature, light, mineral nutrition and water supply which affect development of individual leaves, tillers or plants. It is now neces-sary to consider responses of the grass sward to its environment.

2.7.1   *Photosynthetic efficiency of the sward*

In all green plants the basis of growth is photosynthesis, the process by which green plants form their carbohydrates from atmospheric carbon dioxide and water in the presence of sunlight; from these, together with mineral nutrients, nitrogen and water from the soil, all plant constituents are formed. The quantity of light energy received by a sward is thus of great importance in dry matter production. Fertilizer application and irrigation are means by which the farmer improves the efficiency of use of solar energy by crops and in-creases yield. The photosynthetic efficiency of a plant or sward is the proportion of the received light energy that is converted into plant material. Efficiency of use of light energy is partly an inherent quality of a forage species and variety, but practices that affect the leaf area of the sward also influence the utilization of solar energy.

The efficiency with which light energy is converted by the grass sward will depend on the photosynthetic activity of individual leaves, their arrangement within the crop and the proportion of the light energy falling on a given area that is intercepted by green leaves.

The photosynthetic efficiency of individual leaves decreases as light intensity increases (Cooper 1966 and 1969, Cooper & Tainton 1968). At low light intensities of about 2000 lux the grass leaf can fix around 12–15% of the incoming light energy, but as light intensity increases, leaves of temperate grass species at from 20 000 to 30 000 lux become light-saturated and do not respond to higher light intensities. (Leaves of most tropical grasses have much higher light saturation values.) Mid-summer light intensities in Britain may reach 90 000 lux but photosynthetic efficiencies of leaves at such intensities are of the order of 2–3%. Photosynthetic activity is at an optimum at from 20 to 25°C, decreases rapidly below 10°C and is almost negligible at 5°C. Leaves decline in efficiency with age, and leaves that expand in shade have lower efficiencies than those developed in higher light intensities. These differences correlate with differences in the chlorophyll content and with the anatomical features of sun and shade leaves.

Leaf canopy structure is of importance to the photosynthetic efficiency of crops. The relationships between the growth of a crop and its leaf area and the orientation of leaves have been extensively investigated (Donald 1963, Brown & Blaser 1968). In a grass sward following defoliation leaf area and mutual shading of leaves are at a minimum, the photosynthesis per unit area of leaf at a maximum, but crop growth rate is low. Some light may fall on the ground and not be used. As growth occurs, leaf area increases and although photosynthesis per unit area of leaf declines, owing to increased shading of leaves, the overall efficiency of light utilization and crop growth rate increase. With continued growth all the incident light energy is intercepted by green leaves and crop growth rate becomes maximal and remains so until the respiration of the basal parts of the sward which receive no light becomes a contributing factor. Leaf area is thus of great importance in crop growth. The ratio of the area of leaf to the surface area that supports it, is known as the leaf area index (LAI).

The amount of leaf required to intercept all light is dependent on the orientation of leaves. Thus, white clover, with leaves that tend to be horizontal, has a low optimum LAI while grasses with more upright leaves have higher optima. Grasses that differ in the erectness of leaves similarly have different optimum LAI, the more erect the leaves, the higher the optimum LAI and crop growth rate. Conversely at lower than optimum LAI prostrate grasses have higher growth rates than more erect grasses which gives them advantages in productivity when frequently defoliated (Rhodes 1969). In grass and grass-clover swards the optimum LAI may range from 3 to 9.

Theoretically maximum crop growth rates and yields are obtained when swards are maintained at their optimum LAI. However leaves decline in efficiency with age, and swards must be harvested periodically to prevent losses due to senescence and decay. Moreover, the nutritive value of the crop declines with age. Thus for maximum production suitable defoliation systems must be adopted which maintain the best average LAI for a succession of harvests grown under non-limiting conditions of plant nutrient and water supply. Such systems normally involve from five to eight defoliations during the growing season with growth intervals of four to six weeks.

Genotypes vary in leaf photosynthesis, rate of leaf production and leaf orientation. Successful selection by plant breeding of any or all of these characters would improve the use of light energy and crop yield.

2.7.2   Climate and grass growth

The main feature of the British climate that has determined the high proportion of the agricultural land occupied by grassland is the well distributed rainfall and a moderate range of temperatures over the growing season. But rainfall is not adequate everywhere and considerable variation of importance to the growth of grass occurs between regions and between years.

The growth of forage species is negligible at below 5°C, and the lower temperature threshold for growth can be reasonably taken as 6°C for the onset and the end of the grass growing season. The number of days during which temperature is above this limit give the potential growing days.

Using 6°C as the threshold temperature, and correcting for altitude, maps have been constructed showing the mean length of the growing season in Britain. The coastal areas of Devon, Cornwall, South West Wales and Anglesey have a mean of above 300 growing days while large areas of lowland England have around 250 growing days decreasing to around 200 days in the more elevated areas of the Pennines, the Welsh hills and the elevated areas of Scotland. However, in individual years of late springs and early autumns the growing season may be considerably shortened.

2.7.3   The need for water

All green plants require water since plant nutrients are all taken up and internal physiological processes take place in solution. Carbon dioxide enters through stomata which remain open during daylight only if there is adequate water within the green leaf. They close if a shortage of water occurs, bringing photosynthesis and hence growth virtually to a halt. As long as the stomata remain open evaporation or transpiration of water from the plants continues.

Provided there is adequate moisture in the soil, the rate of transpiration is a function of the evaporative capacity of the environment which is directly related to the duration of bright sunshine, mean air temperature, humidity and wind speed, and from these transpiration can be calculated (MAFF 1954a). Evapotranspiration calculated by this method is applicable to a continuous cover of green vegetation of a reasonably uniform height with adequate soil moisture in the root zone. Evapotranspiration so calculated is known as the potential evapotranspiration. Actual transpiration can be reduced by low soil moisture conditions or an incomplete cover of green vegetation. Potential evapotranspiration is measured, as for rainfall, in terms of depth of water, e.g. mm (or inches) of water.

Maps of the potential transpiration (MAFF 1954a, 1954b) show that the average values for the summer six months range from

460 mm in Essex and Kent to 400 mm in Northern England and Wales. Rainfall maps show average summer rainfall ranging from about 280 mm to over 380 mm for these areas respectively, clearly indicating the disparity between supply and need over a large part of the country. Potential evaporation does not markedly vary from year to year, but summer rainfall does. The frequency with which rainfall does not meet transpiration is expressed in terms of probability. Water held in the soil in the root zone at the start of a drying cycle can meet a part of transpiration needs, approximately 75 mm of water on average soils is added to the rainfall. On this basis, rainfall and soil-held water do not meet grassland needs, and irrigation would be beneficial in England, in eight years out of ten in areas south and east of the line from Dorset to the Wash, and in five years out of ten in a further area north and west to a line from Exeter to Scarborough.

2.7.4 Irrigation of grassland

The methods of calculating the potential evapotranspiration are of great value in determining the need of the grass crop for water. Indeed, the need for no other input is so precisely defined. In a soil at field capacity a grass sward will deplete water at a rate initially equal to the potential transpiration. This will eventually result in a soil water deficit defined as the quantity of water required to return a soil profile to field capacity (the quantity of water in the soil when drainage ceases).

When to irrigate, and how much, are the obvious essentials of an irrigation routine. Many investigations (Low & Armitage 1959, Penman 1962, Reid & Castle 1965, Stiles & Williams 1965) have shown that the highest yields of grass or grass/white clover are obtained from irrigation practices that keep the soil nearest field capacity. Thus when 12, 25, 50 and 70 mm of water were provided each time these soil water deficits had been reached, the more frequent irrigations gave the higher yields. Since over time the same total quantity of water had been used, the more frequent routines also gave the most efficient use of water. Yield and response to water fall markedly with deficits greater than 50 mm. Taking into account the labour and loss of irrigating time in moving irrigation equipment it is likely that irrigation at intervals of between 25 and 50 mm deficit is optimal.

2.7.5   Response of grasses and legumes to irrigation

No differential response to irrigation, or in susceptibility to drought, has been observed between the commonly sown species, ryegrass, cocksfoot, timothy (Stiles 1965), but tall fescue was less susceptible to drought than perennial ryegrass or cocksfoot (Garwood & Sheldrick 1978). White clover is more sensitive to dry weather than grasses and correspondingly shows better responses to irrigation than do the grasses. Lucerne has not shown responses to irrigation in a summer with a soil water deficit of 150 mm and it is unlikely that under British weather conditions droughts of a severity to affect lucerne would occur with sufficient regularity to warrant irrigation.

Growth is greatly diminished when soil water deficits exceed 40–50 mm, a quantity of water available in the top 300 mm of many soils, but grass roots can extract water from a further 300–600 mm depth at rates adequate for transpiration needs (Garwood & Williams 1967a). The retardation and cessation of growth when water is obtained from the deeper soil horizons is primarily due to lack of nitrogen at depths below 200 mm. Growth can be maintained if nitrogen is deeply placed in the horizons from which water is extracted (Garwood & Williams 1967b) but this is not possible in practice. It has, however, led to partial irrigation with the use of nitrogen fertilizer to enable some productive use of subsoil water. Partial irrigation, although giving less total yield than full irrigation, showed better returns per unit of irrigation water, particularly in the presence of increased nitrogen fertilization (Garwood & Tyson 1973).

The influence of irrigation on response to fertilizer nitrogen has been variable. Over a period of four years, response to N of a ryegrass-white clover sward was not affected by irrigation (Table 2.1). The effects of N and irrigation were nearly additive, although during short periods within a growing season both positive and negative interactions occurred. Munro (1958) and Garwood & Tyson (1973) reported positive interaction between N and irrigation during periods of irrigation within a season.

The response to irrigation has varied widely with most values being within the range 15–25 kg DM per mm of water per ha in those years with a potential water deficit greater than 100 mm. Irrigation of a grass-white clover sward increased yield by the same amount as an

TABLE 2.1. Annual yield of perennial ryegrass–white clover as influenced by irrigation and fertilizer nitrogen. (After Stiles 1961.)

(kg N ha^{-1} yr^{-1})	Not irrigated (4 year mean t DM ha^{-1})	Irrigated
0	5·7	9·7
130	6·3	10·9
260	8·7	12·2
520	11·4	15·8

application of 300 kg per ha of N, but it is unlikely that irrigation would be used to the exclusion of N since in practice there would be a strong incentive to maximize production.

The benefits of irrigation are not to be measured only by increased grass productivity. The more uniform production of grass between years allows more accurate planning of stock-carrying capacity and the area needed for conservation and thus permits a reduction in the safety margin which is normally allowed against the risk of drought.

2.8   THE INFLUENCE OF CUTTING FREQUENCY ON YIELD

The yield of grassland and other perennial herbage crops is the total of a number of harvests taken during the growing season, but the number of harvests and the height of stubble left after each cutting greatly influence the total yield. In the grasses, maximum yield is obtained when the first cut is taken shortly after ear emergence and a further two or three cuts taken at intervals of approximately eight weeks. Increasing the frequency of cutting progressively depresses yield. A typical outcome is illustrated in Table 2.2. That yield is inversely proportional to the number of harvests is partly related to the photosynthetically more efficient leaf area indices of the less frequent cutting, and also significantly to the higher growth rates associated with the uninterrupted stem elongation and inflorescence development of the primary hay harvest which constitute the major proportion of the total production for the year. The relevance of this to grazing and conservation is referred to in Chapters 4 and 5.

Numerous experiments have been conducted to determine the optimum height above ground level for cutting. With perennial

TABLE 2.2 Influence on grass yield of frequency of cutting at different levels of fertilizer nitrogen. (After Cowling *et al.* 1962.)

(kg N ha^{-1})	Twice weekly cutting	8 cuts during season	3 cuts during season
	(grass sward t DM ha^{-1})		
0	1·12	1·03	3·76
112	2·02	2·35	6·65
224	3·14	4·48	9·30
448	5·15	8·62	13·58

ryegrass, cocksfoot and timothy highest yields have resulted from cutting at a height of 25 mm, yields decreasing above or below this level (Roberts & Hunt 1936, Blood 1963, Reid 1966).

The frequency and timing of cutting have a marked influence on the yield of lucerne in any one year, on yields in the following year and the longevity of the crop. Cutting before the early bud stage in late May reduces the rate of regrowth, while second and third regrowth periods of less than six weeks growth reduce productivity, but periods of eight weeks or alternating six and eight week periods are satisfactory. Three cuts during the growing season, adequately spaced, produce a last harvest towards mid-September allowing time for further growth before the end of the growing season. This ensures that the lucerne plant enters the winter with a strong root and crown system and good reserves of carbohydrates that ensure winter survival, and a high yield at the first harvest in the following year. The removal of the last growth in November or December by light grazing has a minimal effect on future productivity (Green 1955, Jones 1955a, Jones 1955b).

Frequency of cutting has a dominant effect on total yields of grasses and legumes. However, cutting managements to produce maximum dry matter yields are not often those most suited for animal production systems since the nutritive value of herbage in terms of digestible energy or protein content is inversely related to stage of growth and the length of the growing period (Chapter 3).

2.9   THE SEASONAL GROWTH CURVE

The rate of growth for all grass species varies enormously during the year. Using an overlapping sequence of successive cuts at intervals of three or four weeks, curves of daily growth rates can be constructed (Anslow & Green 1967). When fertilizers and irrigation were provided so that growth was not limited all perennial grasses showed a similar growth pattern through the growing season (Figure 2.4). Typically, measurable growth occurs in March and the rate of growth accelerates rapidly through April reaching a peak daily growth rate some time in May, depending on species and variety. At peak, daily growth rates of 80 to 100 kg per ha are normal. Subsequently, the growth rate declines with about equal rapidity for a period of four to five weeks to a rate about half that at peak. During the next month, growth rates recover and in early August reach a second peak which is, however, considerably lower than that attained in spring. For the remainder of the season growth rates decline reaching non-measurable proportions in November.

This form of growth curve is displayed by most species, although the mid-summer trough in rate of growth in some years is not

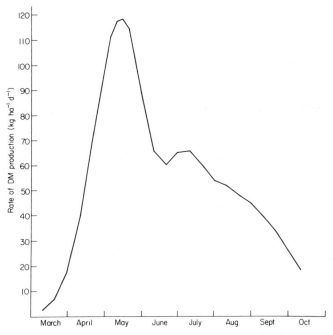

FIGURE 2.4. Growth rate of perennial ryegrass cut at intervals of three and four weeks. (After Anslow & Green 1967.)

pronounced. Amongst the species, timothy regularly shows the mid-summer trough and it is least in evidence with Italian and hybrid ryegrasses. Other species are in intermediate positions.

The rates of growth outlined (Figure 2.4) apply only to the frequency of cutting adopted to construct the curves. If growth is not interrupted from spring to ear emergence, daily rates of 180 kg DM per ha are common. Nevertheless, growth curves constructed from frequent cutting are valuable in tracing differences in the yield capacity of species and varieties and in indicating the particular seasons at which differences arise (Corrall *et al.* 1979).

2.10   FERTILIZER AND SOIL CONDITIONS

It is to be expected that the soil environment in respect to its drainage status, acidity, plant nutrient and fertilizer input individually and in combination have a dominant effect on grassland productivity.

2.10.1   *Drainage*

Grassland may tolerate a degree of imperfect drainage which is not acceptable for arable cropping. Nevertheless, surveys have shown that soils poorly or badly drained have lower proportions of preferred species (perennial ryegrass, cocksfoot, timothy, white clover) than better drained soils and that poor drainage is a factor contributing to the deterioration of sown swards (Hopkins & Green 1979). In badly drained situations, *Deschampsia caespitosa*, *Alopecuris geniculatus*, *Juncus spp.* and creeping buttercup (*Ranunculus repens*) are prevalent. Poor drainage imposes limitations on the use of grassland in wet periods and greatly increases the effect of grazing animals on soil compaction and poaching. Poaching is often the most serious consequence of poor drainage, impairing the utilization of grassland, accelerating sward deterioration. It is unusual that all grassland on a farm is poorly drained and much can be done by the complementary use of better drained fields to carry livestock during wet periods to reduce the danger of poaching on the less well drained fields.

2.10.2   Soil reaction

British soils under grassland range in pH from marked acidity below 4.0 to moderately alkaline exceeding pH 7. The desirable grasses and clover species require a minimum pH of about 5.5 for maximum productivity, but lucerne and sainfoin are not likely to thrive at less than 6.5 through a considerable depth of soil. They are, therefore, normally grown only on calcareous soils. Grassland may need periodic liming, more frequently in the higher rainfall areas, to maintain a suitable soil reaction. The use of ammonium nitrate at high rates markedly increases the leaching of Ca and the need for lime.

2.10.3   Soil nutrient status

Soils show much variability in their ability to supply plant nutrients. All are inadequate sources of nitrogen for grass, but many soils can provide the greater part of the P and K, particularly when these fertilizers have been used in the past. Soil analysis is a useful guide, particularly for recognizing marked deficiencies and to form a basis for a fertilizing programme. This will also be influenced by whether the grassland is grazed or cut for silage or hay, since one tonne of grass dry matter contains approximately 4 kg P* and 20 kg K* when these nutrients are available in amounts that do not limit production; repeated cutting and removal of crops from high yielding, intensively fertilized grassland removes large quantities of all plant nutrients.

2.10.4   Phosphorus

On grassland that in recent years has been regularly receiving P, where soil analysis does not show a deficiency, maintenance dressings of 14 to 18 kg P per ha per annum should suffice. Phosphates are neither leached from soils nor taken up by grasses or legumes in quantities greater than their needs. Thus fertilization in excess of current requirements does not lead to nutrient losses and it is satisfactory to apply phosphorus every second or third year in appropriately larger quantities. In proportion to the amount of cutting

* 1 kg P = 2.29 kg P_2O_5; 1 kg K = 1.2 kg K_2O

and removal of herbage an additional input of 4 kg P per ha per t DM removed should be adequate to maintain the soil P status. A programme of phosphorus manuring at these levels would prevent deficiencies or excesses, but the situation should be checked by periodic soil analysis.

On old neglected grassland or upland pasture where little or no phosphate has been used or where soil analysis shows a very deficient phosphorus status, initial dressings of 30 to 45 kg P per ha are needed rapidly to improve the situation. Inputs during the next three or four years could be reduced to the level of maintenance dressings.

Fertilizer phosphate, even if water soluble, is rapidly removed from solution in the soil and is converted into insoluble forms. For this reason phosphate does not move in the soil although it will continue to be a source of plant-available phosphorus. It is thus preferable that heavy dressings applied to correct initial deficiencies are cultivated into the soil.

2.10.5 *Potassium*

A maintenance and replacement K fertilizing policy is not as satisfactory as for P for several reasons. Analysis indicates the amount of exchangeable (plant-available) K in the soil but in addition soils contain large amounts of so-called non-exchangeable K reserves which replenish the exchangeable K as the latter is taken up by the plants. Normal soil analyses do not indicate the rate at which exchangeable K becomes available. Soils vary greatly in the rate at which non-exchangeable K is transformed to exchangeable K. Some soils high in clay content release K at a sufficient rate to meet the needs of grass at the highest rate of production, while on light sandy soils the rate of supply of exchangeable K is low. Grasses and legumes take up K, not in relation to their need or growth rate, but according to the quantity available in the soil. Thus with high soil availability the K content of herbage may be in excess of their requirement, so called luxury uptake. A K content of 20 g per kg herbage dry matter is considered adequate to maintain maximum production, a lesser content implies deficiency of the nutrient, and greater contents an excess which is not accompanied by increased growth and is thus a waste of fertilizer. Moreover, high K levels in herbage affect the availability of Mg to plants and animals and have been implicated in the incidence of hypomagnesaemia. Potassium application to grassland should therefore be closely related to the current needs and guided by soil and herbage analyses.

Soils which, on analysis, show a deficiency of K may require from 60 to 80 kg K per ha as an initial dressing. Subsequent dressings should aim to maintain K levels to meet production requirements, depending on whether the grass is grazed or cut and removed, and also on the inherent soil reserves. Under grazing conditions, virtually all the K is returned in the excreta, although its spatial distribution may be uneven and dairy cows will deposit some off the field. From 15 to 40 kg K per ha per annum is adequate to meet the needs of grazed grassland, the higher amounts being appropriate to intensively managed pastures receiving high quantities of N.

For cut swards, about 20 kg K should be applied per tonne DM harvested. Alternatively, the input of K on cut swards may be adjusted to the use of fertilizer N. Allowing for normal responses of grass swards to N, each 3 kg of N needs to be supported by 2 kg K or by 1·5 kg K on soils known to be better than average sources of K.

A programme of K fertilizing as outlined above may nevertheless lead to excessive use of K, not accompanied by an increase of yield, but producing herbage with high K values. In such circumstances, to achieve more economical use of K periodic sampling of the herbage would be advisable with appropriate action taken if the amount of K in the herbage departs significantly from 20 g per kg dry matter (Clement & Hopper 1968).

2.10.6 *Nitrogen*

The soil is an inadequate source of nitrogen for grass. The inclusion of white clover both by its own contribution to yield but more significantly as an additional source of nitrogen will often double yield compared with a grass sward receiving no nitrogen. Nevertheless, maximum yields of grass require such high levels of N that the possibility of the survival of white clover is much reduced. A multitude of independent experiments have clearly demonstrated the large increases in herbage yield and in potential stocking rates that result from high inputs of nitrogen at virtually all sites (Whitehead 1970). However, there are substantial differences between sites in dry matter response per unit of N, in maximum yields and in the N input required for maximum yield. These differences arise from environmental differences between sites and other differences in the management of the experiments.

Recent investigations uniformly managed at 21 sites with grass swards with no clover, cut at monthly intervals illustrate both the general form of response and the substantial variation that occurs between sites (Morrison *et al.* 1980). The mean response curve to input of N from this study is presented in Figure 2.5. The curve is of the inverse quadratic form showing that response per unit of nitrogen declined at a relatively low rate until inputs of N were high, but then with further N declined at a rapid rate to reach a maximum yield and then a yield reduction. The form of the curve gave a good fit for all sites but between individual sites there was a large range of values around the mean (Table 2.3). The mean maximum yield of 11·9 t per ha required a mean input of 624 kg N per ha. The observed range of values was, however, very large, reducing the relevance of mean values to an individual site. The mean response

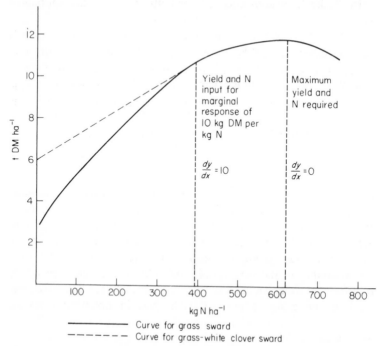

FIGURE 2.5. Mean response of grass and grass-clover swards to N fertilizer.

TABLE 2.3. Mean annual yields and responses to fertilizer N (4-year averages).

	Mean	Range
Maximum DM yield (t ha^{-1})	11·9	6·5–15·0
N required for maximum yield (kg ha^{-1})	624	446–750
DM yield at 10 : 1, kg DM : kg N (t ha^{-1})	10·9	5·4–14·4
N required for 10 : 1 limit (kg ha^{-1})	386	260–530
Response kg^{-1} N at 300 kg ha^{-1} (kg DM)	23	14–29
DM yield with no N (t ha^{-1})	2·6	0·6–5·7
% recovery of fertilizer N at 300 kg ha^{-1}	70	51–87

per kg N at an input of 300 kg per ha was 23 kg DM (range 14–29). In practice, maximum yield is of little interest owing to the low dry matter returns for nitrogen as the maximum is approached. Assuming that a DM : N return of 10 : 1 is an acceptable response, a reduction in yield of 1 tonne was accompanied on average by a reduction in input of 238 kg N.

The increase in the amount of N harvested in the grass is less than the amount of fertilizer applied. The input/output ratio is customarily known as the apparent recovery. Some of the nitrogen is retained in the roots and stubble not harvested, and eventually will be incorporated in the soil organic matter. Nitrogen may be leached in periods of excessive rainfall, but over the greater part of lowland Britain there is little or no through-drainage of water between spring and autumn and leaching is not an appreciable factor in the recovery of fertilizer N. Gaseous loss of N as a result of denitrification which proceeds most rapidly in the presence of living grass roots (Woldendorp *et al.* 1965) is a further cause of loss of N fertilizer applied to grassland. In the investigations quoted above, the mean annual apparent recovery of N varied from 51 to 87 per cent and had a much greater influence on response to N than other factors of the environment. Dry matter yield at an input of 300 kg N per ha was correlated with the apparent recovery of N ($r = 0.78$) and with rainfall ($r = 0.53$).

The inclusion of white clover in a sward raises yield in the absence of fertilizer N and reduces the response to N until white clover is eliminated (Fig. 2.5). Owing to the increased competition from grass, white clover usually disappears with inputs of 150–250 kg N per ha. Responses on grass/clover swards are of the order of 10 to 15 kg DM per kg N and for swards receiving less than

150–200 kg the presence of white clover enhances yield. All these values vary widely depending on the abundance of white clover in a sward, which can be influenced by the cutting and grazing management, moisture supply and also by all the factors that affect response of the grass sward to N.

Response to N *under grazing.* The response of grass growth to fertilizer N may be affected by the recycling of excreta N, the treading and biting action of the grazing animals and the efficiency of grazing achieved. With sheep grazing, response to fertilizer N up to 200 kg N per ha was enhanced by grazing compared to cutting (Shaw *et al.* 1966). In a series of experiments at six sites designed to investigate grass yield under cutting and cattle grazing at high levels of N use (200, 400 and 600 kg N per ha), yields were higher under grazing than cutting at two sites at an input of 200 kg N per ha. At higher levels of N grass yields were less under grazing than cutting at all sites and no significant response was obtained on any site on grazed grass to inputs above 400 kg N per ha. On average, yields of grass under grazing were 84, 68 and 61 % of cut grass at inputs of 200, 400 and 600 kg N per ha respectively. Maximum yields of grass were less under grazing than cutting and less fertilizer was required for maximum production (Jackson & Williams 1979).

Somewhat similar responses, measured through the animal, have been reported by Holmes (1968) and Gordon (1974) for dairy cows, and by Holmes (1974) for beef cattle. These showed a linear response in grazing days up to 300 kg N per ha for cows and 500 kg N per ha for growing beef cattle, with declining responses above these levels. There was considerable variation around the response equations.

Further research and development is needed to increase knowledge of the relationships between soil and fertilizer nitrogen, the grazing animal and the environment to allow appropriate stocking rates to be defined with more accuracy. (The targets shown in Table 7.3 are an attempt in this direction.)

2.10.7 *Minor and trace elements*

In lowland Britain, there are no recorded mineral deficiencies that affect grass growth. A deficiency of molybdenum in white clover has been reported under acid hill conditions which disappeared when lime was applied. The content of magnesium in grass is frequently low but no yield benefits have been recorded as a result of adding Mg to fertilizer, although an increase in the Mg content could benefit livestock. The possibility that trace element deficiencies may exist on some sites should not be ignored. Dramatic changes in productivity have followed the correction of such deficiencies in Australia and elsewhere.

2.11 POTENTIAL PRODUCTION FROM GRASS

The potential productivity of a grass sward would be realized under conditions of unrestricted supplies and uptake of water and plant nutrients on a sward where the area of leaf at all times of the year was adequate to intercept fully the incident light energy. In such conditions it has been calculated that a ryegrass sward in Britain is capable of a potential production of 27 t DM per ha and in small plots a production of 25 t DM per ha was achieved (Cooper 1970).

Over a range of sites in England and Wales under natural rainfall, with N fertilizer input non-limiting and the input and uptake of P and K showing no evidence of deficiencies of these elements, the highest yield recorded was 17·9 and the lowest 6·5 t DM per ha. Variation in rainfall during the growing season accounted for 25–30 per cent of the variation in yield, and difference in the apparent uptake of nitrogen at an input of 300 kg N per ha accounted for 60–65 per cent of the variance in yield.

It is important to practice and research to recognize the restraints that militate against growth, productivity and the realization of potential yields. Improved inherent utilization of light energy is a matter of plant breeding and would entail improvement in selected genotypes of such factors as the photosynthetic rate, in the configuration of the leaf canopy to improve the utilization of light energy at high light intensity and a high leaf area index, and the ability to continue active photosynthesis at low soil moisture levels and other related factors (Cooper 1969).

The other constraint to the realization of potential yield of existing varieties is in the efficiency of use of nitrogen. The processes involved in the non-recovery of nitrogen are well documented but the characteristics which bring about the marked differences are poorly

understood and not yet quantified. A knowledge of these characteristics would indicate the prospects of improving soil conditions to
enhance the recovery of nitrogen by grass swards.

2.12   COMPETITION BETWEEN HERBAGE SPECIES

When two or more species grow together in a community, they
interact one with the other, each species seeking to obtain its requirement of those factors needed for growth. Competition is for specific
environmental factors that affect growth and development, water,
plant nutrients and light. Its effects are expressed as dynamic
changes in the relative growth of the individual species.

The competitive characteristics of species may change at different
stages of growth from the seedling to the vegetative and reproductive condition and also with environmental conditions of water
supply, soil fertility, temperature and light. Utilization management
may also change the relative competitive ability.

Much of the early information on species competition was
obtained from work on seed mixtures (Davies 1928). Seedling
vigour is closely related to seed weight and while seedling competition may not occur at normal sowing densities, the sooner a seedling is established, the sooner it tillers and begins to exploit the
environment. Species and varietal differences in seed weight and
rate of tillering are thus of importance in determining competitive
ranking. From mixed sowings the ranking in decreasing order of
competitiveness is Italian ryegrass, perennial ryegrass, cocksfoot,
timothy, meadow fescue and tall fescue. In the early development of
sown seeds, red clover can establish well but suffer in competition as
the ryegrasses begin to tiller rapidly. The degree of competition
depends upon soil nitrogen, with lower nitrogen favouring clover.

Italian ryegrass, owing to its rapid growth, and extended autumn
and early spring growth can become very aggressive to perennial
ryegrass and red clover unless held in check by grazing or early
cutting. On the other hand, broad red clover can dominate the
developing sward, particularly in the autumn after sowing under a
cereal nurse crop when a lush growth of red clover requires grazing
to allow the development of the ryegrasses.

Competition between species can be readily appreciated but
stresses detrimental to the survival of the species are also possible in
single-species swards, most frequently in ryegrass swards. When wet

autumn and winter conditions prevent grazing of successfully established swards and the crop is allowed to grow on to a large and dense silage cut in the following spring, regrowth can be slow after cutting, new tiller development poor and swards become open and allow the ingress of seedlings of indigenous grasses such as annual and rough-stalked meadow grasses. Dense grass crops inhibit the development of new tillers, the tiller buds remaining dormant, and the longer they are inhibited the fewer will develop and the poorer their vigour when conditions for tillering are restored. The uppermost buds on the stems develop into new tillers and these, in extreme conditions, may fail to develop their adventitious roots leading to a condition known as aerial tillering. The same course of events may be observed at other times of the year, most frequently as poor tiller development and regrowth after large crops, usually induced by high fertilizer N, have been harvested. Thus, while rapid tiller development confers competitive ability on a species it also may aggravate within-plant competition.

Competition most commonly occurs amongst plants for water, nutrients, and light. Competition for water and nutrients is equated with root competition and is more likely to occur at early stages of plant development, while shoot competition for light occurs at later stages. Determination of the nature of the competition, root or shoot, and the response of the individual plant in the community to competition stress require sophisticated experiments (Donald 1958, 1963, de Wit & den Bergh 1965).

There has been little research directly related to competition between species in older associations of mixed swards either leys or permanent grass. However, many agronomic studies of response to fertilizers, grazing and cutting have noted changes in botanical composition resulting from the altered competitive conditions.

Rotational grazing, with judicious manuring, increases the proportion of perennial ryegrass and white clover with a reduction of *Agrostis*, rough-stalked meadow grass, Yorkshire Fog and herbaceous weeds (Fenton 1931). With fertilizing and increased fertility, grazed swards tended to pass through the same phases of botanical change (Fenton 1934). The order of progression with increasing fertility and productivity was from *Festuca rubra* to *Agrostis* dominance followed by an increasing contribution of perennial ryegrass and white clover with rough-stalked meadow grass (*Poa trivialis*).

Similar species succession have been observed on hill pastures initially of low fertility consisting of either *Molinia* or *Festuca/Agrostis* swards. With lime and complete fertilizer, *Molinia* and *F. ovina* soon disappeared to be replaced partly by *Agrostis*, white clover, rough-stalked and smooth-stalked meadow grass with the ultimate appearance of perennial ryegrass, cocksfoot and timothy. Successful improvement in a reasonable period of time was dependent on grazing, the taking of hay greatly reduced the rate of change (Milton & Davies 1947).

Controlled grazing experiments with swards containing perennial ryegrass, cocksfoot, *Agrostis* and white clover showed that the maintenance of perennial ryegrass required periodic grazing with intensity of grazing adjusted to the seasonal production of the grass. Over-grazing in winter and spring with under-grazing in May and June at the time of maximum growth, increased *Agrostis* while cocksfoot increased with long rest periods from grazing in early autumn (Jones 1933a–e). More recent work is reviewed by Dibb & Haggar (1979) and by Hopkins (1979).

2.13   SOWN GRASSLAND OR LEYS

In recent years, British agricultural statistics recognize two categories of lowland grassland, (i) that sown during the last few* years and (ii) all other grassland, excluding rough and hill grazing, which are recorded separately.

The sown grasslands occupy 2 m ha in the UK and mainly comprise short duration leys within arable rotations. Short duration leys composed of Italian and hybrid ryegrasses also feature on intensively managed grassland farms. In addition, sown grassland includes a proportion of leys intended for a longer duration than five years, particularly in south-west England and lowland Wales. A sample survey in the south of England showed that slightly more than 80 per cent of the leys were established from ryegrasses with or without a smaller contribution of cocksfoot and/or timothy (Morrison & Idle 1972). In a survey in England and Wales, the average contribution of sown species declined from over 80 per cent in the second to 65 per cent in the fourth year, with a lower contribution where drainage was not

---

* Four in England and Wales, seven in Scotland.

satisfactory. Soil texture did not influence the persistency of the sown species (Green 1974).

Leys provide grazing and conserved fodder for ruminant animals. They also improve soil fertility in some aspects that are not possible with other crops. There is a gradual accumulation of organic matter and nitrogen. As a consequence, soil structure improves, confers stability to soil crumbs and increases the porosity and water-holding capacity of soils. Organic matter accumulates each year by the death and decay of root and stubble, and is greater under grass than legume leys. Of the grasses, perennial ryegrass increases organic matter and the development of water-stable soil aggregates more than cocksfoot, timothy or meadow fescue (Clement & Williams 1964, 1967).

The rate of accumulation of organic nitrogen is influenced by the relative abundance of grass and legume, whether leys are cut or grazed and by the use of N fertilizer. Medium duration leys of lucerne accumulate more nitrogen than grass/white clover swards, but the one year red clover ley is of high value in relation to its duration (Heard 1965). The influence of fertilizer N used on grass/white clover swards depends on whether they are cut or grazed. When swards are wholly cut fertilizer N has little effect on soil nitrogen status—the fertilizer does no more than balance the loss of white clover—but under grazing, the nitrogen status increases in proportion to the use of fertilizer nitrogen. The realization of the accumulation of fertility is dependent on ploughing and arable cropping (including grass leys) and is reflected by savings in the requirements of subsequent crops for fertilizer N (Table 2.4).

TABLE 2.4. Residual value of grass/white clover leys in terms of fertilizer N (kg per ha). (After Williams 1966.)

	1st crop wheat	2nd crop kale	3rd crop barley	Total
3 year, grazed (low N[1])	56	70	28	154
3 year, grazed (high N[2])	84	70	28	182
3 year, cut	28	43	28	99
1 year ryegrass/red clover	28	13	Nil	41

[1] Low N = mean 0 and 80 kg N annually to ley
[2] High N = mean 160 and 320 kg N annually to ley
    Cut sward, N fertilizer to ley not significant

2.14   GRASS AND LEGUME SPECIES FOR SOWING

Plant breeders have selected within each species, varieties that possess physiological and morphological characters within well defined limits. To distinguish between varieties within a species the mean date of ear emergence is adopted for classification purposes (NIAB 1978, The Scottish Agricultural Colleges 1979). Other characters of agronomic significance are associated with the date of ear emergence. Within a species, early heading is broadly associated with early spring growth and a less densely tillered plant, and since persistency and sward longevity depend on tillering capacity, the later heading varieties which have greater tillering capacity are more suitable for long duration leys.

Perennial ryegrass (Lolium perenne) possesses many favourable properties. It is easy to establish from seed and rapidly develops into a closed sward soon capable of being grazed. It is aggressive to other species, including weeds, and there is little yield benefit from the inclusion of other species other than white or red clover. Seed is easily harvested, yield is high and the cost of seed is proportionally low. Yield of digestible matter is higher than for other perennial grasses and the species is capable of responding to high fertility. Under comparable management conditions, the digestibility of perennial ryegrass is not exceeded by any other grass species. It is not surprising, therefore, that the species has received the greatest attention by plant breeders in Western Europe. Currently 32 varieties are on the list recommended for use in England and Wales (NIAB 1979a) and a larger number in Scotland, many varieties being common to both lists (The Scottish Agricultural Colleges 1979). The dates for ear emergence range from May 8 for the earliest heading varieties to June 14 for the latest heading in central England, and from May 22 to June 29 in Scotland for the same varieties. Latitude, through day-length, influences the initiation of flowering, while the temperatures prevailing during the two months before normal heading date affect the rate of development of the inflorescence and ear emergence. Differences in temperature may alter heading dates by six to eight days in extreme seasons. The significance of ear emergence in the grasses is that digestibility of herbage declines with maturity (Chapter 3) and the stage of development as indicated by heading is more appropriate than the calendar date. Not all varieties have the same digestibility at ear emergence. With the very late varieties, digestibility at ear emergence is about the same as that in the early varieties about a week after ear emergence (D values $\simeq 67$). A knowledge of the heading dates is essential for the control of the digestibility of conserved fodders and the choice of varieties with suitable differences in heading dates makes it possible to plan a longer season of silage making with material of similar digestibility.

Italian ryegrass (*Lolium multiflorum*) together with tall fescue is the earliest to start growth in spring. It is two to three weeks earlier than early varieties of perennial ryegrass, but ear emergence is two weeks later. An early spring grazing may be followed by a conservation cut by the time of ear emergence. It is fully productive for 18 to 24 months from sowing and under good growing and management conditions for a further 6 to 12 months, but with a yield reduction of the order of 20 per cent. Hybrids with perennial ryegrass resemble the Italian ryegrass parent. They yield slightly less but are more persistent.

Westerwolds ryegrass may be regarded as a short-lived Italian ryegrass capable of rapid establishment and growth. Following spring sowing it will flower in the same year and behave as an annual. Most bred varieties persist into the second year. It is useful where high production is required within 3 to 6 months from sowing.

Tetraploid varieties of perennial and Italian ryegrass and their hybrids. Tetraploidy has not improved yield. Seed size is almost double that of the diploids and individual tillers are frequently larger but fewer giving rise to more open, less persistent swards. The water and water soluble carbohydrate contents are slightly higher and they are more palatable than the comparable diploids.

Cocksfoot (*Dactylis glomerata*) thrives best under rotational grazing. Continuous hard grazing reduces its vigour, while under lax grazing it becomes coarse and unpalatable. At all stages of growth its D value is about four to five units lower than perennial ryegrass (Table 2.5). It is less productive than perennial ryegrass when harvested at stages of growth of equal digestibility. These characteristics have contributed to the marked decline in the use of cocksfoot in recent years. However, it is useful for light sandy soils under low rainfall

TABLE 2.5. Annual yield and mean digestible organic matter and nitrogen contents; monthly cutting, mean of two years. (Irrigated: 612 kg N per ha.) (After Corrall *et al.* 1979.)

	Yield (t DM ha^{-1})	D value	DOM (t ha^{-1})	%N
Perennial ryegrass (mean 2 varieties)	12·7	70·6	9·0	3·00
Timothy (mean 4 varieties)	12·3	68·5	8·4	3·14
Cocksfoot (mean 3 varieties)	13·8	65·0	9·0	3·10
Tall fescue (mean 3 varieties)	13·1	67·4	8·8	3·11

conditions where ryegrass does not do well. When used, it should be sown as the dominant species in the mixture or as the only grass species. Mixtures with timothy and meadow fescue have been successful. Cocksfoot shows good growth in late summer and early autumn which left to late autumn or early winter can extend the grazing season for non-productive livestock.

Timothy (*Phleum pratense*) is not as productive as perennial ryegrass and has traditionally been regarded as a hay grass. The heading dates for early varieties are in the first week of June and some three weeks later for late varieties. Cuts taken around ear emergence are heavy yielding and form a very high proportion of the total annual yield. Growth is poor in mid-summer, but recovers to give better growth in late summer. To obtain forage of high digestibility (D value = 67) for silage, cutting should take place about one or two weeks before heading for early and late varieties respectively. Although timothy suffers severely in competition with perennial ryegrass, a low proportion of a late multi-tillering variety is often sown with ryegrass in long-term grazing leys. While yields may not be improved, timothy is sought after by grazing animals and the general palatability of the sward is improved. Timothy seedlings initially survive as small plants and gradually develop in later years. Timothy sown with red clover is suitable for two-year hay leys, while mixtures of timothy, meadow fescue and white clover have proved to be productive under grazing conditions with low input of nitrogen.

Meadow fescue (*Festuca pratensis*) has never been used extensively, and only recently has gained a useful role in mixture with timothy and white clover. Owing to its poor competitive ability it fails to establish to any worthwhile extent with ryegrass. It is the most suitable grass to sow with lucerne on loams and heavy soils, contributing well to the mixed herbage without becoming aggressive to lucerne. Its digestibility is similar to ryegrass.

Tall fescue (*Festuca arundinacea*) is a perennial grass with the earliness and seasonality of growth of Italian ryegrass. It is coarse-leaved and not readily eaten by livestock except in the spring. Its digestibility is generally higher than that of cocksfoot (Table 2.5) while its fibre content is not as high as the physical nature of the plant might suggest, being similar to perennial ryegrass. Seedling establishment and sward development of the species is slow with the result that frequently yields are better in the second than in the first harvest year. The species has been successfully used in long-term swards for grass drying. It dries rapidly and may be of value for hay.

Red clover (*Trifolium pratense*) is a short-lived perennial, easily established from seed on a wide range of soils. There are early and late varieties. The former, previously known as broad red clover, flower in the first week of June and the later group some two to three weeks thereafter. Early varieties do not usually last for more than 18 months from sowing, but late varieties will persist for two to three years. They are normally harvested for conservation and to get satisfactory quality, about 63 D, the first cut is taken at the early flowering stage. A lower digestibility value is permissible with red clover, sainfoin and lucerne than with grasses since the voluntary intake and the net energy content, at equal digestibility, are materially higher in the legumes. Three cuts are possible during the season, but the first harvest is much the heaviest, particularly with the late red clovers. In arable soils clover rot (*Sclerotinia trifoliorum*) is widely prevalent and causes much death of plants in the first winter after sowing. Stem eelworm (*Ditylenchus dipsaci*) is also common. These diseases caused much reduction in yield before resistant varieties became available. A high degree of resistance to clover rot which first appeared in certain tetraploid varieties greatly improves yields on infected soils. Certain older varieties and land races of the late group possess good resistance to stem eelworm as do some recently produced varieties of early red clover. At present no variety of red clover has a high degree of resistance to both diseases. In the absence of stem eelworm, tetraploid red clovers persist and yield well in the second year. They are poor seed yielders and seed is correspondingly expensive, but this defect may, with further plant breeding, be overcome by the production of diploid varieties possessing high resistance to both maladies, when even early red clover could be expected to yield equally well in the second harvest year.

The attraction of red clover is its high protein content and a yield which approaches that of grasses receiving high dressings of N fertilizer. Its yield is about 20 per cent less than lucerne but in contrast to lucerne it can be grown on practically all soils with no problems of rhizobial inoculation.

Red clover, best grown with a small admixture of ryegrass, is well suited for conservation as silage. Large quantities of red clover/ryegrass hay are harvested at present, but field drying presents difficulties and loss of leaf can be high.

The crop is suitable for grazing and could contribute much to this in the summer but there is the attendant risk of bloat, more particularly with cattle. The presence of oestrogenic substances may necessitate the avoidance of grazing with ewes prior to oestrus but it is eminently suitable grazing for fattening lambs.

White clover (*Trifolium repens*). Classification of white clover is based on leaf size, and varieties are grouped as small-, medium small-, medium large-, or large-leaved. Small-leaved varieties, typified by Kent wild, white clover, are productive and persistent under hard grazing and are most suitable for upland conditions where much of the grazing is by sheep. Medium small-leaved, e.g. S 100 and Grasslands Huia, are widely used for general purposes and the medium large-leaved varieties such as Blanca are suited to light grazing with occasional cutting and are likely better to survive competition from grass receiving some nitrogen fertilizer. Medium small-leaved white clovers are truly persistent and the medium large-leaved are suited for medium duration leys.

White clover, sown with grasses, has a dual role. It makes its own contribution to the herbage produced but its more important role is the contribution of nitrogen for the benefit of grass growth and an increase in the protein content of the sward.

The fertilizer value of white clover has been variously estimated as from 135 kg to 200 kg N/ha. The inclusion of white clover in seed mixtures is justified unless the sward is to receive large quantities of fertilizer N. The harvested or grazed produce of white clover is entirely leaf and digestibility is very high, D values of 72 to 75, with a crude protein content of 26 to 28 per cent being typical of produce from monthly cutting. White clover is more sensitive to dry weather than grasses and its potential value is greater under high than low rainfall conditions. Clover rot (*Sclerotinia*), where present, seriously reduces the contribution of white clover in mixed swards. Some varieties show resistance to infection, none is immune, and currently it is a character which is receiving attention in plant breeding programmes.

Alsike clover (*Trifolium hybridum*) is a perennial used in mixture with grasses and other clovers. It is recommended for acid conditions in high rainfall areas and for soils of low fertility which are unsuited to the more productive red clovers.

Lucerne (*Medicago sativa*) requires soils that are well drained and alkaline or near alkaline throughout the soil depth and it is mainly restricted to calcareous soils. Under these conditions, a healthy and weed-free crop will persist under appropriate management for many years and will give consistent high yields because of its virtual immunity to dry weather. To ensure effective nodulation in lucerne, the seed should be inoculated with the appropriate strain of lucerne rhizobium.

Lucerne varieties are distinguished by the time of flowering but under British conditions the early flowering type outyields all others and is the only type recommended (NIAB 1979b). Varieties of the early group flower in the second week of June but to obtain an acceptable digestibility the first cut needs to be taken at the early bud stage in the last week of May when the expected D value would be 62–64 and subsequent cuts at six to eight week intervals give D values of 56–60. Some varieties of lucerne resist infection by *Verticillium* wilt and stem eelworm and should be used in districts where these are known to be present, particularly if lucerne is expected to remain for more than two years. Resistant varieties are up to 5 per cent lower yielding than the best of the non-resistant, but a modest infection can cause greater loss of yield.

Although lucerne is frequently sown as a pure crop, in time, self-sown grasses, typically rough-stalked meadow grass, become prevalent and competitive to the crop, without adding much to yield. For these reasons small quantities of a non-aggressive grass, preferably an early type of meadow fescue or timothy, may be sown with lucerne largely to control unsown grasses. Cocksfoot is not generally recommended except on light sandy soils and under low rainfall conditions. Now that suitable herbicides (e.g. carbeta-mide and propyzamide) are available to control the ingress of grass there may be less advantage in growing a grass with lucerne.

Lucerne has never been an important crop in Britain. It occupied, in 1979, about 12 800 ha having declined from a maximum of 40 000 ha during the last two decades. It has been consistently used for artificial drying in the lower rainfall areas, but for the generality of farms the crop has not gained wide acceptance. For this, various reasons have been given, the chief of v .iich are the difficulties in-volved in ensiling or making hay of the crop. However, with wilting and suitable additives, ensiling problems are being overcome. For consistent success in making hay, barn drying facilities are essential. The incidence of disease need not be a deterrent now that resistant varieties have been developed. Owing to its reliability in dry sum-mers, it is valuable as grazing provided it is strip grazed behind an electric fence and cattle are prevented by a back fence from grazing the new regrowth. Bloat is a problem, but anti-bloat agents included in feed or water may overcome this.

Sainfoin (*Onobrychis viciifolia*) was once widely grown on the chalk and oolitic limestone soils in England, but it is now reduced to a small area. Two major types are recognized, giant and common sainfoin. Formerly, distinctive local varieties particularly of common sainfoin, were also recognized, but few if any have been maintained. Both types of sainfoin are sown in the spring under a cereal crop, the giant lasting for eighteen months, but common sainfoin is expected to last from three to five years. Giant sainfoin was cut for hay. The regrowth produced inflorescences and provided either another hay cut or seed crop. Common sainfoin was usually cut for hay at the flowering stage and the regrowth which produced no flowers in the aftermath was folded with sheep. Seed was harvested from the first cut in the third or fourth year. Well-made sainfoin hay is held in high esteem, especially for horses. Recent investigations have shown that in the first growth in the latter half of May and early June, the digestibility of sainfoin is similar to that of an early ryegrass and higher than that of lucerne, and that the voluntary intake is higher than that for lucerne or red clover. Moreover, probably because of its tannin content it does not induce bloat.

Trefoil (*Medicago lupulina*), a biennial, is much less productive than red clover but was used as an alternative where clover rot was prevalent and has also been used as a short-term, green manuring crop. The relative importance of the various herbage legumes may be inferred from the amount of seed used.

Red clover, white clover and alsike clover account for 33, 46 and 7 percent by weight respectively, with lucerne accounting for 6 per cent.

2.15   SEED MIXTURES

Increased fertilizer usage, the availability of varieties bred for specific characteristics and a better appreciation of competition between plants have justified the recent trends towards the use of simple seed mixtures. It is now common practice to establish a sward from a single grass species, with or without a legume. Some species formerly used in small quantities are no longer included in seed mixtures. The improved varieties of the aggressive ryegrasses are also a factor. The ryegrasses account for over 80 per cent of seed sown, with timothy, cocksfoot and meadow fescue accounting for 8, 5 and 3 per cent respectively. Concurrent with the use of simple seed mixtures and the dominance of the ryegrasses there has been an increase in the number of varieties of each species.

The sale of seed of herbage species is restricted by law to that of certified, named varieties entered in a UK National List or in a Common Catalogue of the Community (EEC). For national listing, the requirements are that a variety must be distinct, uniform and stable and have values for cultivation or use which in comparison with other plant varieties in the National Lists constitute an improvement. New additions thus require statutory performance testing. In addition to authenticity of variety, seeds sold must also comply with statutory minimum standards of purity, germination and freedom from weeds.

As an aid to farmers, lists of recommended varieties are issued annually by the National Institute of Agricultural Botany (NIAB

1979a, b) for England and Wales and by the Scottish Agricultural
Colleges (1979) for Scotland. The recommended lists are composed
of the best yielding varieties, grouped according to heading dates,
together with information on their persistency, winter hardiness and
resistance to disease.

In Table 2.6 some outline seed mixtures are presented as a basis
for discussion. The last column gives the amount of seed required to
establish a crop of that species sown alone under average conditions. Mixture No. 1 is a typical red clover and Italian ryegrass one
year ley which, however, if it included persistent tetraploid red
clover would produce well for a further year. This mixture would
normally be sown under a cereal crop. Mixture No. 2 indicates the
use of Italian ryegrass in an 18 to 30 month ley to provide herbage
both early and late in the year and to be managed intensively with
high inputs of nitrogen. Substitution of part of the Italian ryegrass
by hybrid ryegrass would ensure high production in the second
year. A lower seed rate would be suitable if established under a
cereal nurse crop. Medium duration leys to last a minimum of three
years or long duration leys of indefinite duration may well be
established from perennial ryegrass and white clover (mixture
No. 3). It is important, however, to choose varieties of appropriate
persistence using early varieties for the shorter duration and persistent varieties only in long duration leys. This mixture can be varied
by the inclusion of a persistent variety of timothy.

TABLE 2.6. Typical seed mixtures (kg seed per ha).

| | | | | Mixture No. | | | |
	1	2	3	4	5	6	(a)
Italian ryegrass	14	34					25–35
Perennial ryegrass			20		10		16–22
Timothy				7	4	(4)	10–24
						or	
Cocksfoot					5	(4)	15–20
						or	
Meadow fescue				14		(4)	16–20
Tall fescue							14–20
Red clover	9				4		10–14
White clover			2	2	2		–
Lucerne						16	16–18

(a) Seed rate for pure sowings of species.

The timothy-meadow fescue mixture (No. 4) is suitable for dairy farms. These non-aggressive grasses allow good development of white clover although the mixture is also suited to high use of fertilizer nitrogen. In dry areas about 5 kg of cocksfoot could be added to the mixture.

Mixtures of perennial ryegrass, timothy, cocksfoot, red and white clovers are frequently used (mixture No. 5). This form of mixture, called the Cockle Park type, now appears to be complex but, when first advocated, it represented a marked simplification compared with earlier mixtures. It was successful under a wide range of conditions before the introduction of bred varieties which accentuated the aggressiveness of perennial ryegrass.

In medium duration leys, whether to include white clover is dependent on the intended use of nitrogen fertilizer. If the intended annual input of nitrogen is above 200 kg per ha from the time of establishment, white clover may be omitted particularly under the lower rainfall conditions. White clover is normally included in mixtures for long-term pastures. For detailed suggestions for seed mixtures for a wide range of circumstances the reader is referred to the current advisory literature (MAFF 1979c).

2.16 The establishment of leys

2.16.1 Germination

The germination of seed requires a favourable temperature and an adequate supply of water and air in the soil. Subsequent seedling growth depends on the continuation of these favourable factors. Grass and clover seeds are capable of good germination at relatively low temperatures, e.g. 5–10°C. The ryegrasses germinate most readily, while cocksfoot, timothy, meadow fescue and tall fescue require slightly higher temperatures. For satisfactory rates of growth after germination all species require higher temperatures. Under British conditions it is apparent that seeds will germinate in the field for much of the year, but environmental conditions may restrict development owing to the incidence of poor moisture conditions during the summer and low temperature in winter.

2.16.2 Time of sowing

Sowing in Spring as soon as soil conditions allow the preparation of a suitable soil tilth for the small seeds, is most favoured in the lower rainfall areas, allowing the maximum time for seedling establishment before the onset of summer drought. Sowing in March or April, but avoiding very early sowing for tall and meadow fescue, timothy and lucerne, will allow development of sufficiently mature plants of all species to withstand dry summer conditions. In high rainfall areas sowings may be made much later and are successful even in mid-summer. In the lower rainfall regions, grass and clover seeds may be successfully sown again in August and September. Germination and establishment is then dependent on current rainfall and August sowing may fail because of delayed autumn rain. The legumes are most at risk from late autumn sowing. Although they germinate well, small plants fail to survive the winter for a variety of reasons including soil disturbance by freezing and thawing and the depredations of small fauna and plant pathogens. Lucerne needs to be sown not later than the latter half of July or early August to ensure a sufficiently strong plant to give full growth the following year. Red and white clover need to germinate by the end of August in central England and earlier in northern parts. Ryegrasses can be sown well into September without undue risks.

2.16.3 Method of sowing

Ideal methods of sowing should give uniform distribution of seed, placed at a depth in the soil appropriate to the seeds and soil moisture conditions. It is important that the soil tilth is sufficiently fine and consolidated after sowing to make good contact with the seeds for the rapid uptake of water and later to allow the transmission of water to the seedling roots. A fine seed bed also gives better control of depth of sowing. Optimum depths of sowing under average field conditions range from 10 mm, for small-seeded species such as white clover and timothy, to about 25 mm for the larger seeded grasses and legumes. The appropriate depth also varies with soil moisture conditions, shallow sowing being successful when there is adequate moisture, and deeper sowing with less favourable conditions. In the latter situations seeds need to be placed at a depth that reduces the chances of alternating dry and moist soil during seedling establishment. It follows that in the higher rainfall districts the sowing of seed by broadcast methods and then covering by light harrowing gives good results. This is also satisfactory in the lower rainfall areas, provided that the seeds are covered to a satisfactory depth, but drill sowing gives more uniform and better control of depth and, provided the drills are no more than 10 cm apart, a satisfactory closed sward is soon formed. Drilling, however, increases competition if there is a mixture of species, and seeds which require shallow sowing may be sown too deep. However, drilling can place seed into the moist soil layer under dry conditions and this may outweigh other disadvantages. Soil consolidation by rolling is usually advisable before broadcasting or drilling and should be repeated after sowing.

2.16.4 *Nurse and cover crops*

The practice of sowing grass and clover seeds in the spring under a cereal is becoming increasingly hazardous with modern high yielding and heavily fertilized cereal crops. A lodged cereal crop generally causes a failure of undersown grass and clover. Undersowing is most successful with the easily established ryegrasses and red clover sown under spring cereals but some reduction in the cereal seed rate and amount of N fertilizer used may be needed. It is preferable that the seeds are sown early immediately after the cereal is drilled. Other cover crops may be used. A mixed cereal crop, which may include forage peas and vetches harvested early for silage is suitable.

On arable farms, autumn sowing of seeds is increasingly becoming the normal practice. After an early-ripening cereal crop, such as winter barley, there is adequate time to establish a strong plant of grass and clovers before winter.

The establishment of long duration leys warrants extra care to achieve rapid establishment of a closed and actively tillering sward. Sowing without a cereal nurse crop will allow appropriate management. With spring sowing of seeds, a grazing nurse crop is helpful. This could be a low seed rate of barley, e.g. 50–60 kg per ha or of Westerwold or Italian ryegrass at 10 kg per ha. These allow grazing, some six to eight weeks after sowing, when the developing seedlings will benefit from the soil consolidation and the defoliation will encourage the tillering of the grasses. The early grazing should be intermittent. Sheep may be preferable to cattle for first grazing but the latter do no harm if the surface soil is dry. Barley and Wester-wold will have the least competitive influence on the developing seeds. Italian ryegrass will persist to the following year and although having little influence on perennial ryegrass, it may not be desirable with meadow fescue and timothy. Rape (*Brassica napus*) at a low seed rate is used for summer sowings in high rainfall areas, but it should not be allowed to develop into a tall crop before grazing. It provides useful feed for weaned lambs.

Grass is commonly sown on arable land after a sequence of crop-ping but it may also be sown following the ploughing up of old pasture. This is referred to as *direct reseeding*. Another possibility is that the old pasture is ploughed, cropped for one year with a forage crop, referred to as a *pioneer crop*, which is grazed off. This procedure encourages more complete breakdown of the turf so that a better seed bed can be prepared for the important long-term pasture.

In discussing the establishment of leys, the time of sowing, methods of seeding, the use of a nurse crop and early management, the aim has been to outline means of reducing the risks of poor establishment to a minimum. The hazards of establishment vary widely as will the necessity for practices to circumvent such hazards.

2.17   PERMANENT GRASSLAND

2.17.1   *Definition*

The term permanent grassland does not clearly define a type of grassland. It describes land maintained perpetually as grassland without the intervention of ploughing and reseeding. Such grass-land exists. Unfortunately it is not separately recorded but is included in the category of grassland of five years old and over, of which there are about 5 m hectares in the UK (Table 1.1). A survey of grassland in England and Wales indicated that of the 3·16 m ha of grassland of 5 years old and over, 23 per cent was from 5 to 8 years old, 22 per cent from 9 to 20 years and 55 per cent was more than 20 years old (Green & Williams 1975). Long-term grassland occupied a large proportion of the agricultural land in the higher rainfall areas. In all districts much of the old grassland occupies land with limitations to its cultivation, including ploughing and mowing or grazing, as a result of poor drainage, gradient or surface

TABLE 2.7. The proportion of grassland in different usability classes (%).

Usability (ease of management)	Age of grassland	
	More than 20 years	Less than 20 years
No limitation to management	38	72
Moderate limitation to management	37	20
Severe limitation to management	25	8

irregularities (Table 2.7). The most common limitation was poor drainage which also reduced the proportion of useful grasses, mainly perennial ryegrass (Green 1974).

2.17.2 Grades of permanent grassland

Permanent pastures have been classified according to their botanical composition particularly the abundance of perennial ryegrass or the dominance of *Agrostis* or red fescue (*Festuca rubra*). Field studies have shown that productivity measured by stock-carrying capacity and performance was positively correlated with the abundance of perennial ryegrass, white clover, soil pH and P status (Neenan *et al.* 1959). For survey purposes (Davies 1941, Stapledon *et al.* 1945) swards containing ryegrass were divided into three grades in which ryegrass contributed more than 30 per cent, from 15 to 30 per cent, and less than 15 per cent to the ground cover. In these swards white clover is always present and *Poa trivialis*, rough-stalked meadow grass, is abundant. The other better grasses such as cocksfoot, timothy and meadow fescue, although they are frequently present, do not contribute in significant amounts to the herbage of permanent grassland. As the proportion of perennial ryegrass decreases, that of *Agrostis* increases and it is most frequently the dominant grass in third-grade ryegrass pastures.

The *Agrostis* swards, in which ryegrass and other better grasses are absent or present in only insignificant amounts, are widespread and extensive. They are capable of subdivision according to soil reaction. Those on acid soils have a restricted flora and acid-tolerant species are present such as Yorkshire fog (*Holcus lanatus*), sweet vernal (*Anthoxanthum odoratum*), sorrell (*Rumex acetosa, R. acetosella*) and others. On neutral and calcareous soils the dominance of *Agrostis* is less pronounced, and dicotyledonous weeds are more abundant including some calcicolous species.

These grades and types of permanent grassland are not discrete classes but subdivisions that cover a continuous range from one extreme to the other. No areas are exclusively occupied by any one grade of pasture. In a district one grade will be the most prevalent but better and poorer grades will also be present. Cartographic representation on this principle (Davies 1941, Stapledon *et al.* 1945) showed a dominance of first-grade ryegrass swards on two small localities in the Welland Valley in Leicestershire and Northampton-shire, and in Romney Marsh, Kent, while second-grade pastures were the most plentiful type of sward over contiguous areas, with an additional area in Cheshire. These are areas of fertile soils mainly of heavy texture, but the most significant feature was the efficient utili-zation of the sward under a grazing management that ensured that grass was consumed at its highest nutritive value. Although these high quality swards were developed under a system of continuous grazing, stock numbers, particularly for fattening cattle and sheep, were carefully adjusted throughout the growing season to provide an adequate intake of grass of high nutritive value to maintain a high level of liveweight gain. Areas of predominantly third-grade ryegrass or *Agrostis* ryegrass swards are widespread.

Changes in manuring and management and the adoption of re-seeding have altered the quality of much of the permanent or old grassland. Thus in 1939 (Davies 1941) ryegrass was dominant on about 8 per cent whereas in 1971 it predominated over 25 per cent of the old grassland (Green 1974). Nevertheless, *Agrostis* still dominates about half of the old grassland.

2.17.3   *The management of permanent grassland*

The management given to permanent grassland is highly variable both within and between localities. In England, Wales and North-ern Ireland, about one quarter is mown annually, usually once for hay or silage, but only half this proportion in Scotland. The overall average inputs (1973) of fertilizer at 59, 24 and 15 kg per ha of N, P and K respectively were approximately half those applied to leys. In any one year, about 4 per cent of the area received lime and 21 per cent an application of farmyard manure.

Permanent grassland occupies the largest proportion and area of land in the west and north of Britain, regions less suited to arable farming. The climate is favourable to the growth of herbage but is not the easiest in which to make hay or in which to use pasture without damaging both the crop and soil structure by poaching. Nevertheless, this large area, including really old grass and also that which has been sown for more than ten years, represents a resource which is much underused. The most ready means of improving productivity is by correcting soil deficiencies of lime, phosphate and potash allied with good utilization through grazing and conservation. Under high rainfall conditions it is important to recognize the virtues of permanent swards and the protection they afford against poaching. An undisturbed soil under old grass develops a useful structure which improves its permeability to water. With a continued and regular application of P and, where necessary, K fertilizer, sward productivity will be greatly increased, white clover will increase as will the proportion of the better grasses. The use of fertilizer N is not precluded but initially it should be used selectively to increase grass growth for grazing at specific times and for conservation. Hay is often the major form in which grass is conserved, but the quality of the swards themselves would improve if earlier, more nutritious but less heavy crops were taken and the wider adoption of ensilage would aid the better grasses and the maintenance of white clover.

2.17.4 *Renovation of pasture*

Improvement of permanent grassland by fertilizing and improved utilization management is possibly the most economical means of raising farm productivity in the higher rainfall areas on poorly drained soils. However, over a third of the old grassland is on soils presenting little or no impediment to cultivation, and ploughing and reseeding may be worthwhile. The use of herbicides for partial or complete destruction of grass swards and direct drilling or broadcast sowing of seeds with a minimum of surface cultivation may be alternatives, Allen (1979), Haggar & Squires (1979). Nevertheless, the present low productivity of grassland and the dominance of poor grasses and low clover content is primarily due to failure to manage grass as a crop. An adequate liming and fertilizer policy in conjunction with good grassland utilization is essential to improve existing grassland and to maintain the presence of sown grasses.

In the recent resurgence of interest in permanent grass it has been emphasized that with good management its yield may be comparable to that of leys and it incurs lower costs (Mudd & Meadowcroft 1964). Moreover, the productivity of the 'weed' grasses is not much below that of sown pastures provided that soil deficiencies are corrected and nitrogenous fertilizers are applied (Dibb & Haggar 1979).

2.18   ROUGH AND HILL GRAZINGS

The rough and hill grazings occupy land above the limits of cultivation and enclosure which in England occurs at an altitude of from 250 to 300 metres but at a lower elevation in Scotland. In addition, heath rough grazings occur on infertile soils at low elevation. Rough and hill grazings occupy nearly a half of the total agricultural area of Scotland, one-third of Wales, one-ninth of England and one-sixth of Northern Ireland, making a total of about 7 million hectares.

The combination of soils and climate has a more decisive influence on the vegetation developed on the hill grazings than on that of permanent grassland at lower elevations (Table 2.8). Grazing is far less intensive, mostly with sheep and a few cattle, and fertilizers are rarely used. With the exception of small areas of lime-bearing rocks, the upland soils are acidic and with the high rainfall a large proportion of the hill land is peat clad, frequently to a great depth.

2.18.1   The fescue pastures

These form the link between the vegetation of the permanent grassland of the lowlands and that of the uplands. The downland fescue pastures were at one time extensive on the chalk and oolitic formations of southern England, but at present they are greatly reduced, many having been ploughed for cereal cropping. Those remaining are mainly on steep valley sides and escarpments. These floristically rich fescue pastures are threatened by the lack of sheep grazing under which they were developed and maintained, and are being invaded by *Brachypodium pinnatum* and scrub.

The mountain fescue pastures are essentially pastures of hillsides, often steep, with thin, well-drained, acid soils with some accumula-

TABLE 2.8. Summary of the main soil and vegetation types of the hills (HFRO 1979).

Soil	pH	Vegetation type	Principal species
Brown earth freely drained	5·3–6·0	*Agrostis-Festuca* grassland high grade or spp. rich. Herbs abundant	*Agrostis tenuis* *Festuca rubra* *F. ovina* *Poa* spp. *Trifolium repens*
Gleys poorly drained	5·3–6·0	As above with wet-land spp. *Carex, Juncus*	*Carex* spp. *Juncus* spp.
Brown earth freely drained	4·5–5·2	*Festuca-Agrostis* grassland low grade or spp. poor	*Agrostis* spp. *Festuca ovina* *Pteridium aquilinum*
Gleys poorly drained	4·5–5·2	As above with *Nardus* and wet-land spp. *Carex, Juncus*	*Nardus stricta* *Carex* spp. *Juncus* spp. *Deschampsia caespitosa*
Podsols Peaty podsols freely drained	4·0–4·5	*Nardus* or *Deschampsia* *Festuca* grass heath or *Calluna* shrub heath	*Nardus stricta* *Deschampsia flexuosa* *Festuca ovina* *Calluna vulgaris* *Vaccinium* spp. *Erica* spp.
Peaty gleys poorly drained	4·0–4·5	*Molinia* grass heath or *Calluna/Molinia* heath	*Molinia caerulea* *Festuca ovina* *Deschampsia flexuosa* *Calluna vulgaris*
Deep blanket peat poorly drained	3·5–4·0	*Trichophorum/Eriophorum/ Calluna* bog	*Trichophorum caespitosum* *Eriophorum* spp. *Calluna vulgaris* *Molinia caerulea* *Sphagnum* spp.

tion of undecayed root and tiller bases. On the more fertile patches, red fescue *Festuca rubra* and *Agrostis* are abundant constituents but elsewhere sheep's fescue, *F. ovina*, is dominant, and at higher elevations with thin peat development, *Nardus stricta* occurs. Other grasses often present are heath grass (*Sieglingia decumbens*) and sweet vernal (*Anthoxanthum odoratum*).

The fescue pastures afford the best summer grazing on hill land and are dry and healthy. Where physical conditions of slope and access permit, they are capable of considerable improvement by liming, phosphate manuring, fencing and controlled grazing. However, with decreasing management large areas have been invaded by bracken (*Pteridium aquilinum*) and gorse (*Ulex* spp.) at the lower and *Nardus* at higher elevations.

2.18.2   *Moorland pastures*

Nardus moor. Nardus stricta occupies the drier hill slopes on very acidic soil with a development of a shallow layer of peat. This tussocky grass, commonly called mat grass or white bent, has a system of horizontal rhizomes and tough basal sheaths. Areas dominated by it are the least useful of the natural grazings. Sheep's fescue (*F. ovina*), in variable quantities, is almost always present, as are small areas of heath rush (*Juncus squarrosus*) which is sought after by sheep during the winter months. Other species usually present are *Deschampsia flexuosa, Galium hercynicum, Potentilla erecta* and stunted *Calluna* and *Vaccinium* spp.

Molinia moor. Extensive areas dominated by *Molinia caerulea* develop on wet peaty soils on moderate or slight gradients. Although growing under wet soil conditions *Molinia* does not thrive in stagnant water. Small quantities of other grasses typically present include *Agrostis tenuis* and *canina, F. ovina* and *Nardus* and heath plants such as *Calluna vulgaris, Erica* spp. and *Juncus articulatus*.

Molinia starts growth at the end of May or early June, but this is rapid and luxuriant. Sheep are unable to keep pace with the growth but it affords good grazing for hill cattle from June to early September, which also maintains the grass in a better condition for sheep. With the onset of winter the leaves are shed and blow in the wind, hence its common name of flying bent. Burning at intervals of about seven years helps to maintain *Molinia* moors in a good condition. *Molinia* is rapidly reduced by heavy grazing.

Molinia-Nardus moorland. Although *Molinia* and *Nardus* moorland occur extensively in Britain with dominance of one or other of the two species over appreciable areas, there are also extensive areas of the mixed *Molinia-Nardus* plant associations. The heterogeneity is associated with mixed topography, and springs and seepage of ground water giving rise to mountain flush bogs.

Heather moor. Well developed heather moors occur on relatively shallow, but not excessively wet peat. Little real distinction can be made between lowland heaths dominated by heather and the upland heather moor. The most extensive heather moors occur on the drier eastern slopes of the Pennine hills in Yorkshire and Durham and similarly in Scotland. Local topography and soil variations in a heather moor give rise to small associations of and admixtures with *Nardus, Molinia, P. aquilinum, Vaccinium* spp., *Erica* spp. and *Empetrum nigrum.* Where the peat is poorly drained, cotton grass (*Eriophorum vaginatum*) and deer grass (*Trichophorum caespitosum*) will appear.

Heather moors provide pasturage for sheep, particularly valuable in the early part of the year when young shoots are available. In snow it may be the only accessible feed. Nevertheless access to grass moors in conjunction with heather moors is considered beneficial to the management of the sheep flock. Heather moors need to be appropriately managed to maintain the plant in young vigorous condition. This is achieved by regular burning at intervals of five to ten years which rejuvenates the heather. Left unburnt it grows tall, grey or stick heather, which sheep find difficult to enter and provides less new growth. Heather when burnt after a suitable interval of five to ten years regenerates from the stools, but stick heather on burning is apt to be killed. Regeneration is then from seed, of which there is great abundance in the soil but seedlings are more sensitive to grazing than are regenerating stools and the return of heather is slow. If such burnt areas are small they may attract sheep in such intensity as to prevent regeneration of heather when reversion either to *Nardus,* or on the better areas to bracken, may be the consequence of burning. On wet peat heather moor development can be assisted by open ditch draining to reduce cotton and deer grass. Heather moors apart from being valuable for hill and mountain sheep are essential for grouse. Fortunately the type of heather best suited for sheep is also that best for grouse.

On average, only 15% of the annual growth of heather is grazed by sheep. Work at the Hill Farming Research Organisation has shown that 40% of the annual growth may be grazed without affecting new shoot production. The heather was then maintained in a more juvenile condition and the intervals between burning could be extended (Grant *et al.* 1978).

Cotton and deer grass moors. Eriophorum vaginatum and *Tricho-phorum caespitosum* form the typical plant association of deep blanket peat under high rainfall conditions. In the most boggy areas *Eriophorum angustifolium* is present. These moors are the least valuable for sheep grazing although sheep seek the young basal sheaths of the developing inflorescence (draw moss) in early spring. Cotton grass moors occupy extensive areas of the highest ground in the Pennines and are distributed throughout Britain on deep, wet peat.

2.19 WEEDS OF GRASSLAND AND THEIR CONTROL

2.19.1 *The weeds of grassland*

Practically all grass swards, particularly those of long standing, contain grass species whose productive potential is less than that of better species which could exist in the prevailing conditions, although they are readily eaten by livestock. Such grasses, notably *Agrostis* spp. and the meadow grasses (*Poa* spp.) may and often do contribute more to the total production than do perennial ryegrass, cocksfoot or timothy. The former species may be considered as undesirable weeds. Nevertheless, species of the same category as *Agrostis* would not be classed as a weed in a hill grazing composed largely of fine-leaved fescues and *Nardus*. Other grass species which are grazed only under duress, such as tussock grass (*Deschampsia caespitosa*), are easily defined as weeds. The concept of weed status amongst gramineous species that are edible to livestock is thus largely a matter of a ranking order within a given environment. The control of weed grasses involves cultural and management practices that prevent the initial establishment of the less desirable grass species or reduce their contribution to swards where they are already present. These practices favour the development of the more desirable species and are detrimental to the undesirable species. The development of herbicides that exhibit selectivity between grass species is a new field of research that shows promise of success in respect to the control of the initial ingress of unsown grass species into sown swards and to a degree of control in established swards, although much can be done by the traditional methods of grazing and burning.

Broad-leaved weeds in grassland are frequently present in abundance. Many species may occur in impoverished grassland and these largely disappear with fertilization and improved management, however, some persist under fertile conditions to impede grazing and compete with the better grasses. These include buttercups (*Ranunculus* spp.), creeping and spear thistles (*Cirsium arvense* and *C. vulgare*), curled and broad-leaved docks (*Rumex crispus* and *R. obtusifolius*) and ragwort (*Senecio jacobaea*). The latter is poisonous to livestock particularly in hay. To these must be added the common rush (*Juncus effusus*) on poorly drained soils and bracken (*Pteridium aquilinum*) which is also harmful to cattle if eaten. All these may be largely controlled by herbicides and permanently reduced if accompanied by improved fertilization and management.

Some weeds are partial parasites of grasses, namely yellow rattle (*Rhinanthus crista-galli*), eyebright (*Euphrasia officinalis*), red bartsia (*Odontites verna*) and lousewort (*Pedicularis palustris*). These are rarely of agricultural consequence and are readily eliminated by fertilization and improved management. Broomrape (*Orabanche* spp.) is a root parasite of red clover and leguminous crops incapable of a separate existence. It is not uncommon in red clover on chalk soil.

While herbicides are not widely required on grass swards, many are now available which control weeds and undesirable species in grassland. The more commonly used herbicides are referred to in the following sections. For more information as to their use and efficacy, dose rates and other details the reader is referred to the Weed Control Handbook (Fryer & Makepeace 1978 and later editions).

2.19.2   *Controlling broad-leaved weeds in established swards*

The majority of these weeds are controlled by a spray application of the hormone type of herbicide (MCPA or 2,4-D). It needs, however, to be supported by a state of fertility that ensures vigorous growth and efficient utilization of the pasture and attention to drainage, without which weeds would re-establish. Spraying is usually carried out when the weeds are actively growing. For buttercups, other than bulbous buttercup, spraying in late spring or early summer before flowering is most appropriate but it may be better to spray bulbous buttercup in the autumn when the new leaves appear. For the control of creeping thistle it is most appropriate to spray in the early flower bud stage, while a change of management to mowing, especially a silage cut, will increase the effectiveness of herbicides. Established docks in grassland are most effectively controlled by spraying with asulam when the leaves are well expanded. Many grasses are temporarily checked but it may be safely used with ryegrass and clovers, although cocksfoot and Yorkshire fog are severely checked.

Although not strictly broad-leaved weeds, rushes may be controlled by MPCA or 2,4-D spraying when well grown, and are largely eliminated if treatment includes cutting, improved fertility and attention to drainage.

Asulam gives good control of bracken when sprayed at or near full frond expansion. In the year of treatment, yellowing and distortion of the fronds may occur and the bracken dies back normally but there is little or no regrowth the following year. It is essential that spraying is followed by a programme of fertilizer application, some cultivation and reseeding and adequate stock control to prevent re-incursion of bracken.

On established grassland where it is necessary to safeguard the contribution of white clover to the swards, MCPB or 2,4-DB herbicides should be used or mixtures with a smaller proportion of MCPA or 2,4-D.

2.19.3   *Control of grass weeds in established swards*

Differences exist between grass species in their response to herbicides although at present neither the range of herbicides nor the degree of selectivity is comparable to that available for the control of broad-leaved weeds. Thus a small dose of dalapon in June or July is much more toxic to creeping bent, Yorkshire fog and *Poa* spp. than to perennial ryegrass.

To be effective, swards must contain as much perennial ryegrass as susceptible grasses and little or no red fescue since this is not affected and may rapidly increase. Tussock grass (*D. caespitosa*) is not affected but this species can be controlled by spot treatment with dalapon.

In established perennial ryegrass swards autumn application of ethofumesate or methabenzthiazuron gives good control of *Poa* spp. and of seedling blackgrass (*A. myosuroides*).

2.19.4   Grass control in established legume crops

Grasses readily colonize legume stands and increase particularly after the first harvest year. They are particularly troublesome in lucerne that is intended to last several years. Late winter application of paraquat, when the legumes are dormant, gives good control of *Poa* spp. and chickweed. Carbetamide will, in addition, give useful control of ryegrass and blackgrass. Propyzamide, applied in late winter, has also proved useful in controlling grass weeds in these crops.

2.19.5   Controlling weeds in newly sown swards

Erect annual weeds in newly sown swards without a cover crop may be controlled by mowing but this is ineffective with rosette type and prostrate weeds (shepherds purse, cleavers, knotgrass). In grass-only swards a wide range of herbicides may be used such as those based on MCPA, 2,4-D, mecoprop, dichlorprop and mixtures of these and other herbicides to deal with particular weed species. Grass seedlings are tolerant to these herbicides after the development of three leaves.

A few herbicides, for example methabenzthiazuron and ethofumesate, can be used to control the seedlings of grasses such as *Poa* spp., blackgrass and Yorkshire fog in ryegrass swards.

Broad-leaved weeds in establishing grass-legume mixtures may be controlled by the use of MCPB and 2,4-DB. Legume seedlings are tolerant to these herbicides after the development of the first trifoliate leaf. However, 2,4-DB is slightly more toxic to red clover than MCPB and MCPB is not recommended for use on lucerne.

2.19.6   Chemical sward destruction for reseeding

In many situations the chemical destruction of a sward as an alternative to ploughing will have attractions and advantages. In open swards free of plant debris seed may be direct drilled without cultivation or a normal seedbed prepared by shallow cultivation. The presence of a thick mat requires more cultivation, rotovating being particularly suitable. Further destruction of the mat will take place if left over winter. Spraying is most effective when swards present a short cover of green growing herbage.

Paraquat gives a rapid desiccation of the turf and an effective kill of most grasses, but control of fine-leaved fescues, tussock grass and cocksfoot requires heavy doses. Split applications are more effective against resistant species. Deep-rooted broad-leaved perennial weeds are best controlled by previous application of appropriate herbicides. Glyphosate is foliage-absorbed, rapidly translocated throughout the plant, and effective against all grasses which are generally killed at lower dose rates than broad-leaved species. After paraquat, reseeding may be carried out preferably about ten days after spraying, but glyphosate is slow-acting and a two to four week interval is recommended.

Dalapon, although effective against grasses, gives poor control of broad-leaved weeds which must be dealt with by other herbicides. It is also slow-acting, persists longer in the soil, and reseeding is not recommended earlier than six weeks after spraying. It is most frequently used in the autumn followed by sowing in the spring.

2.20   DISEASES AND PESTS OF HERBAGE CROPS

Herbage crops are hosts to many invertebrate pests and diseases caused by fungi and viruses. Some are known to reduce yield, persistency or herbage quality, but the influence on yield and performance of many pests and diseases is uncertain and assessment of their influence on productivity is difficult. The pests and diseases dealt with below are the most important occurring in Britain. Further information on diseases of grass and legumes is given by Sampson & Western (1954). Their distribution and prevalence are dealt with by Moore (1959) and their control in grass and fodder crops by Gair & Roberts (1969). The life history of pests and their control are given by Jones & Jones (1964) and Edwards & Heath (1964). The diseases and pests of herbage seed crops and their control are to be found in publications on this subject (MAFF 1968, Welsh Plant Breeding Station 1978).

2.20.1   *Fungal diseases of grasses*

Rusts. The causal agencies, *Puccinia* spp. and *Uromyces dactylidis* invade all herbage grasses but rust is most common in ryegrasses in the southern half of Britain and prevalent in warm summers and autumns. Rust in ryegrass is less abundant under good conditions for growth, including high nitrogen fertilization and frequent defoliation. Severely affected herbage is unpalatable to livestock. Some ryegrass cultivars show a degree of resistance to common rust, and cultivars of timothy and cocksfoot resistant to timothy rust and stripe rust respectively are available.

Choke (Epichloe typhina) is a systemic fungus, infecting many grasses but more common in cocksfoot, timothy and fescues. The presence of infection is apparent when a stromatic sheath binds leaves together, frequently preventing ear emergence. The disease is not of significance in herbage crops, but reduces yield of seed. It most frequently occurs in seed crops of cocksfoot. If present in the early years, it will cause serious reductions in yield after the third year. There are no adequate control measures.

Powdery mildew (Erisyphe graminis) may infect most grasses and may temporarily reduce growth and affect yield. It may be controlled by appropriate systemic fungicides.

Blind-seed disease of ryegrass (Gloeotinia temulenta) is the most common cause of unexpectedly low germination in apparently normal samples of perennial ryegrass and, less frequently, Italian ryegrass. The disease is most common in the wetter and cooler areas of Britain. The spores infect the developing ovules, early infection destroys the embryonic tissue, but later infection may not destroy the embryo and these latter seeds, if sown, spread the disease. For seed production, it is important to sow seed from a healthy crop. The fungus can be destroyed by hot water treatment of infected seed.

Ergot (Claviceps purpurea) attacks most grasses. A proportion of the ripe seed is replaced by horn-shaped black or purplish black ergots that normally are longer than the glumes. They are most numerous in inflorescences developed late in wet seasons, are rarely numerous in seed crops and most are removed in seed cleaning. Ergots, if eaten by livestock in sufficient quantities, are poisonous (Woods *et al.* 1966). The simple expedient of topping pastures late in the seasons will give adequate protection.

Damping-off diseases caused by a number of fungi of the genera *Drechslera, Cylindrocarpon, Fusarium, Pythium, Rhizoctonia* may cause seedling deaths in all herbage grasses. These are seed- and soil-borne pathogens that may affect establishment of grass and clover seeds. Control can be obtained by dressing the seed with captan or difolatan but the general need of fungicidal seed dressings has not yet been established (Michail & Carr 1966, Carr 1967, Tribe & Herriott 1969).

A number of fungi cause lesions on grass leaves. *Drechslera* spp. cause leaf spot and net blotch in ryegrass and *Mastigosporium* leaf fleck in cocksfoot and timothy. These diseases rarely cause damage and are reduced under conditions of vigorous growth and efficient utilization which prevent accumulation of herbage by under-utilization.

2.20.2   *Fungal diseases of herbage legumes*

Clover rot (*Sclerotinia trifoliorum*) is a most serious disease of herbage legumes, particularly of red clover. It is present in the majority of red clover crops in the arable areas of England, but less prevalent elsewhere (Lester & Large 1958). Its significance in reducing the contribution of white clover in leys is becoming increasingly apparent. It also causes reduction in stands of giant sainfoin and causes death of stems in lucerne. In red clover, the disease becomes evident in the autumn as necrotic spots on the leaves. The fungus spreads within the stems and into the crowns causing the death of individual plants. The disease perennates by the production of sclerotia in the stems and crowns which drop on the soil, producing sporulating bodies and spores in the following summer. The sclerotia persist in the soil for many years. Fungicides such as quintozene and benomyl may give good control. In practice, the best control is obtained by choosing varieties most resistant to clover rot in the case of red and white clover.

Verticillium wilt (*V. albo-atrum*) is a common disease where much lucerne is grown, causing wilting of entire stems and death of whole plants. The disease incidence increases with the age of the crop and can severely impair yield. The fungus is retained in dead tissue, in soil and the seeds may carry spores. Resistant varieties are available.

Powdery mildew (*Erysiphe polygoni*) commonly occurs in red clover, sainfoin and crimson clover, most severe in the autumn, affecting yield and palatability of herbage. Downy mildew (*Peronospora trifolium*) occurs on all herbage legumes. Scorch of red clover (*Kabatiella caulivora*), although not common, may severely affect crops in wet seasons. Leaflets of affected plants hang down giving a shrivelled, scorched appearance. Yield of herbage and seed can be severely affected. The disease is carried over from year to year on decayed plant debris. Species of *Pseudopeziza* cause leaf spot in all herbage legumes, occasionally causing leaf loss in late autumn.

2.20.3 *Pests of grasses*

Grassland normally harbours a wide range of pests and their influence on the productivity and persistency of sown species is not well understood. The damage caused to individual plants may be compensated for by increase of growth of adjacent plants and so go unnoticed. It is only when damage is extensive or intensely local that sward destruction becomes obvious. The build-up of above-ground pests is observable before the occurrence of serious damage, but the depredations of underground pests are unsuspected until the damage is obvious. Both types of pests are more readily noticeable during the establishment of sown swards.

Of the root-feeding pests, wireworms, the larvae of click beetles (*Agriotes* and *Althous* spp.) are most abundant in old swards. Their effect is rarely observable in established swards, but they may cause seedling death in new sowings. Good cultivations and well consolidated seed beds minimize damage. Leatherjackets, the larvae of craneflies (*Tipula* spp.), damage the roots of most grasses, severing them just below the soil surface. They are most active in the spring, causing the death of many plants in severe cases.

Chafer grubs, the larvae of chafer beetles, cause damage similar to that of leatherjackets. Normally this occurs in rough pasture in small areas and rarely on well managed swards. The caterpillars of the Antler Moth occasionally cause substantial damage to upland pastures in the North of England.

The general control of invertebrates in grassland by the use of the pesticide aldrin on a series of sites increased annual yield of ryegrass dominant swards by between nil and 30 per cent (Henderson & Clements 1977). The degree of response was connected with the population, on the control plots, of aphids (*Aphididae*), plant-sucking bugs (*Jassidae, Delphacidae, Cercopidae*), and stem-boring flies and their larvae. The last were considered to be particularly involved. Of the grasses, the ryegrasses, smooth-stalked meadow grass, *Agrostis* and red fescue harbour large populations of dipterous stem-boring larvae, but cocksfoot, timothy and tall fescue relatively few (Jepson & Heard 1959). Differences between varieties of the ryegrasses have been demonstrated (Henderson & Clements 1979, Clements 1980).

The larvae of the cocksfoot moth (*Glyphipterix cramerella*) attack seed crops causing minute holes in seeds and stems and reduce seed yields. Although common, infestation is rarely serious and build-up of harmful populations of the moth is prevented by burning of stubble and straw after harvest. Grass seed midges attack the seed heads of most grasses, but only infrequently reduce seed yield (except in meadow foxtail). Many species of aphids infest the cultivated grasses, but only assume importance with the build-up of harmful populations in seed crops. If necessary, aphids may be controlled by organophosphorus insecticides. The presence of timothy flies (*Amacerosoma* spp.) is indicated by parts of the inflorescence being stripped bare of florets where the larvae have fed while the inflorescence is still within the leaf sheath.

2.20.4 *Pests of herbage legumes*

Stem eelworm (*Ditylenchus dipsaci*) causes severe disorder in red clover and lucerne and also attacks white clover, trefoil, crimson clover and sainfoin. Eelworm is soil- and seed-borne. In established plants, eelworm causes stunting and swollen stem bases, nodes and petioles. Soil-borne infestation normally occurs in patches whereas seed-borne infestation is scattered. Seed infection can be controlled by fumigation with methyl bromide. Soil-borne infestation is long-lived. In such cases, varieties resistant to eelworm which are available in red clover and lucerne, should be chosen.

Pea and bean weevils (*Sitona* spp.) in districts growing beans and peas can cause damage and death of germinating seeds of clovers and lucerne by eating the cotyledons and juvenile leaves. Prompt insecticidal treatment at the cotyledon stage will give control. Seedling establishment of herbage legumes may also be affected by wireworms, slugs and leatherjackets, but good cultivations and the preparation of a good seed bed do much to minimize their effects.

Clover seed weevils (*Apion* spp.) on occasion cause seed losses in red and white clover. Adult beetles feed on the foliage and deposit eggs in the flower buds and the larvae devour the ovules. Seed crops of red clover should be isolated from hay crops. Cutting or grazing of the first growth of early and late red clover reduces the incidence, but further reduction is obtained by treating with DDT no later than two weeks after cutting the first growth in the case of early red clover, but immediately after the final grazing or topping on late flowering red clover.

2.20.5 *Virus diseases of grasses and herbage legumes*

The viruses of cocksfoot mottle and cocksfoot streak have on occasion caused considerable reduction in yield of cocksfoot swards and the barley yellow dwarf virus has been found in most cultivated grasses. Ryegrass mosaic virus is common in Italian and perennial ryegrass in the South of England and perhaps elsewhere. A high incidence will reduce crop growth. A number of viruses have been reported in white and red clover, lucerne and sainfoin, but there is little evidence to assess their effect on yield. Clover phyllody is caused by a mycoplasmic infection transmitted by leaf hoppers and common in white clover. The inflorescences of infected plants are transformed into leafy structures that set no seed. Small-leaved white clovers are less affected than larger-leaved varieties.

FURTHER READING

DAVIES W. (1960) *The Grass Crop.* Spon, London
FORBES T. J., DIBB C., GREEN J. O., HOPKINS A. & PEEL S. (1980) Factors affecting the productivity of permanent grassland. *The Permanent Pasture.* Grassland Research Institute, Hurley.
HODGSON J. *et al.* (eds) (1981) *Sward Measurement Handbook.* British Grassland Society, Hurley.
HUBBARD C. E. (1968) *Grasses.* Penguin Books, Harmondsworth, Middlesex
LANGER R. H. M. (1972) *How Grasses Grow.* Edward Arnold Ltd., London.
MILTHORPE F. L. & IVINS J. D. (eds) (1966) *The Growth of Cereals and Grasses.* Butterworth, London
PRINS W. H. & ARNOLD G. H. (eds) (1980) *The role of nitrogen in intensive grassland production.* Centre for Agricultural Publishing and Documentation. Wageningen, Netherlands.
SPEDDING C. R. W. (1971) *Grassland Ecology.* Clarendon Press, Oxford
SPEDDING C. R. W. & DIEKMAHNS E. C. (eds) (1972) *Grasses and Legumes in British Agriculture,* Bulletin 49, Commonwealth Bureau of Pastures and Field Crops. Commonwealth Agricultural Bureaux, Farnham Royal
THOMAS J. O. & DAVIES L. J. (1964) *Common British Grasses and Legumes,* 4e. Longman Group Ltd., London

Chapter 3

The feeding value of
grass and grass products

The value of a forage for animal production, its feeding value, is the product of the concentration of nutrients contained in the forage (nutritive value) and the amount of forage an animal will eat (voluntary intake). The more nutrients an animal eats in excess of its maintenance requirements, the more nutrients are available for the deposition of tissue or the secretion of milk, and the greater is the gross efficiency with which the animal converts food into animal products. This is particularly true for ruminant animals eating forage diets because in many instances the nature of the forage can limit the animal's intake.

Various attempts have been made to resolve the relative importance of intake and nutritive value in determining the feeding value of forages. It may be concluded that intake contributes at least equally with nutritive value in determining the feeding value of forages, and both are determined by the structure and chemical composition of pasture plants.

3.1   THE STRUCTURE AND CHEMICAL CONSTITUENTS OF PASTURE PLANTS

3.1.1   *Structure*

The grass harvested by the grazing animal or when the sward is cut comprises leaf blades and leaf sheaths, the latter forming a pseudo-stem. As the tillers enter the reproductive phase, the stem or peduncle elongates, carrying the inflorescence and ultimately the seeds above the leaf canopy. In the forage legume, leaflets, petioles, stem and inflorescences are readily distinguished, although in white clover the true stem is prostrate and stoloniferous, only the petioles standing erect above it. The proportion that each morphological part of these plants contributes to the whole varies considerably with season and stage of growth but in general the proportion of leaf indicates the approximate nutritive value of the crop.

As the leaf canopy increases to exclude all light at ground level, the lower leaves begin to senesce and die. In Figure 3.1 these changes in the proportions of leaf, dead leaf, stem and inflorescence are illustrated for Italian ryegrass from the data of Wilman *et al.* (1976).

Histologically the plant comprises tissues varying from the parenchyma tissue of the leaves which have thin cell walls and are packed with cytoplasm and actively synthesizing chloroplasts, to the very thick-walled elongated cells of the sclerenchyma tissues, associated with the water and nutrient conducting vessels of the vascular bundles. These together provide the skeleton of both leaves and stems. Again the proportions of these tissues in each organ vary with age; the proportion of the thick-walled tissues increases as the plant matures.

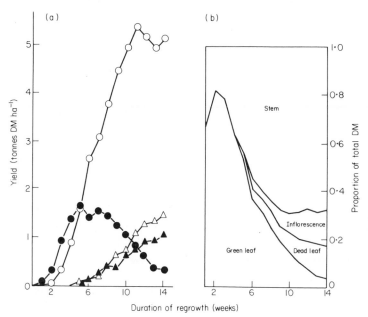

FIGURE 3.1. The morphological development of a crop of S22 Italian ryegrass over fourteen weeks after a cut in late April (after Wilman *et al.* 1976). (a) Dry matter yields: ○, stem; ●, green leaf; ▲, dead leaf; △, inflorescence. (b) DM proportional contribution of morphological fractions.

3.1.2   *The chemical constituents of pasture plants*

A useful nutritional and a simple empirical chemical division of plant material is into the cell contents (CC) and the cell walls (CW). This is achieved chemically by refluxing the dried ground plant material with a detergent solution at a neutral pH, when the cell contents are dissolved and the cell walls remain (Van Soest & Wine 1967b). The cell contents include the nucleus, cytoplasm and plastids containing most of the plant's proteins, peptides, amino acids, nucleic acids and lipids. In addition, the minerals and organic acids together with the α-linked carbohydrates, glucose, fructose, sucrose, fructans and starches are concentrated in the cell contents. Although chemically dissimilar, the contents of the cell are nutritionally similar in that they are all almost entirely digested by the enzymes of the animal's digestive system.

The cell wall fraction of the plant contains pectic substances which make up the middle lamella and function as an intercellular cement and the structural polysaccharides, hemicellulose and cellulose, which are incorporated into the cell wall as it thickens with age. None of the domestic livestock secrete enzymes capable of degrading hemicellulose or cellulose but the symbiotic microorganisms living in the reticulo-rumen and caecum of ruminants and herbivores do secrete polysaccharidases.

As plants mature, lignin, a polymerous complex of three phenyl propanoid alcohols, is deposited in the cell walls in increasing quantities. The lignin confers rigidity on the plastic matrix of polysaccharides. Lignin itself is extremely stable and is only slowly degraded in nature by oxidative processes, brought about by saprophytic, wood-rotting fungi. Lignin not only encrusts the cell wall polysaccharides but also forms chemical bonds which prevent the cell wall matrix from swelling, a prerequisite for the penetration of microbial polysaccharidases. The result of the localized lignification of the cell walls in certain tissues is to render parts of the cell wall fraction unavailable to microbial digestion.

3.2   FACTORS AFFECTING THE CHEMICAL COMPOSITION OF HERBAGE PLANTS

3.2.1   *Maturity, stage of growth*

The major changes in composition occurring in pasture plants are those that accompany maturation, illustrated schematically in

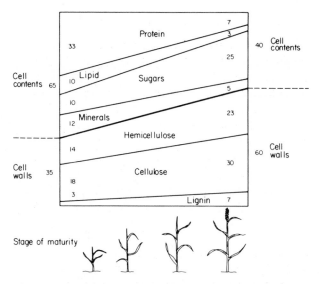

FIGURE 3.2. Schematic representation of the changes in the chemical composition of grasses which accompany advancing maturity.

Figure 3.2. As the grass plant matures, the proportion of cell walls and its constituent fractions increases and the cell content fraction decreases. The proportion of protein, lipid and mineral matter in the dry matter decreases as the plant matures, but the non-structural carbohydrates, mainly fructans, in the stem, stem base and inflorescence increase. The proportion of the crude protein that is true protein or amino-acids varies from 70 to 90% and the composition of the total amino-acid fraction is remarkably constant in both grasses and legumes at all stages of maturity.

3.2.2 *Variation in composition between species*

Leguminous forages have a lower content of cell walls than grasses at comparable stages of growth, a higher pectin content (4–7%, grasses 1–3%); a markedly lower ratio of hemicellulose to cellulose (0·5–0·7 : 1, grasses 0·7–0·9 : 1) and higher lignin contents. Relative to grasses, legumes contain a higher proportion of crude protein, organic acids and mineral elements and a lower proportion of water-soluble carbohydrates, but the presence of amylopectins in the legumes results in similar levels of total non-structural carbohydrates in grasses and legumes (Smith 1972).

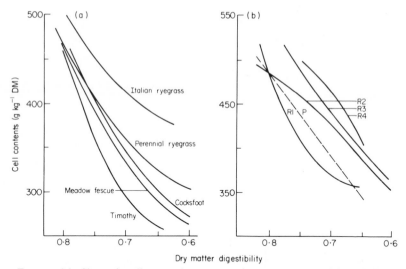

FIGURE 3.3. Change in cell content in grasses as the crop matures and digestibility declines. (a) Primary growth of five grass species. (b) Primary growth (P) and regrowths of S24 perennial ryegrass initiated following cutting of the primary growth on 12 April, R1; 26 April, R2; 24 May, R3, and 7 June, R4.

At immature, leafy stages of growth most grass species have similar ratios of cell walls to cell contents. One notable exception among the temperate grass species is Italian ryegrass (*Lolium multiflorum*) which has a distinctly higher proportion of cell contents (mainly fructans) than other grass species. This characteristic of Italian ryegrass persists as the grasses mature. Timothy (*Phleum pratense*) develops a higher proportion of cell walls than do perennial ryegrass, cocksfoot or meadow fescue at the more mature growth stages (Figure 3.3a). Characteristic and heritable differences in the proportions of crude protein and water-soluble carbohydrates and specific mineral element concentrations exist between species and varieties. Chemical composition may, therefore, be changed by selection, but this may often be accompanied by undesirable changes such as reduced seed production or increased incidence of disease (Cooper 1973).

3.2.3 Environmental factors

Increased light intensity increases the water-soluble carbohydrates (WSC) in grasses, as does decreasing day and night temperature, especially at high light intensities. Conversely, high light intensity and high ambient temperatures increase the proportion of cell walls in the plant and their degree of lignification. Increasing nitrogen supply increases the proportion of crude protein and reduces the proportions of WSC and cellulose in grass plants (Waite 1970). Irrigation has no effect upon chemical composition.

In practice, the factors affecting chemical composition interact with cutting or grazing management to produce regional and seasonal changes in the chemical composition of the harvested crop, which result as much from changes in leaf/stem ratio as from environmental factors. Thus in Figure 3.3b the initiation of regrowth by defoliation of the primary growth of S24 in early April failed to remove the inflorescence primordia and resulted in a very stemmy regrowth and a crop with a significantly lower cell content, typical of hay crops taken after an early bite. Successive regrowths initiated by later defoliation of the primary growth removed most of these primordia and produced leafier crops with progressively higher cell contents.

A major feature of grass and legume crops is their extremely variable chemical composition. The variation induced by management decisions on stage of growth at harvest and by soil and climatic factors is several times greater than the variation between varieties and between species within the grasses. To understand the significance of these changes upon the nutritive value of forages it is necessary to consider the processes of digestion in ruminant animals.

3.3 DIGESTION IN THE RUMINANT

3.3.1 *The ruminant digestive tract*

Ruminant animals are characterized by the development of a forestomach comprising three diverticula or compartments anterior to the true stomach, the abomasum (Moir 1968). Food eaten by the animal is subjected to preliminary chewing which ruptures cell walls releasing considerable quantities of the cell contents. Saliva is secreted into the mouth in large amounts and mixed with the food to form a bolus which passes down the oesophagus into the rumen, the first and largest of the forestomach's compartments. Digesta pass freely between the rumen and the second compartment, the reticulum, in response to cyclic muscular contractions.

Passage into the third stomach, the omasum, through the reticulo-omasal orifice is restricted to fluids and small food particles in suspension. The necessary reduction in particle size is achieved largely by the regurgitation of digesta from the rumen into the mouth where saliva is added again and the digesta are subjected to prolonged chewing or rumination prior to being reswallowed. The reflex mechanism of regurgitation which initiates rumination is a response to the physical stimulus of coarse fibrous food particles in the rumen. As rumination proceeds it reduces particle size eventually removing the stimulus for regurgitation.

The reticulo-rumen serves as a large reservoir in which to store bulky food consumed throughout the day. Within the reticulo-rumen the digesta are maintained at a near constant temperature, in anaerobic conditions, and amply supplied with a sodium phosphate buffer, the saliva, maintaining a pH between 5·5 and 7·0. This and the flow of nutrients and water through the organ combine to create a favourable and relatively constant environment in which bacteria and protozoa develop. These micro-organisms grow and multiply, degrading the protein, structural and non structural carbohydrates to supply the energy required for the synthesis of the microbial biomass. The waste products of the microbial metabolism are volatile fatty acids, which are absorbed from the rumen to provide the major source of energy for the host animal, ammonia, absorbed and converted into urea, and methane and carbon dioxide largely eliminated from the rumen by belching.

Undigested feed constituents, lipids, proteins and carbohydrates, together with a proportion of the micro-organisms synthesized in the rumen, pass via the omasum into the acidic conditions in the abomasum and the alkaline conditions in the small intestine where host enzyme secretions continue the process of digestion, reducing feed and microbial proteins to amino-acids and α-linked polysaccharides to glucose. These, together with the long-chain fatty acids derived from dietary lipids, are absorbed from the small intestine. Any β-linked structural carbohydrates pass unchanged through the small intestine into the large intestine where they and any undigested residues of ruminal micro-organisms are subjected to a second anaerobic microbial fermentation centred largely in the caecum. This fermentation too produces volatile fatty acids (VFA) and ammonia which are absorbed, but any microbial biomass synthesized is excreted in the faeces together with undigested feed residues as there is no further host animal enzyme secretion in the colon and rectum.

3.3.2 *The bacteria and protozoa in the rumen*

The bacteria in the rumen numbering 10^{10} per ml of rumen contents utilize carbohydrate, protein and lipids contained in the food entering the rumen as a source of energy from which, together with simple inorganic forms of nitrogen and minerals, they synthesize the lipids, polysaccharides and protein of their own biomass (Hungate 1966). The protozoans are found in smaller numbers (10^6 per ml). Some types ingest both feed particles and bacteria and many utilize cellulose, but as very few protozoa can tolerate pH values of less than 5·5, they are generally much reduced in animals consuming concentrate diets which result in a marked increase in the proportion of propionic acid produced within the rumen.

3.3.3 *Microbial fermentation in the rumen*

The processes occurring in the rumen are therefore primarily the culture of a diverse population of microorganisms and the first objective of feeding ruminants must be to maintain this culture. The end products of this fermentation useful to the host animal are the microbial biomass synthesized and the volatile fatty acids. Energy balances of fermentation in the rumen indicate that some 15–25% of apparently digested energy is lost as heat of fermentation and methane, leaving 75–85% available as VFA and microbial biomass to meet the animal's energy needs.

Although the fermentation in the rumen results in some losses, the bacteria, notably the genera *Bacteriodes*, *Ruminococcus* and *Butyrivibrio*, secrete enzymes capable of degrading cellulose and hemicellulose to their constituent sugars and ultimately to VFA's. These symbiotic bacteria therefore confer a major advantage on herbivores and ruminants.

3.3.4 *The degradation of dietary constituents*

A proportion of the cell walls increasing from 10% in young, immature, leafy herbage to 70% in the most mature, stemmy herbage, is rendered unavailable by its association with the indigestible lignin. Normally 90% of the cellulose and 70% of the hemicellulose potentially digestible is degraded in the rumen. The rate of fermentation of the cell wall constituents is relatively slow and if conditions in the rumen, such as the development of a low pH, do not favour cellulolytic activity or if the rate of passage out of the rumen is increased by fine grinding or high levels of feeding, cell wall digestion may not be complete before the material leaves the rumen.

The sugars and starches in herbage cell contents are rapidly and almost completely fermented within the rumen, yielding VFA, so that little of the α-linked glucose polymer present in herbage and cereal grains reaches the small intestine.

Lipids are hydrolysed by bacteria in the rumen to glycerol and long-chain fatty acids. The former is reduced to VFA and any double bonds in the latter are largely saturated by the reducing conditions in the rumen and absorbed in the small intestine, contributing some 7–10% of the apparently digested energy.

Proteins in solution are readily degraded by bacterial proteases yielding amino-acids which may in turn be degraded to VFA and ammonia, although the intermediate formation from some amino-acids of C_4 and C_6 branched-chain fatty acids appears to be essential for the growth of some cellulolytic organisms. The pool of ammonia in the rumen formed by the degradation of dietary protein and non protein nitrogen in the diet (the ruminally degraded protein, RDP) is added to by urea entering in the saliva and across the rumen wall, and is utilized by the bacteria as the basis for the synthesis of their own proteins. Any excess ammonia is absorbed and converted to urea by the ruminant.

As with the cell wall fraction, not all protein in the diet is degraded by bacteria in the rumen. A proportion, the undegraded dietary protein (UDP), passes into the abomasum together with a portion of the microbial protein synthesized, and thence into the small intestine where both fractions are digested to amino-acids and absorbed in this form.

The quantification of the processes occurring as a result of fermentation in the rumen is being actively pursued by research workers at the present time with the objective of determining how the nutrients actually absorbed relate to the nature of the diet. However, our current measures of nutritive value and nutrient requirements are based upon the apparent digestion and utilization of the constituents of the diet as measured by input–output studies on the animal and its symbiotic micro-organisms.

3.4 MEASURES OF NUTRITIVE VALUE, DIGESTIBILITY

All ruminant animals have requirements for energy, protein, some specific nutrients and a variety of minerals and vitamins. Their requirements for these nutrients will depend upon their stage of development, size, type and level of production. If grass is to be the sole feed of the animal, then the herbage consumed must contain all the nutrients to match the animal's requirements or the desired level of performance will not be achieved. The nutritive value of a forage cannot therefore be expressed simply as one value but must ideally give the concentration of all the required nutrients contained in the forage. The useful energy and, to a lesser extent, the protein, are the nutrients showing most variation in their concentration in forages. They are also the most costly nutrients to purchase as other feeds. While minerals and vitamins are often needed to supplement the diet of a high-producing animal, forage feeds generally contain adequate amounts of these nutrients to meet the requirements of growing animals. Ruminant animals can derive energy from all the organic constituents in their diet and hence the organic matter content (dry matter – minerals) roughly approximates to the gross energy content of the diet. However, not all the organic matter in forages is digested by the ruminant animal or its symbiotic micro-organisms. It follows that a first approximation to the useful energy in forages is its concentration of digestible organic matter.

3.4.1 *The digestibility of forages*

The simplest nutritional balance between input and output that can be determined with an animal is to measure the quantity of food or dry matter consumed and the faeces voided over a fixed time period. The difference between these two values is the amount digested and, when expressed as a percentage of the amount consumed, this is termed the coefficient of digestibility of dry matter (DMD). Values for forages vary between 50 and 80%. They may be expressed as decimals, i.e. 0·5 and 0·8

$$\text{DMD} = \frac{\text{DM consumed} - \text{DM defaecated}}{\text{DM consumed}} \times 100. \quad (3.1)$$

Similar coefficients of digestibility may be determined for organic matter (OMD), cell walls, cell contents or crude protein.

3.4.2 D-value (*digestible organic matter in the dry matter, DOMD*)

The organic matter digested (DOM) expressed as a percentage, not of the organic matter consumed, but of the dry matter consumed, is not a true coefficient of digestibility and the term D-value was coined to describe it.

$$\text{D-value} = \frac{\text{OM consumed} - \text{OM defaecated}}{\text{DM consumed}} \times 100$$

$$= \frac{\text{DOM consumed}}{\text{DM consumed}} \times 100. \quad (3.2)$$

This term was developed for use in practice where forage feeds, particularly silages, are often contaminated with minerals from soil. The relationship between the major measures of digestibility, DMD OMD and D-value is shown in Figure 3.4.

The unit for feeding is generally dry matter which includes all mineral contaminants, while the energy yielding part is the organic matter. It was considered best to combine the two fractions; in this way D-values are always less than organic matter digestibility by an amount depending on the ash or mineral content of the herbage.

3.4.3 True and apparent digestibility

The constituents of the cell wall fraction of forages, cellulose hemicellulose and lignin, are chemicals found only in plants. They do not occur in animals or bacteria. The cell walls found in an animal's faeces must therefore have originated from the forage consumed by the animal and the coefficient of digestibility measured is a coefficient of true digestibility.

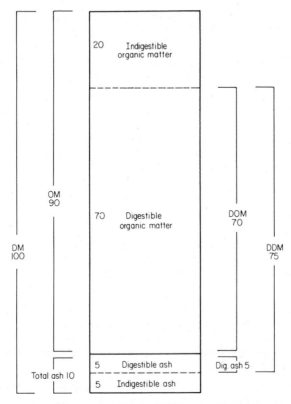

FIGURE 3.4. The relationship between digestible and indigestible plant constituents (after MAFF 1979d). DM, Dry matter; OM, Organic matter; DOM, Digestible organic matter; DDM, Digestible dry matter; DMD, Dry matter digestibility; OMD, Organic matter digestibility.

$$DMD = \frac{\text{Wt of DDM}}{\text{Wt of DM}} \times 100 = \frac{75}{100} \times 100 = 75\%$$

$$OMD = \frac{\text{Wt of DOM}}{\text{Wt of OM}} \times 100 = \frac{70}{90} \times 100 = 77.7\%$$

$$\text{D-value} = \frac{\text{Wt of DOM}}{\text{Wt of DM}} \times 100 = \frac{70}{100} \times 100 = 70\%$$

In contrast, the cell contents of plants and their constituents, crude protein, lipids, sugars and minerals, also occur in the animal tissues and microbial biomass, and it is not possible to distinguish simply between the chemicals originating from the plant, bacteria or the animal. In fact, most of the cell content in an animal's faeces is bacterial and animal in origin and so the coefficient of digestibility is termed the coefficient of apparent digestibility.

3.4.4   *Digestion of cell contents*

Van Soest & Moore (1966) demonstrated that a precise rectilinear relationship existed between the apparently digested cell contents (DCC) and cell content of grass and legume herbages. The equation describing this line when the parameters are expressed as g per kg feed DM is:

$$DCC = 0.98 \; CC - 129 \qquad RSD \pm 14.8. \qquad (3.3)$$

The slope of the line, 0·98, is close to 1·00 and indicates that the true digestion of the cell content fraction approximates to 1·0, or 100%.

The negative intercept of 129 g apparently digested cell contents when cell content in the herbage is zero indicates that for every kg of dry matter consumed 129 g of cell content material of bacterial and animal origin appears in the faeces. While this value is reasonably constant for mature wether sheep, variation has been demonstrated in lactating cows in response to changing digestibility of the diet (Van Soest & Wine 1967a) and the concept has been challenged on theoretical grounds by Aerts *et al.* (1978).

3.4.5   *Cell wall digestibility*

The true digestibility of the cell wall fraction of herbages varies considerably, declining as the plant matures and lignified tissues develop. Van Soest (1967) showed that cell wall digestibility (CWD) is related to the degree of lignification when this is expressed as the acid detergent lignin × 100/acid detergent fibre (L). The relationship is curvilinear but can be transformed to a linear function by relating cell wall digestibility (expressed as a decimal) to the logarithm to the base 10 of the degree of lignification (L).

$$CWD = 1.473 - 0.789 \log L \qquad RSD \pm 0.042. \qquad (3.4)$$

Much of the curvilinearity is accounted for by the differences between grasses and legumes. Legumes have high lignin contents but this does not seem to depress the digestibility of the cell walls as much as an equivalent quantity of lignin in grasses. The contribution of the cell wall fraction to the dry matter digested, the digestible cell wall (DCW), is simply the product of the cell wall content (g per kg DM) and cell wall digestibility.

3.4.6   *The contribution of cell wall to the total dry matter digested*

The DMD of a herbage is the sum of the apparently digested cell contents (DCC) and the digestible cell walls, DMD = DCC + DCW. In Figure 3.5 the changing proportions of cell content and cell wall and their contribution to digested dry matter as the plant matures are shown schematically. As the plant matures, cell wall content increases, but cell wall digestibility declines simultaneously so that the digested cell wall tends to remain relatively constant. At the same time, cell content declines and as the endogenous secretions remain constant the apparent digestibility of the cell content fraction quickly declines, causing the apparently digested cell content to decline even more rapidly.

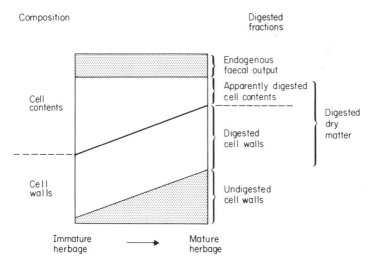

FIGURE 3.5. Schematic representation of the changes in composition, cell content and cell wall and their digestion, as a grass plant matures.

Cell walls contribute only 20–40% of the DOM in legumes, in marked contrast to the grasses in which the contribution ranges from 45–65% with only the immature stages of Italian ryegrass falling below this range. Within the grass species, Italian ryegrass is characterized by the lowest proportion of DCW in the DOM, Timothy has the highest proportion and perennial ryegrass is intermediate.

3.4.7 Changes in the D-value of primary growth herbage

The leafy growth initiated in the spring has a very high D-value in all grass species, 74–77% in the sown grass species. As the crop grows and DM yield increases, stem formation is initiated and the

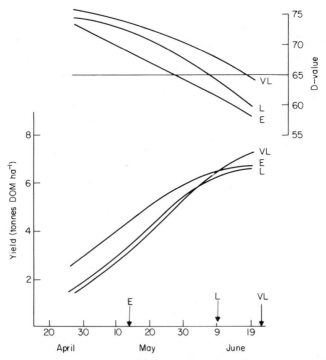

FIGURE 3.6. Changes in the D-value and yield of DOM (t per ha) of Early (E), Late (L) and Very Late (VL) flowering varieties of perennial ryegrass during primary growth.

ratio of leaf to stem declines rapidly, causing the cell wall content and its degree of lignification to increase. The net effect of these changes is to produce a characteristic pattern of decline in the D-value of the whole crop. The timing of this pattern of change of D-value is peculiar to each grass species and variety being largely determined by the earliness or lateness of flowering (Figure 3.6). For any one variety it is repeated annually, the actual timing being affected only by the locality and the relative earliness or lateness of the spring in that locality.

Typical patterns of decline of D-value for the major grass and legume species are shown in Figure 3.7. Amongst the grasses, cocksfoot is characterized by a lower initial D-value than the other species, while Italian ryegrass and Timothy show a slower rate of decline, 3·0 units D-value per week, than do the other species, which decline at a rate of 3·5 units per week.

Amongst the legumes, white clover is unique, with a very high D-value which declines at the rate of only 0·8 units of D-value per week. The erect legumes, red clover, lucerne and sainfoin, commence

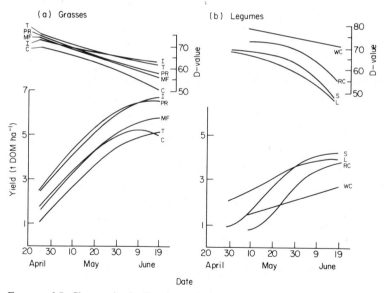

FIGURE 3.7. Changes in the D-value and yield of DOM (t per ha) of (a) grass species, and (b) legume species, during primary growth. I, Italian ryegrass; T, Timothy; PR, Perennial ryegrass; MF, Meadow fescue; C, Cocksfoot; WC, White clover; RC, Red clover; L, Lucerne; S, Sainfoin.

growth later and have a lower initial D-value than grasses. Their rate of decline of D-value is slower than grasses but much faster than white clover, being 2·5, 2·5 and 2·8 units per week for red clover, sainfoin and lucerne.

The whole crop D-value depends upon the leaf : stem ratio of the crop. On average the rate of decline of D-value for the leaf lamina, leaf sheath and stem of ryegrass during primary growth is 1·5, 3·0 and 5·5 units per week.

3.4.8   The D-value of regrowth herbage

The practice of taking an early bite from a pasture before putting it up for hay or silage removes leaf while leaving the stem primordia intact. The resulting crop for conservation is of lower yield and much stemmier, and shows a more rapid decline in D-value than uninterrupted primary growth. Progressively later defoliation of the primary growth removes stem primordia now carried above ground level and so produces leafier regrowths characterized by a slower rate of decline of D-value. Leafy crops developing in early summer, because of the higher temperature and light conditions, do not develop the high D-values found in the early spring growth but, because of the lack of stem development, the rate of decline of D-value is much slower than primary growth—of the order of 1·5 to 2·0 units D-value per week.

3.4.9   The D-value of grazed herbages

Animals grazing a sward, be it rotationally grazed or continuously grazed, select herbage of higher D-value than the herbage on offer (Table 3.1). Cattle achieve some degree of selection even at high grazing intensities, but only at the expense of reducing their intake.

There is evidence to suggest that cattle grazing any well-managed, productive grass sward will select herbage of higher D-value (75) in the spring than in mid season (69) or in the autumn (71). The inclusion of white clover in a grass sward in significant quantities increases the D-value of the herbage on offer, and sheep in particular exert a positive selection for white clover.

While stage of growth, climate and management are the major determinants of D-value, choice of variety can assist in the determination of the date during primary growth when the crop

TABLE 3.1. The organic matter digestibility (OMD%) (determined *in vitro*) of herbage on offer and consumed by cattle, strip grazing or continuously stocked, on a grass sward (Tayler & Deriaz 1963).

| | Strip grazed | | Continuously stocked | |
	Herbage on offer	Herbage eaten	Herbage on offer	Herbage eaten
April	77	83	62	80
May	76	79	67	76
August	62	70	60	74
September	60	70	60	74

achieves a desired D-value. Alternatively, the use of three varieties of ryegrass, as illustrated in Figure 3.6, allows a period of one month (15 May to 15 June at Hurley) during which herbage may be harvested at between 68 and 65 D-value.

3.5 ENERGY AS A MEASURE OF NUTRITIVE VALUE

The basic unit of energy is the joule, equivalent to 0·239 calories. In nutrition it is convenient to use a much larger unit, the megajoule (MJ), equal to one million joules.

Complete combustion of a food in oxygen produces carbon dioxide and water and releases as heat the total energy contained within the food. The heat released per kg DM is termed the gross energy (GE), heat of combustion, calorific value or energy value (EV) of the food. The sum of the energy value of the constituents of a feed equals the EV of the feed. Ash or mineral constituents have no energy value but each organic constituent has a specific value. Carbohydrates have varying values averaging about 17·5 MJ per kg. Protein and fats too have various values depending upon their exact chemical composition but averaging one and a half and two and a half times the value of carbohydrates.

The processes of digestion and metabolism whereby an animal obtains its energy are not achieved with complete efficiency and energy is lost in the process in a variety of forms (see Figure 3.8). These losses of energy can be measured. Deduction of the energy contained in the faeces leaves as the residue the digested energy (DE). Further deduction of the energy value of the methane produced during digestion and the urine excreted leaves a residue

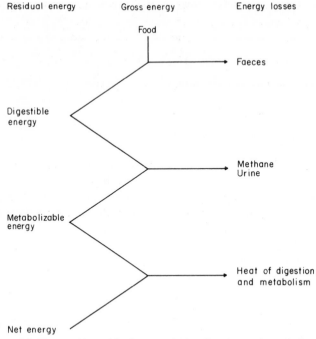

FIGURE 3.8. The partition of food energy during digestion and metabolism by an animal.

termed the metabolizable energy (ME). This term is illogical because the energy lost as heat of fermentation precedes absorption while the energy lost as the urine arises as the result of metabolism. The difficulty of directly measuring the heat of fermentation is the basis of this anomaly. When the heat increment (HI) resulting from the digestion and metabolism of feed is determined and subtracted from the metabolizable energy, the residue remaining is the net energy made available to the animal. Each of these residual energy values has been used as a measure of both the energy value of feeds and to express the energy requirements of animals.

3.5.1   *The energy value of herbage*

Because of their varying chemical composition, the EV of herbages varies also. The equation given below was developed at the Oskar Kellner Institute in East Germany to predict the EV of feeds (MJ

THE FEEDING VALUE OF GRASS

per kg DM) from a knowledge of their proximate composition as crude protein (CP), ether extract (EE), crude fibre (CF) and nitrogen free extract (NFE) and their average energy values.

$$EV = 0.0226 \text{ CP} + 0.0407 \text{ EE} + 0.0192 \text{ CF} + 0.0177 \text{ NFE}$$

$$RSD = \pm 0.2 \text{ MJ per kg DM.} \tag{3.5}$$

3.5.2 Digested energy and the energy value of digested organic matter

Although widely used as a close approximation to energy value, the D-value of a herbage is not simply related to digested energy because of the variable chemical composition of herbages of the same D-value. However, herbages contain very little lipid and their content is highly correlated with the crude protein content of the herbage. Hence for fresh grasses there is a linear increase in

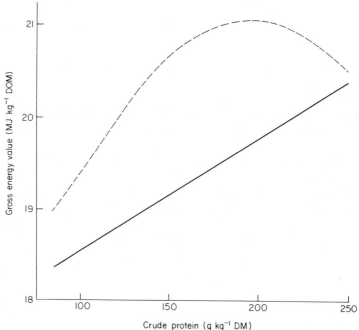

FIGURE 3.9. Relationship between the energy value of digested organic matter and crude protein content for fresh grass (———) and silages (-----).

the energy value of DOM with increasing crude protein content (see Figure 3.9). During the process of ensiling, the low energy value sugars are fermented to CO_2, water and acids of lower energy value, and the higher energy value polysaccharides, protein and lipids are thereby concentrated. The energy value of the DOM of silages is, therefore, higher than that of the grass from which it was made and appears to show a curvilinear relationship with crude protein content. The digested energy (MJ DE per kg DM) may therefore be accurately predicted in forages from a knowledge of D-value *in vivo* and crude protein content (g CP per kg DM).

Grass:

$$DE = 0.1866 \text{ D-value} + 0.00866 \text{ CP} - 0.920 \tag{3.6}$$

$$RSD = \pm 0.175 \text{ MJ DE per kg DM}$$

Silages:

$$DE = 0.2136 \text{ D-value} + 0.041 \text{ CP} - 0.000103 \text{ CP}^2 - 4.219 \tag{3.7}$$

$$RSD = \pm 0.279 \text{ MJ DE per kg DM}$$

As a rough guide, for forages of 120–150 g CP per kg DM, DE can be assessed as $0.19 \times$ D-value.

3.5.3   *Metabolizable energy*

The unit proposed in the Agricultural Research Council's Technical Review No 2—Ruminants, 1965, and in Technical Bulletin 33 Energy Allowances and Feeding Systems for Ruminants (MAFF 1975) for equating the energy supplied by a diet to the ruminant animal's requirement, was metabolizable energy (ME).

Since the losses of energy as methane and urine vary around 19% of the DE, ME can be predicted simply as

$$ME \text{ (MJ per kg DM)} = 0.81 \text{ DE} \tag{3.8}$$

or by transformation of equations derived to predict DE

$$ME = 0.15 \text{ D-value} \tag{3.9}$$

$$ME = 0.151 \text{ D-value} + 0.0070 \text{ CP} - 0.745 \text{ (fresh grass)} \tag{3.10}$$

$$ME = 0.173 \text{ D-value} + 0.0333 \text{ CP} - 0.000083 \text{ CP}^2 - 3.41 \text{ (silages)}. \tag{3.11}$$

Directly derived equations based upon the digested proximate constituents of the diet have been published as indicated below

$$ME = 0{\cdot}0152\ DCP + 0{\cdot}0342\ DEE + 0{\cdot}0128\ DCF + 0{\cdot}0159\ DNFE.$$

(3.12)

3.5.4 Net energy

Subtraction of the total heat output of the animal from the metabolizable energy consumed leaves the residual net energy available to the animal. The efficiency with which metabolizable energy is used by the animal depends on the process for which the energy is used. Thus separate efficiencies represented by the term k can be identified for maintenance (km), growth (kf) and lactation (kl). For maintenance and growth metabolizable energy is used more efficiently as the ME concentration of the diet is increased. In contrast kl does not vary very much with ME concentration (see Table 3.2). In the current ME system in use in the UK, these variations in efficiency are taken into account in the definition of the animal's requirements. Transformation of the ME system into a variable net energy system simplifies the calculations required to formulate a diet and is illustrated in detail in MAFF Bulletin 33 for cattle and sheep.

While the system described above has proved extremely sound for mixed forage/concentrate diets and for milk production, its use for forage diets and for growing animals needs further refinement. Recent research has established that the relationship between kf and ME concentration is different for all-forage diets and mixed diets. Furthermore, kf, at a given ME concentration, is higher for legumes than for grasses and higher for grass grown in the spring than for

TABLE 3.2. Variation of the efficiency of use of metabolizable energy with physiological function and with the concentration of ME in the diet.

ME concentration in the diet (MJ kg⁻¹ DM)	Efficiency of use of metabolizable energy of mixed diets for:		
	maintenance km	growth kf	lactation kl
9	0.69	0.39	0.62
12	0.74	0.52	0.62

grass grown in mid season or autumn. The inclusion of a family of relationships relating kf to ME concentration with separate lines predicting higher values of kf for diets containing high crude protein content has been suggested as one empirical solution to overcome this problem (Blaxter & Boyne 1978).

3.6   PROTEIN VALUE OF GRASS AND GRASS PRODUCTS

The crude protein (CP) in herbage is determined as nitrogen and then, because most nitrogenous compounds in plants contain on average 16% N, the total is multiplied by 6·25 to estimate crude protein. Normally 70–90% of the total N in herbage is in the form of proteins, the remainder being non protein nitrogen (NPN) as peptides, amino acids, amines and inorganic nitrate. The amino acid composition of the protein extracted from the leaves of grasses, legumes or any green leaf is remarkably constant. The total N content of grass herbage declines from 4–6% N in the dry matter of young leafy tissue, to 1–2% in the mature flowering plant. Frequent defoliation maintains a high N content. The N content of legumes is significantly higher than the content in grasses; white clover has a higher N content than other legumes and Italian ryegrass tends to have a lower and cocksfoot a higher N content than other grasses.

However, the supply of N to the grass plant as soil N or fertilizer N has a much greater effect on the plant N content than does the species of grass. Some two weeks after N is applied to a sward the herbage may contain as much as 6% total N and 0·6% NO_3-N. These values will decline to 2·5% and to less than 0·1% by the sixth week after N application.

3.6.1   *Digestible crude protein*

The unit currently used to measure protein value is the content of digestible crude protein. As already shown, the crude protein in fresh herbage is really 100% digestible and it appears to be reduced with advancing maturity only because total crude protein declines and the endogenous secretion remains constant per unit DM consumed. This plus the fact that rumen micro-organisms can synthesize protein from non protein nitrogen (NPN) compounds and inorganic nitrogen indicates that neither crude protein nor digestible crude protein is a good indicator of the protein supplied by the diet to a ruminant animal. In Table 3.3 the data presented indicate that

TABLE 3.3. The amino acids consumed, apparently digested and absorbed from the small intestine when sheep were offered the dried herbage of lucerne or sainfoin (Thomson *et al.* 1971).

| | Diet | |
| | Lucerne | Sainfoin |
	g total amino-acid d^{-1}	
Consumed	135	132
Apparently digested	94	69
Absorbed from the small intestine	68	114

sheep fed the dried herbage of sainfoin and lucerne consumed similar quantities of amino acids and apparently digested more amino acids when offered the lucerne, but absorbed more amino acids when offered sainfoin. The reason for this and similar observations lies in the dual source of the protein entering the small intestine. A satisfactory system of protein evaluation must take account of both the dietary protein escaping degradation in the rumen and the microbial protein synthesized there.

3.6.2   Tissue protein

Several new systems of protein evaluation have been proposed recently, based upon the evidence accumulating on the measured flow of protein from the rumen to the small intestine.

The system proposed by a group convened by the Agricultural Research Council has been outlined by Roy *et al.* (1977). It closely resembles a system outlined by Miller in 1973, and is based upon the protein or more exactly the amino acid available to the tissues for protein deposition. Thus tissue protein (TP) is the measure of both the protein requirement of the animal and the protein value of a feed.

The basis of the system is illustrated in Figure 3.10. The crude protein (CP) comprising true protein (PN) and non protein nitrogen (NPN) consumed by the animal is partially degraded by bacteria in the rumen to ammonia. The proportion escaping degradation and passing into the small intestine is termed undegraded dietary protein or UDP. The proportion degraded is termed the rumen degradable protein or RDP. The ratio of RDP to CP is termed the degradability of the protein (dg = 0·85 in Figure 3.10) and it follows that UDP = CP $(1 - dg)$.

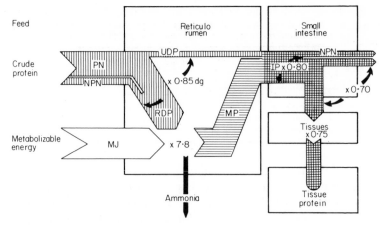

FIGURE 3.10. The degradation of dietary protein, synthesis of microbial protein, and their subsequent fate in the small intestine and tissues.

The degradability of the proteins in foods is variable depending in part upon their natural constitution and in part upon the processing to which they have been subjected.

Provided there is sufficient RDP available in the rumen to meet the requirements of the micro-organisms, the net outflow of microbial protein (MP) from the rumen is dependent upon the energy available for fermentation in the rumen. This can be related approximately to the metabolizable energy consumed and the maximum microbial protein entering the small intestine can be calculated as

$$\text{MP (g)} = 7.8 \times \text{MJ of ME.} \qquad (3.13)$$

The protein entering the small intestine (IP) comprises microbial protein and undegraded dietary protein so that

$$\text{IP} = \text{MP} + \text{UDP.}$$

Only a portion (80%) of the protein entering the small intestine yields amino acids and only 70% of these are digested and absorbed from the small intestine. The protein absorbed into the tissues is utilized with an efficiency of 75% to provide tissue protein (TP) for deposition in the body or secretion as milk. Hence

$$\text{TP} = \text{IP} \times 0.80 \times 0.70 \times 0.75 \qquad (3.14)$$

$$\text{TP} = 0.42 \text{ IP}$$

$$= 0.42 \text{ (UDP} + \text{MP)}$$

$$= 0.42 \text{ (CP } (1 - \text{dg)} + 7.8 \text{ ME)}.$$

If the rumen degradable protein g is less than 7·8 times the ME consumed, MJ, then MP = RDP and the supply of MP can be increased by increasing RDP up to a value of 7·8 × ME. Simple inorganic forms of N such as urea will achieve this.

Should the animal's requirement for tissue protein be higher than that supplied by the diet, then this can be supplied either by increasing the ME consumed by feeding a supplement such as barley which will increase the supply of MP, or by feeding a protein supplement of low degradability such as herring meal to increase the supply of UDP. These alternatives are illustrated in Table 3.4, which shows that either 100 g barley or 16 g of herring meal can result in the supply of an additional 4·5 g of tissue protein.

TABLE 3.4. Calculations to illustrate the tissue protein which might be derived from the supply of 100 g of barley or 16 g herring meal.

	Rumen degradable protein (RDP)	Undegraded dietary protein (UDP)	Microbial protein (MP)	Intestinal protein (IP)	Tissue protein (TP)
			g protein		
Barley 100 g (11 g CP, dg 0·9 ME, 1·25 MJ)	9·9	1·1	9·8	10·9	4·58
Herring Meal 16 g (10·9 g CP, dg 0·3 ME, 0·2 MJ)	3·3	7·6	3·3*	10·9	4·58

* MP = RDP when RDP is less than 7·8 g per MJ of ME.

The appetite and requirements for TP and ME in ruminants are generally such that increasing the ME concentration of the diet with supplements of barley usually supplies the required balance of TP : ME. The high-yielding cow in late pregnancy and early lactation and the rapidly growing weaned calf of 3–6 months of age are, in certain instances, exceptions to this generalization and may require the addition of proteins of lower degradability to their diets.

3.6.3 The degradability of forage proteins

In the ARC tissue protein system a specific constant degradability is assumed for the protein present in each feed or in classes of feeds (Table 3.5). However, the evidence is not yet sufficiently clear to justify a more complex assumption and will be difficult to obtain, as

TABLE 3.5. Proposed classification of feeds on the basis of the degradability (dg) of their protein (Roy *et al.* 1977).

| | Degradability | | |
Class	Range	Value adopted	Examples
A	0·71–0·90	0·80	Hay, silage Barley grain
B	0·51–0·70	0·60	Flaked maize Cooked soya bean meal
C	0·31–0·50	0·40	Fishmeal
D	< 0·31	—	Dried sainfoin

direct *in vivo* determination of protein degradability is beset by many technical problems.

Many of the constants assumed in the tissue protein system of evaluation may well prove to have significant and predictable variation. The system is, like the ME system, theoretically sound and can therefore be improved by added refinement as further evidence is produced.

3.6.4   *Fresh grass and hay*

There is insufficient evidence to establish clearly a degradability of the crude protein in fresh grass but it seems certain to be fairly high, in excess of 0·70. Degradability is increased by wilting during which auto-degradation of both protein and carbohydrates occurs. Thus both wilting prior to ensiling and the normal processes of sun-curing hay increase the degradability of the protein, and sun-cured hay is generally assumed to have a value of 0·90.

3.6.5   *Silage*

The process of ensiling leads to some degradation of dietary protein to NPN forms including ammonia, and consequently increases protein degradability to 0·85 or even higher in poorly fermented silages where decarboxylation as well as deamination occurs. Furthermore, the readily fermentable carbohydrate is lost during ensiling leading to a reduction in the energy fermented in the rumen and to a reduced synthesis of microbial protein. While wilting prior to ensiling may improve the general fermentation, it does not appear to increase the supply of protein to the small intestine. This may account for the increases in intake observed in response to wilting without concurrent increases in production (Demarquilly & Dulphy 1977).

Formaldehyde forms weak links with proteins which are resistant to rumen micro-organisms but may be broken down by the animal's digestive enzymes. With levels of application of around 3 g HCHO per 100 g CP, protection of the protein and an increased supply of amino acids to the tissues seems to be possible, but higher levels of application reduce microbial protein synthesis and the digestibility of the protein entering the small intestine (Siddons *et al.* 1979).

3.6.6 *Dehydration and pelleting*

The temperature developed in plant tissues during artificial dehydration decreases protein solubility markedly, increasing the supply of both UDP and MP to the small intestine, while at the same time rendering a small portion of the grass protein indigestible and therefore leading to a reduced apparent digestion of crude protein (Table 3.6). The effect can vary with the nature of the drying process but generally is quite marked, so that dried grasses and legumes are valuable sources of protein of low degradability.

Pelleting, either by further increasing protein denaturation or increasing the rate of passage of material out of the rumen, reduces protein degradation still further, but while this occurs on all pelleted diets, it probably is not significant when pellets are added to a basal

TABLE 3.6. Effect of dehydration on the net flow of microbial and undegraded dietary protein into the duodenum of sheep (Beever *et al.* 1974).

	Fresh grass	Dried grass
	amino acids $(g\ d^{-1})$	
Consumed	125	120
Apparently digested	94	86
Entering the duodenum		
microbial origin	30	47
dietary origin	68	101
total	98	148

diet of hay or silage, although the changes wrought by dehydration will persist.

3.6.7 *Naturally occurring tannins*

Many tropical forage legumes and some temperate species such as sainfoin and birdsfoot trefoil contain tannins in their cell contents which, when released by chewing, react with proteins reducing their availability to rumen micro-organisms and hence their degradability. This markedly increases the supply of amino acids to the tissues. The same legumes are noted for the absence of bloat in animals grazing them, presumably in part because of the insolubility of their proteins.

The degradability of the proteins in forage feeds determines firstly the adequacy of the balance of RDP : ME for the adequate nutrition of the rumen micro-organisms, and secondly the amount of UDP passing to the small intestine. It is therefore the critical quality of proteins in terms of their influence on protein supply. Table 3.5 indicates current views concerning the classification of food proteins on the basis of their degradability.

3.7   PREDICTION OF THE NUTRITIVE VALUE OF FORAGES

Simple laboratory procedures to determine the energy and protein value of forages have been sought over many years. The fairly regular changes in the chemical composition of herbage that accompany their decline in digestibility have led to the use of simple correlations, mainly based upon fibre analyses.

More recently, a mechanistic approach has been developed on the basis of the isolation of not so much pure chemical fractions as nutritionally uniform entities within the plant. This approach as exemplified by the work of Van Soest & Moore (1966) has been described earlier. While to date the nutritional entity approach has not provided the simplicity needed for routine advisory analysis, it has shown the need to keep the predictions based upon a simple chemical determination within the limited and appropriate range to which they can be safely applied (Osbourn 1978).

Before considering in detail the methods adopted for estimating energy and protein value, it is interesting to compare the similarity of the bases of our units of energy and protein value. Three points of similarity are apparent:

(1) Both systems have a summative basis. Thus the use of DMD as the basis for ME is achieved basically by a summation of the apparently digested cell contents (DCC) and the truly digested cell walls (DCW). The basis for arriving at tissue protein value is similarly a summation of the microbial protein and undegraded dietary protein entering the small intestine.
(2) In both systems one of the two parts summated is estimated from an apparently universal constant applicable to all feeds. These constants are 129 g faecal cell contents per kg DM consumed for the prediction of DCC (p. 82) and 7·8 g microbial protein per MJ of metabolizable energy consumed for the prediction of MP (p. 94).
(3) In both systems the second of the two parts summated is estimated as the product of the chemical fraction and its variable biodegradability, i.e. $DCW = CW \times CWD$, and
$$UDP = CP\ (1 - dg).$$

The major problem has been, and still is, to find a simple and universal method of assessing the variable biodegradability of cell walls and crude protein. Not surprisingly there is a great similarity in the laboratory methods that are in use or under examination to predict this.

3.7.1 *Estimation of the energy value of the standing crop*

Each grass or legume variety has its own distinctive and repeatable pattern of change of D-value during primary growth in the spring which is related to stage of growth and to the calendar date over broad bands of latitude. The date by which a variety reaches a particular D-value is progressively later as the crop is located further northwards. There is further variation due to the earliness or lateness of the season. Charts to predict D-value, N content and moisture content for a range of varieties are available as NIAB Farmers Leaflet No 16 (NIAB 1979b) and GRI Technical Bulletins Nos 8 and 26, and in the UK information is available from the advisory services.

These predictions based upon date or stage of growth assume that the sward was tightly grazed the previous autumn and not

TABLE 3.7. The use of growth stage and leafiness to predict the D-value of any predominantly ryegrass pasture during the main conservation period (after Walters 1976).

| Growth stage | Percentage leafiness | | | | |
| | 10 | 20 | 30 | 40 | 50 |
			D-value		
Flower-head, pre emergence (16–20 cm above ground)	—	—	69	72	75
Flower-head just emerging	—	—	67	70	73
Flower-head 3/4 emerged	—	63	66	69	—
Head free of flag leaf	—	61	64	67	—
Floret stalks elongating	57	60	62	—	—
Anthers visible	55	58	61	—	—

grazed at all prior to being put up for conservation. In fact this form of management is rarely practised, and the scheme proposed by Walters (1976) to use both stage of growth and a subjective, visual assessment of leafiness of the crop is a useful method to assess the D-value of the standing crop on any farm. The use of the scheme is illustrated in Table 3.7.

The D-value of regrowth herbage is largely determined by the number of days of regrowth. The average values indicated in Table 3.8 can only be taken as a guide for leafy regrowths. If flowering heads are produced, as they almost invariably are with Italian ryegrass, then the system shown in Table 3.7 should be used.

TABLE 3.8. Approximate D-value of leafy regrowths of swards of grass species at four and six weeks post cutting.

| Grass species | Weeks post cutting | |
| | 4 | 6 |
	D-value	
Perennial ryegrass	74	70
Timothy	72	68
Tall fescue	70	66
Cocksfoot	67	60
Italian ryegrass	66	62

3.7.2 Estimation of the energy value of hay and silage

The time interval between hay and silage making and the start of the winter feeding programme is sufficiently long to permit the conserved crop to be sampled and subjected to chemical analyses to estimate its metabolizable energy content. The errors in sampling are far higher than the errors in chemical analysis or the prediction equations. Normally each batch of hay or silo should be sampled from at least 12 random points and the samples obtained thoroughly mixed and a representative sub sample taken. Silos should not be sampled on the ramp and should be sampled to as great a depth as possible with a core sampler (MAFF 1977a).

3.7.3 Methods based upon chemical analysis

The earlier discussion demonstrated the need to summate the separate nutritional entities and implied that these must, because of their different nature, be estimated separately. The method proposed by Van Soest & Moore (1966) and based upon determination of the cell wall (CW) acid detergent fibre (ADF) and acid detergent lignin (ADL) summates estimates of the two nutrient entities in forages (DCC and DCW) to predict DMD (%)

$$DCC = 0.98 \ (100 - CW) - 12.9 \tag{3.15}$$

$$DCW = CW \ \{1.473 - 0.789 \log (ADL \times 100/ADF)\}. \tag{3.16}$$

This method is precise but far too costly for use in routine assays on commercial samples. It is nevertheless a method which can be used on any forage grass or legume with some confidence and with an error of prediction ± 2.4 percentage units.

The majority of chemical methods in use for routine assessments are based upon assessments of a fibre fraction, crude fibre or modified acid detergent fibre supplemented with estimates of crude protein, ash, date of harvest and the class of forage being assessed.

Thus in the UK a series of relationships has been developed to predict ME from the modified acid detergent fibre content of forage samples (MADF). These equations are based upon derived relationships between D-value and MADF (g per kg DM), transformed using the general assumption that

$$\text{ME (MJ per kg DM)} = 0.15 \text{ D-value.}$$

Derived equations are: '

Fresh grass

general equation	$\text{ME} = 15.9 - 0.019 \text{ MADF}$	(3.17)
regrowths	$\text{ME} = 16.6 - 0.022 \text{ MADF}$	(3.18)
Grass hays	$\text{ME} = 17.1 - 0.022 \text{ MADF}$	(3.19)
Dried grass	$\text{ME} = 14.0 - 0.014 \text{ MADF}$	(3.20)
Legume forages	$\text{ME} = 12.3 - 0.012 \text{ MADF.}$	(3.21)

Separate equations are needed for grasses, legumes, primary growths and regrowths, hays and fresh herbage, because the method is non summative and they would be very inaccurate if applied outside their specific classes of feed, say to an Italian ryegrass sample or a ryegrass/white clover mixture. Within their specific areas of application these methods are reasonably precise and, of course, being based upon one single chemical determination, they are rapid and low cost methods.

Silage samples have proved difficult to incorporate into this system. The inclusion of crude protein content improves the prediction of the energy value of the digested organic matter so that equations based upon MADF and CP content have been developed.

$$\text{Hays ME} = 13.5 - 0.0152 \text{ MADF} + 0.014 \text{ CP} \qquad (3.22)$$

$$\text{Silages ME} = 10.9 + 0.021 \text{ CP} - 0.0047 \text{ MADF} - 0.006 \text{ DM.} \qquad (3.23)$$

Between the north of Scotland (58°N) and the south of England (51°N) the light and temperature regimes are very different and influence the ratio of cell contents to cell walls and the degree of lignification of the cell wall. ME declines more rapidly per unit fall in MADF in the north. Adjustment for latitude or climate might improve the accuracy of prediction of ME from MADF contents (Osbourn 1978).

3.7.4 The use of rumen micro-organisms to assess the biodegradability of cell walls

Tilley & Terry (1963), working at the Grassland Research Institute, developed a two-stage *in vitro* digestion procedure for the prediction of herbage digestibility. Samples of dried herbage were exposed to 48h incubation with a buffered rumen liquor containing rumen micro-organisms and then a further 48h incubation with acidified pepsin (the protein digesting enzyme from the true stomach). This technique contained the essential two stages necessary to solubilize all the cell contents and simulate the biodegradability of the cell wall fraction; summating these two nutrient entities gives a precise prediction of the DM or OM digested. The residual standard deviation of the regression equation predicting DMD was ± 2.3. In a later recalibration of the method against *in vivo* determinations with sheep fed at maintenance, Terry *et al.* (1973) confirmed the original calibration and derived the following relationships to predict digestibility *in vivo* (Y) from *in vitro* estimates (X) for grasses and legumes, primary and regrowth herbage

$$\text{DMD} \qquad Y = 1.01 \, X + 0.27 \qquad \text{RSD} \pm 1.47 \qquad (3.24)$$

$$\text{OMD} \qquad Y = 1.02 \, X + 2.55 \qquad \text{RSD} \pm 1.80 \qquad (3.25)$$

$$\text{D-value} \qquad Y = 0.98 \, X + 5.14 \qquad \text{RSD} \pm 1.68 \qquad (3.26)$$

It should be noted that *in vivo* values are approximately 1.0, 4.5 and 3.0 units higher than the values derived by the *in vitro* procedure for DMD, OMD and D-value respectively.

Assuming $ME = 0.81$ DE then *in vitro* D-values plus CP (g per kg DM) can predict ME (MJ per kg DM) using the following equation:

$$\text{ME} = 0.138 \, \text{D vit} + 0.01 \, \text{CP} + 0.231 \qquad \text{RSD} \pm 0.271. \quad (3.27)$$

This equation can conveniently be used to prepare a two-way table from which, knowing D-vit and CP the ME value can be read (Table 3.9). It should be noted that equation 3.27 predicts a higher

TABLE 3.9. Prediction of the metabolizable energy of herbage from the D-value determined *in vitro* and the crude protein content of the herbage (equation 3.27, Terry *et al.* 1973).

D-value *in vitro*	Crude protein g per kg DM					
	90	120	150	180	210	240
	ME (MJ per kg DM)					
56	8·9	9·2	9·5	9·8	10·1	10·4
60	9·4	9·8	10·1	10·4	10·7	10·5
64	10·0	10·3	10·6	10·9	11·2	11·6
68	10·6	10·9	11·2	11·5	11·8	12·1
72	11·1	11·4	11·8	12·1	12·3	12·6
76	11·7	12·0	12·3	12·6	12·9	13·2

ME value than does the value of 0·15 D value, and for practical purposes D values of 68–70 are equivalent to 11·0 to 11·5 MJ ME per kg DM.

The two-stage *in vitro* technique has been adopted in many countries and with many useful modifications to improve reliability, repeatability, and to reduce the high labour cost of the method. It has proved invaluable in the exploration of the contribution of different plant parts to digestibility, in the selection of material for breeding programmes and in the evaluation of agronomic research, but has in general proved too costly for routine use on commercial samples.

3.7.5   *Other methods of predicting digestibility and ME values*

Because of their simplicity, methods based upon the use of fungal cellulases are being actively examined for the evaluation of routine commercial samples.

Analysis of the spectra produced when infra-red light is reflected from a uniformly ground sample of herbage is being developed to predict crude protein, cell wall and moisture contents and also digestibility of the herbage. This is an empirical process but extremely rapid.

3.7.6   *Laboratory procedures to estimate the protein value of herbage*

We have already seen that the new tissue protein system requires a knowledge of the crude protein content and its biodegradability in the reticulo rumen (dg).

Crude protein as N × 6·25 is routinely assessed by the Kjeldahl procedure and for silages the proportion of NH_3-N is usually assessed as well as an indicator of the nature of the fermentation that has occurred, the extent of protein degradation and as some indication of the likely intake of the feed.

3.7.7   *Assessment of the biodegradability of proteins in forages*

The laboratory methods resemble those used to assess cell wall degradability. Thus the degree of degradation of the protein when contained in a dacron bag and exposed to rumen micro-organisms *in vivo* (Ørskov & McDonald 1979) or *in vitro* seems to be the most reliable, although they have not correlated well with *in vivo* estimates or with simpler methods based upon the solubility of proteins in water, buffer solutions or acid pepsin incubations. Nevertheless the dacron bag technique has provided a useful tool for exploration of the factors affecting protein degradability.

3.8   THE MINERAL CONTENT OF HERBAGE

The mineral elements essential for the normal functioning of both plants and animals are phosphorus, potassium, sodium, calcium, magnesium, sulphur, chlorine, iron, manganese, zinc, copper and cobalt. In addition, animals require iodine and selenium and possibly chromium, vanadium, nickel and tin, and may be harmed by excesses of molybdenum, fluorine, silica, lead and other heavy metals.

The nutrient mineral composition of grassland herbage has been summarized by Whitehead (1966), and these data were used by Butler & Jones (1973) to relate the range of normal mineral content of pasture to the content desirable in herbage consumed by a fattening sheep (40 kg LW gaining 200 g per day eating 1·36 kg DM) and

TABLE 3.10. The mineral requirements of ruminants in relation to the mineral content of pasture herbage (after Whitehead 1966 and Butler & Jones 1973).

Element	Normal content in pasture (range)	Desirable pasture content	
		Fattening sheep	Milking cow
	g element kg^{-1} DM		
Calcium	2–10	5·0	5·2
Phosphorus	2–5	2·5	4·2
Sodium	0·5–10	0·7	1·5
Chlorine	1–20	0·9	1·9
Magnesium	1–4	0·6	1·5
	μg g^{-1} DM		
Iodine	0·2–0·8	0·12	0·8
Iron	50–300	30	30
Cobalt	0·05–0·3	0·1	0·1
Copper	2–15	5	10
Manganese	25–1000	40	40
Zinc	15–60	50	50
Selenium	0·03–0·15	> 0·03	> 0·03

a lactating cow (500 kg LW, yielding 20 kg milk and eating 14·3 kg DM), as calculated by the Agricultural Research Council (1965). This calculation is reproduced in Table 3.10, which indicates that the lower requirements of the fattening sheep will be almost invariably met by the minerals contained in normal pasture; the higher requirements of the milking cow are less likely to be satisfied.

The possibility of the minerals in herbage being in too low concentration to meet a cow's requirements is further increased since the mineral elements are not all available to the animal. Apparent availabilities of 0·3 to 0·4 are commonly reported for the calcium, phosphorus and magnesium in herbage but true availabilities (accounting for endogenous losses) are considerably higher.

When cattle are fed indoors it is a relatively simple matter to supplement their diet with the required minerals, but grazing animals can and do suffer from a number of disorders arising from excesses, deficiencies or imbalances of mineral elements in the herbage, and these are discussed in Chapter 4.

Both sheep and cattle ingest considerable quantities of soil when it contaminates the pasture and ensiled herbage. One deleterious effect of the ingestion of soil is the accelerated wear of the animal's teeth, but soil may well increase mineral intake and absorption, particularly of those elements which are essential to animals but not plants, e.g. selenium.

3.9 THE VITAMINS IN HERBAGE

The vitamin content of herbage has little significance in the feeding of ruminants. Firstly, with the possible exception of vitamin E, fresh herbage contains ample fat soluble vitamins A, E and K to meet the requirements of ruminant animals. Secondly the intestinal bacteria of the ruminating animal normally synthesize adequate quantities of the B vitamins, and the animal itself synthesizes its requirements of vitamin C, and vitamin D, given adequate sunlight. A deficiency of cobalt in the diet induces a deficiency of vitamin B_{12} and the presence of a thiaminase in the diet can reduce the absorption of thiamin, producing a simple deficiency in horses but rather more complex disorders in sheep and cattle. Bracken and horsetails contain such thiaminases and it has been suggested that cerebrocortical necrosis occurring sporadically in sheep and young cattle is caused by fungal infections of ryegrass which produce thiaminases.

Pre-ruminant calves, poultry and pigs are far more dependent upon their dietary supply of vitamins than are ruminating animals. The processes of conservation of forage destroy vitamins, and hence winter feeds contain much lower quantities of vitamins than does fresh herbage.

The suggested requirements for vitamin A, as β carotene, and vitamin D proposed by the Agricultural Research Council in 1965 are given in Table 3.11. Because of the complexity of the inter-relationship between vitamin E, selenium deficiency and the quantities of unsaturated fats in the diets of cattle, which interact to cause muscular dystrophy, no requirements are quoted. The effective prophylactic dose for calves would seem to be at least 20 mg α tocopherol daily. Because of the toxicity of overdoses of selenium, the use of vitamin E to treat muscular dystrophy is recommended.

TABLE 3.11. Requirements of vitamins A and D for cattle and sheep (Agricultural Research Council 1965).

	Daily requirement	
	Vitamin A* (μg β carotene kg^{-1} LW)	Vitamin D (i.u. kg^{-1} LW)
Cattle		
Young calf	80	4
Growing animal	80	2·5
Adult, pregnant	150	10
Adult, lactating	130	10
Sheep		
Growing sheep	50	5
Adult (pregnant, lactating)	100	5

* 5 μg β carotene = 1 μg vitamin A alcohol = 3·3 i.u. vitamin A.

The content of vitamins in feeds has been reviewed by Aitken & Hankin (1970). The values given in Table 3.12 from INRA (1978) illustrate the effects of conservation on vitamin content. It can be seen that β carotene, the main precursor of vitamin A, is well preserved by dehydration but losses can be considerable during haymaking and ensiling. Vitamin D is not present in herbage and is only formed when either the ergosterol in plants or the dehydrocholesterol in the animal's skin is irradiated to give ergocalciferol, vitamin D_2, or cholecalciferol, vitamin D_3.

TABLE 3.12. The content of fat soluble vitamins in herbage feeds mg per kg (after INRA 1978, see Table 5.6).

	Vitamin A as β carotene	Vitamin D_2	Vitamin E as total tocopherols
Lucerne			
fresh	30–60		114–280
hay	15·8	400–2000	38
dehydrated	200–> 320	160–400	148–201
Grass			
fresh	9–127		105–166
hay	3·9–18	400–800	200
silage	8–13	—	38–470
Maize			
silage	1·7	—	46–250

3.10   VOLUNTARY FOOD CONSUMPTION BY RUMINANT ANIMALS

3.10.1   *The importance of voluntary food consumption*

The more food an animal eats, the more it has in excess of maintenance, the higher its level of production and the greater the gross efficiency of conversion of food into animal products.

3.10.2   *The measurement of voluntary intake*

The voluntary intake of an animal varies from day to day, sometimes randomly and sometimes in a distinct cyclical fashion. Furthermore, the amount of the same food consumed by animals of apparently similar weight and condition also varies. To obtain a reasonable estimate of how much animals will eat of a particular food, it is necessary to offer it to several animals *ad libitum* for seven to ten days while they adapt to the diet and then measure the quantities offered and refused daily for at least a further ten days. Tayler & Rudman (1965) showed that intake increased the greater the amount offered in excess of consumption, and for this reason *ad libitum* feeding is defined as providing food in front of the animal at all times but limiting the daily refusal to 10% for convenience or 15% if this is not possible. When measured in this way the coefficient of variation of the estimate of intake varies between 10%

and 16%. A large part of the error variance is associated with differences between animals. By the use of Latin square or reversal designs (Osbourn *et al.* 1966) or the technique of adjusting by covariance the intake of unknown feeds on the intake by the same animals of a standard feed, the coefficient of variation of estimation of intake may be reduced to 4% or less.

The voluntary intake of herbage by grazing animals is generally determined indirectly from the relationship between intake (I), faecal output (F) and the apparent digestibility (D) of dry matter or organic matter (as a decimal), as in the following equation:

$$I = \frac{F}{1\cdot0 - D}. \tag{3.28}$$

Faecal output is determined either by total collection of faeces or, more commonly, by feeding the animals a constant daily amount of an indigestible marker not found in the diet (e.g. chromic oxide) when faecal output is estimated from the daily dose of marker and its concentration in representative samples of the faeces (Raymond 1969).

The digestibility of the herbage consumed is determined either directly using *in vitro* methods on samples of herbage plucked manually or collected from oesophageal fistulated animals (Bath *et al.* 1956), or indirectly using faecal indicator or ratio techniques (see Chapter 4).

3.10.3   *The regulation of voluntary food consumption in ruminants*

The constancy of mature adult weight in most animals is taken as indicative of an efficient long-term regulation of energy balance. This subject has been reviewed by Balch & Campling (1969). Appetite or the physiological drive to eat is greatest in the young animal, declining when measured as energy intake per unit of live weight as the animal grows. Appetite is increased following a period of undernutrition or shearing, during pregnancy, and very markedly during lactation.

Three major attributes of the ingestion of food are postulated as acting upon receptors which connect with the hypothalamus in the brain (Baile & Forbes 1974) thereby signalling satiety.

The products of digestion or, in the ruminant, the products of fermentation in the rumen, have been shown to depress intake.

Receptors responding to increased acetate concentration in the rumen (Martin & Baile 1972), to increased concentrations of propionate in the portal blood and to lactic acid concentration in the duodenum (Bueno 1975) have been identified or postulated.

Stretch receptors responding to distension of the rumen have been postulated in the rumen wall, acting to signal satiety when the load of digesta in the rumen stimulates them (Campling 1970).

Finally, the increase in heat production consequent upon the ingestion of food is believed to act either through temperature receptors in the rumen or the hypothalamus to depress food intake (Anderson & Larssen 1961).

These and possibly further satiety signals are received by the hypothalamus and integrated by the higher centres of the brain with signals from the sense organs and previously learned behaviour to determine the animal's phagic behaviour. It seems probable that the ruminant does not respond either to stretch receptors or chemo-

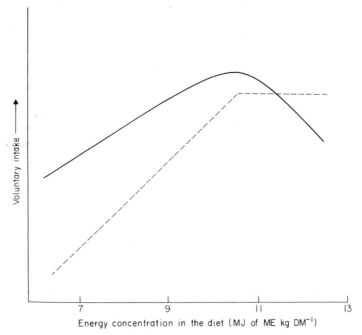

FIGURE 3.11. The influence of dietary energy concentration on the voluntary intake of dry matter (———) and metabolizable energy (– – – – –) by ruminants.

receptors separately but rather to the integration of the signals from all satiety receptors (Forbes 1978).

The voluntary intake of an animal is, therefore, the result of its appetite or physiological drive to eat and satisfy its energy requirements and any restriction imposed upon intake as the result of characteristics of the food which determine its ingestibility. If the animal's energy requirement determines intake, then the intake of energy will remain the same whatever the concentration of ME in the diet, but its intake of dry matter will decrease with increasing ME concentration. In ruminants this occurs when the normal forage and concentrate mixed diet has a high ME concentration (Figure 3.11). However, at lower ME concentrations both ME and DM intake are reduced as ME concentration falls. Assuming the animal's appetite remains constant, this decline in intake must be attributed to a lower ingestibility of the diet. Conrad *et al.* (1964) have suggested that for the lactating cow the point of inflexion above which ME intake is constant comes when ME concentration is greater than about 11 MJ per kg DM, equivalent to an energy digestibility of 68 to 70%. For animals such as dry cows or fat, mature, wether sheep having a much lower energy requirement it seems likely that the point of inflexion will occur at a lower ME concentration.

3.11   FACTORS AFFECTING THE VOLUNTARY FOOD INTAKE OF RUMINANTS

Three groups of factors affect intake.

(1)   Factors affecting the animal's appetite.
(2)   Factors influencing the ingestibility of the diet.
(3)   The manner in which the food is presented to the animal.

3.11.1   *Factors affecting the animal's appetite*

These are factors affecting an animal's requirement such as a change in physiological state or a response to a change in climate.

The most obvious physiological change affecting intake is the increase in size of the growing animal. The appetite of a 100 kg calf may be 2·9 kg DM per day while a 600 kg finished steer may eat 11·6 kg DM per day (MAFF 1975). The adult Jersey and British

Friesian cow may differ in weight by 200 kg, and this affects their appetite. Journet *et al.* (1965) found that appetite increased by 0·74 kg DM per day for every 100 kg increase in live weight in dairy cows.

Fat animals eat less and thin animals more than the animal of normal condition. Appetite is increased slightly during the latter half of pregnancy and very markedly during lactation, although in the dairy cow appetite lags behind the development of milk yield. The higher the milk yield of a cow the greater is its appetite. Partial regression coefficients relating appetite to yield of fat corrected milk (FCM) have varied from 0·13 kg DM per kg FCM on good quality diets (Conrad *et al.* 1964), through 0·25 kg OM per kg FCM for grazing cows (Curran *et al.* 1970) to 0·36 kg DM per kg milk for complete diets (see also p. 130).

The effects of live weight (W, kg) and milk yield (Y, kg per day) on appetite (A, kg DM per day) are expressed in the relationship quoted by MAFF (1975)

$$A = 0·025 \ W + 0·1 \ Y. \tag{3.29}$$

Several similar relationships have been developed and it is noticeable that where the forage component of the diet is offered *ad libitum*, the increased intake in response to increased yield tends to approximate towards 0·2 kg DM per kg FCM.

Monteiro (1972) and Vadiveloo & Holmes (1979b) have developed more complex models for predicting the intake of the dairy cow. These models include the level of concentrate feeding, loss or gain of liveweight and week of lactation or a lag constant to account for the stage of lactation, in addition to liveweight and milk yield as factors determining intake.

The appetite of sheep varies through the season in proportion to day-length, and Forbes *et al.* (1979) have demonstrated clearly that lambs exposed to long days had larger gut fill and appetite than lambs exposed to short days, and this was associated with higher levels of the hormone prolactin in the blood. Heat stress reduces and cold stress increases appetite and the shearing of sheep can increase appetite dramatically.

3.11.2   *Factors influencing the ingestibility of forages*

Ruminant animals offered diets of less than 70% energy digestibility appear to be unable to maintain a constant intake of digested energy. In these situations, where intake and digestibility are positively correlated, animals appear to eat to a constant level of digesta in the rumen (Blaxter *et al.* 1961). Intake is determined by the capacity of the rumen and the rate of removal of digesta from the rumen (Balch & Campling 1969).

Factors influencing the amount of feed and feed residues which may be packed in the rumen or the rate of removal of digesta from the rumen will therefore influence ingestibility of forages and forage-based diets.

Troelsen & Campbell (1968) suggested that lucerne, which breaks down into cuboid particles, occupies less space per unit DM in the rumen than do grasses with their long, thin particles, and that this contributes to their higher intake. A difference between legumes and grasses was also found when tropical legume and grass forages were compared (Thornton & Minson 1973), and white clover was compared with ryegrass (Ulyatt 1971).

Thornton & Minson (1973) have shown that the intake of dry matter (I_D, g per day) by sheep is highly and negatively correlated with the average time dry matter is retained in the rumen (the retention time, R_D, hours)

$$I_D = 1946 - 51 \cdot 06 \, R_D \qquad r = -0 \cdot 93. \qquad (3.30)$$

These observations on tropical forages can be combined with Ulyatt's observations on temperate forages to show that a common relationship exists relating the daily intake of digested organic matter (g) to the retention time of organic matter in the rumen (Ro, hours)

$$DOMI = 1276 - 50 \cdot 7 \, R_o \qquad r = -0 \cdot 96. \qquad (3.31)$$

Digesta are removed from the rumen by onward passage of material into the intestine following physical disintegration by microbial fermentation and absorption and as the result of rumination. Any reduction in the rate of disintegration and passage or the rate of fermentation will increase the retention time in the rumen and decrease intake, and conversely the removal of any such restriction will increase intake. The prevention of rumination by muzzling reduces the rate of physical breakdown and depresses intake. Grinding and pelleting a forage removes the restriction imposed on rate of passage and leads to an increased intake.

Ensiling forages alters their physical nature markedly with the result that they can produce a felt in the rumen which, by interfering

TABLE 3.13. The effect of chop length and additions of formic acid on the intake of silages of grass and lucerne by sheep and cattle. Intake is expressed relative to the intake of fresh forage (from INRA 1978).

| Ensilage | Grasses | | Lucerne | |
| | sheep | cattle | sheep | cattle |
	Relative intake (fresh grass = 1·0)			
Fine chop + formic acid	0·80	0·90	0·76	0·86
Fine chop no additive	0·75	0·82	0·69	0·80
Coarse chop + formic acid	0·42	0·78	0·60	0·74
Coarse chop no additive	0·38	0·71	—	0·68

with regurgitation, reduces the effectiveness of rumination in breaking down forage particles. As indicated in Table 3.13, fine chopping increases the intake of ensiled forages, as does the use of formic acid additives. The latter prevents the type of fermentation which produces either acetic acid or ammonia N, both of which are associated with low intakes of silage. Sheep are more sensitive to fine chopping than are cattle.

The inherent resistance of forages to physical breakdown may be measured crudely in the laboratory (Minson & Cowper 1974). In temperate forages this inherent resistance and the time spent ruminating per kg DM of diet consumed is inversely related to digestibility, and positively and more closely to the cell wall content of the herbage. In tropical grasses (Laredo & Minson 1973), the morphological differences between leaf and stem are so great that the ratio of leaf to stem determines the resistance to breakdown, overriding the general relationship with cell wall content. Thus in tropical forages resistance to physical breakdown seems to be the first factor limiting intake, while in temperate forages differences in resistance to breakdown which invoked 8% more time spent ruminating did not affect intake, suggesting that physical breakdown was not limiting intake and implying that rate of digestion might be more important (Osbourn, unpublished data).

The rate of digestion of organic matter in the rumen is dependent upon its composition. Thus the sugars, proteins and organic acids in the cell contents are rapidly released and fermented, while the structural polysaccharides of the cell wall are much more slowly fermented (Alexander et al. 1969).

Deficiencies of rumen degradable N, sulphur or essential minerals will reduce the activity of rumen micro-organisms, leading to low intakes, which are increased by supplementation. The cellulolytic activity of these same micro-organisms is reduced *in vitro* (Terry *et al.* 1969) and *in vivo* (Osbourn *et al.* 1969) by the development of a low pH in the rumen which leads to a reduced rate of cellulose digestion and a reduced rate of passage of the indigestible material from the rumen. In practice, low rumen pH occurs when large meals of cereal grain are offered to animals and this may reduce intake.

The changes in chemical composition which accompany maturation in forages lead to increased lignification, an increase in the proportion of the slowly digesting cell wall fraction and so to a reduced overall rate of cell wall digestion and removal of digesta from the rumen.

As both resistance to physical breakdown and rate of digestion of the cell wall fraction are reduced as a forage matures and its digestibility declines, intake is positively correlated with digestibility in stall-fed animals. However, distinctly separate relationships were found for the primary growth of perennial ryegrasses, Italian ryegrasses and legumes (Osbourn *et al.* 1976a). These indicated that with herbage of a given digestibility the voluntary intake of these three groups of forages would be in the ratio $1 : 1.12 : 1.27$. The overall correlation between intake and digestibility was poor, $r = 0.57$. A much higher correlation, $r = -0.88$, was obtained between intake and the cell wall content of the grass and legume forages.

3.11.3   *The method of presentation of forage to the animal*

The intake of animals consuming conserved forage diets may be reduced if the time of access to the feed is reduced either directly or indirectly by severe competition for space at the feeding face. Even under the most advantageous conditions it seems probable that animals self-feeding at a silo face will eat less than animals fed in troughs or mangers. Combining all the concentrate and forage ingredients of a diet into an intimate mixture using a mixer trailer may give rise to high voluntary intakes by dairy cows (MAFF 1978a), although Gill (1979) could find no evidence suggesting a positive effect upon intake.

The intake of grazing animals may equally be influenced by the

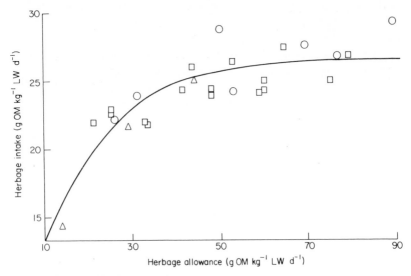

FIGURE 3.12. The effect of herbage allowance on the intake of herbage by ○ calves, △ beef cows, and □ dairy cows.

manner in which the herbage grows and presents itself to the animal. In general, intake is influenced primarily by the amount of herbage on offer to the animal (see Figure 3.12). In a strip or paddock grazing system, daily intake is reduced gradually as the daily allowance of herbage is reduced until a point is reached when further reduction of the herbage on offer causes a marked decline in voluntary intake. This sort of relationship has been demonstrated for ewes, suckler cows, dairy cows, growing cattle and lambs (Gibb & Treacher 1976, Le Du & Baker 1977, Baker & Baker 1978, Gibb & Treacher 1978, Baker *et al.* 1979). Only suckling calves and lambs are buffered against this by their dams' milk supply.

A similar principle operates on a continuously grazed sward, but here the grazing pressure is related to the average height of the sward and reducing this below a height of 5 cm will severely restrict intake. Stobbs (1973a) showed that in addition to the amount on offer, the structure of plants and the sward could influence the quantity of organic matter ingested per bite and he suggested that reducing bite size to less than 0·3 g OM would restrict intake as cattle seldom exceed 36 000 bites per day.

3.12 Effects of supplements upon the intake of forages

The effect of supplements is dependent upon the nature of the forage and the supplement, and the extent to which the mixed diet meets the requirements of the rumen micro-organisms for active growth and the requirements of the animal for nitrogen and energy.

3.12.1 *The interaction between cereal-based supplements and forage quality*

The major supplements in use are rolled barley, a highly digestible source of starch containing some 100 g crude protein per kg dry matter, or mixtures of cereal grain and oil cake meal containing some 120–160 g CP per kg DM. Other supplements include dried sugar beet pulp, brewers grains, citrus pulp, oilseed meals and molasses with and without urea and mineral additions. Often cereal supplements are used simply as the carrier for essential minerals. The general effects of such supplements on the intake of hays of low, medium and high digestibility are illustrated in Figure 3.13 taken

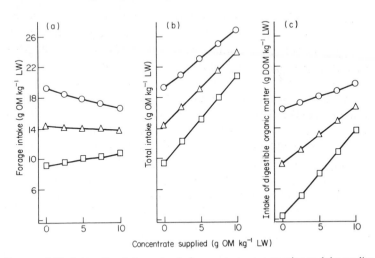

FIGURE 3.13. Interaction between level of concentrate consumption and the quality of hays: effects of level of concentrate consumption by finishing cattle on (a) forage organic matter intake, (b) total organic matter intake, and (c) total digestible organic matter intake (after Vadiveloo & Holmes 1979). ○ high, △ medium, and □ low digestibility hay.

from the observations of Vadiveloo & Holmes (1979a) on 16-month-old cattle weighing 350 kg initially. With the low quality hay containing less than 80 g CP per kg DM, increasing the level of concentrate increased the intake of hay by 0·17 kg OM for each kilogram of concentrate offered. Total intake increased by 1·17 kg OM and DOM by 1·12 kg for each kilogram of concentrate consumed. In contrast, with the highly digestible hay, the consumption of concentrate depressed hay intake by 0·24 kg per kg concentrate and increased total and digestible organic matter intakes by 0·76 kg and 0·34 kg respectively. A similar if more extreme interaction between concentrate supplements and hay digestibility was reported for sheep by Blaxter & Wilson (1963).

3.12.2   *The effect of nitrogen in the supplement upon forage intake*

In the previous two studies and specifically in studies of the effects of supplements containing varying levels of N and energy on the consumption by cattle of straws (Andrews *et al.* 1972), it was demonstrated that the intake of roughages containing less than 80 g N per kg DM was increased by supplements which contained sufficient N to increase the N content of the mixture. If the ME value of low quality hays and straws is assumed to be 7 MJ per kg DM and N degradability is 0·70, this observation agrees closely with the ARC Working Party's proposal that 7·8 g CP are required for every megajoule of ME consumed for maximum microbial activity.

Egan (1965) demonstrated that improving the protein status of an animal could increase its intake of forage beyond that achieved by increased supplies of non protein nitrogen. Increasing the supply of amino acids to the small intestine of calves consuming maize silage by the use of a protein of low degradability, increased the intake of the silage. Similar responses appear to occur with supplements of fishmeal offered to calves consuming grass silage.

3.12.3   *Replacement rates of concentrates for forages*

The change in intake of forage produced by unit change in intake of a supplement is termed the substitution or replacement rate (R) of the forage by the concentrate. The effect of unit change in supplement intake on 1-R with forages of varying digestibility is illustrated

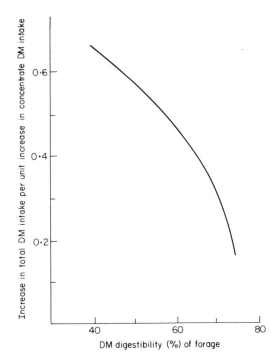

FIGURE 3.14. The influence of forage quality on the supplementary effect of concentrates (after Holmes 1976).

in Figure 3.14 (after Holmes 1976) for situations where N is not limiting microbial activity and supplements depress forage intake.

Clearly, this interaction results in the supplementation of forages of high digestibility having much less effect upon total intake and the intake of digestible organic matter than supplementation of a forage of lower digestibility.

Leaver (1973) showed that replacement rates are not constant for all levels of concentrate intake but rise with increasing level of concentrate intake. The relationship developed by INRA (1978) also indicates a curvilinear response to the proportion of concentrate in the diet (C)

$$R = 0.637 + 1.134 \text{ OMD} - 0.655 \text{ VEF} + 1.262 \text{ C} - 1.182 \text{ C}^2 \tag{3.32}$$

multiple correlation coefficient $= 0.799$,

where R is the replacement rate of forage by concentrate, OMD is the digestibility and VEF the ingestibility of the forage, when consumed alone. The term VEF is calculated in such a way that its value increases from 1·0 to 3·0 as the intake of forage declines.

3.12.4 *Effects of cereal supplements on the digestion of fibre*

The consumption of cereal-based supplements depresses the digestibility of the fibre in the diet as a result of a reduction in the cellulolytic activity in the rumen micro-organism which reduces both rate of disappearance and rate of passage of material from the rumen. Both *in vitro* (Terry *et al.* 1969) and *in vivo* studies (Osbourn *et al.* 1969) suggest that this is associated with the low pH developed in the rumen following the ingestion of rapidly fermented starch or sugars. The depression in cellulose digestion induced by consuming concentrates is greater with forages of high than low digestibility (Vadiveloo & Holmes 1979a), suggesting that the interaction observed for intake is related to the same interaction affecting digestion of the cell wall constituents and related to rumen pH.

3.12.5 *Effect of the chemical composition of forages and supplements upon replacement rates*

In Section 3.12.1 the digestibility or energy value of the forage was isolated as the major determinant of replacement rate when nitrogen was not a limiting factor. However, two forages of similar digestibility but dissimilar chemical composition and intake can have different replacement rates. The long, dried herbage of Italian ryegrass has a much higher water-soluble carbohydrate content and lower cell wall content than does the herbage of timothy of equal organic matter digestibility. Sheep consumed some 15% more Italian ryegrass herbage than they consumed of the timothy. When both herbages were supplemented with the same cereal-based concentrate, replacement rates of 0·99 and 0·59 were obtained for Italian ryegrass and timothy respectively (Osbourn *et al.* 1976b).

Replacement rates are lower for silages than for hays of similar digestibility (Osbourn 1967). This may be associated with both the lower intake of silage diets and their lower content of water-soluble carbohydrate.

A supplement such as non molassed sugar beet pulp which contains relatively little readily fermentable carbohydrate but is nevertheless highly digestible, produced with long, dried herbage of timothy a replacement rate of 0·4 compared to the replacement rate of 0·6 with kibbled barley (Osbourn et al. 1976b). These and previous observations suggest that the presence of rapidly fermentable carbohydrate in both forage and supplement may, via their combined effects on cellulolytic activity and rates of removal of digesta from the rumen, influence replacement rates.

3.12.6   The effects of buffering and bypassing the rumen

If the depression of forage intake by carbohydrate supplements is in part due to their effect upon rumen pH and cellulolytic activity, then the addition of alkali to buffer rumen pH or the bypassing of the rumen with a supplement digestible in the small intestine might improve the intake of forages, as Kaufmann (1969) has suggested. Bhattacharya & Warner (1967) showed that the intake of pellets of barley and dried grass could be increased by additions of sodium bicarbonate. Ørskov & Fraser (1975) demonstrated that processing barley grain led to a decrease in rumen pH and a higher replacement rate for dried grass than did unprocessed grain. The treatment of barley grain with sodium hydroxide also reduced its replacement rate with hay when offered to cattle.

3.12.7   The mechanisms determining replacement rate

The possible mechanisms are illustrated in Figure 3.15 in which the intake of three forages of high (H), medium (M) and low (L) digestibility are plotted against the intake of a supplement B. The ME values of the forages are 12, 9 and 6 MJ per kg DM. The concentrate has an ME value of 13 MJ and the animal consumes 8 kg DM daily of concentrate B. If the animal were to eat to a constant energy intake of 96 MJ (12 × 8), then points EL, EM and EH would represent the daily dry matter intakes of the three forages and the interrupted lines converging on B would be the replacement lines constrained by the energy values of the feeds. Forage H has nearly the same ME value as the concentrate B and its intake is not restricted by fill in the rumen. The line EH–B represents the decline in forage intake as concentrate intake increases and the replacement rate is 1·0. The intakes of forages M and L are limited by fill to 6 and

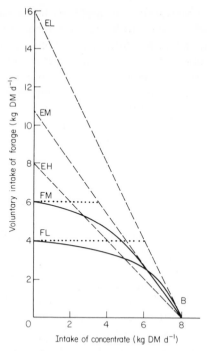

FIGURE 3.15. Schematic representation of the mechanisms influencing the effect of level of consumption of a concentrate (B) on the intake of dry matter of forages of high (H), medium (M) and low (L) digestibility. E – – – – – B assuming animals eat to a constant energy intake; F · · · · · · assuming animals eat to constant rumen fill; F –––––– B assuming energy, fill and other factors such as cellulolytic activity in the rumen influence forage intake.

4 kg DM daily (points FM and FL). If the consumption of concentrate did not influence fill in the rumen then the intake of forages M and L would remain constant as represented by the dotted lines until they met the lines representing isocaloric intakes when they would decline steeply in response to further increments of concentrate B.

Any effect that concentrate B might have in reducing cellulolytic activity and the rate of removal from the rumen of the cell wall material of forages M and L, would lead to a reduction of forage intake from that described by FM and FL but would be constrained to be below the dotted and interrupted lines previously described for each forage.

The solid curvilinear lines joining FM and FL to B represent the probable result of such interference with cellulolytic activity and agree with the curvilinear form proposed by Leaver (1973).

The scope for increasing forage and total intake by means of buffering or bypassing the rumen is limited to the deviation between the solid curved line and its prescribed dotted and interrupted lines, and would be at a maximum for each forage at that level of supplementation where bulk regulation is replaced by isocaloric regulation. If digestibility is also restored, the advantage of achieving such 'maximal' intakes might not be insignificant.

3.12.8 *Supplementation at grazing*

As might be expected, the supplementation with barley of animals grazing and selecting a highly digestible forage diet is invariably associated with high replacement rates. Values of 0·79 to 0·84 were recorded for ewes by Milne *et al.* (1979) and of 0·87 to 0·95 for steers by Tayler & Wilkinson (1972). Greenhalgh (1975) has suggested that a supplement at grazing should be of high energy value but less palatable than grass so that it can be used to extend a limited amount of grazed grass in order to maintain stocking rate and achieve high levels of utilization and animal production per hectare (see also Section 4.12.9).

FURTHER READING

BAILE C. A. & FORBES J. M. (1974) Control of feed intake and regulation of energy balance in ruminants. *Physiol. Rev.*, **160**, 214

BLAXTER K. L. (1962) *The Energy Metabolism of Ruminants.* Hutchinson, London

BUTLER G. W. & BAILEY R. W. (1973) *Chemistry and Biochemistry of Herbage.* 3 vols. Academic Press, London and New York

JOURNET M. & REMOND B. (1976) Physiological factors affecting the intake of feed by cows—a review, *Livestk Prod. Sci.*, **3**, 129–46

MAFF (Ministry of Agriculture, Fisheries and Food) (1975) *Energy Allowances and Feeding Systems for Ruminants.* MAFF Technical Bulletin No. 33. HMSO, London

MAFF (Ministry of Agriculture, Fisheries and Food) (1979a) *Nutrient allowances and composition of feeding stuffs for ruminants, LGR 21.* HMSO, London

MAFF (Ministry of Agriculture, Fisheries and Food) (1979b) Grass as a feed. Grassland Practice No. 7, Booklet 2047. HMSO, London

McDONALD I. W. (1968) The nutrition of grazing ruminants. *Nutr. Abstr. Rev.*, **38**, 381–400

McDonald P., Edwards R. A. & Greenhalgh J. F. D. (1973) *Animal nutrition* (2nd e.) Oliver & Boyd, Edinburgh.

Mertens D. R. (1977) Dietary fibre capacity: relationship to the rate and content of ruminal digestion. *Federation Proc.*, **36**, 186–92

Miller I. L. (1973) Evaluation of feeds as sources of nitrogen and amino acids. *Proc. Nutr. Soc.*, **32**, 79

Osbourn D. F. (1978) Principles governing the use of chemical methods for assessing the nutritive value of forages—a review. *Anim. Fd Sci. Technol.*, **3**, 265–75

Raymond W. F. (1969) The nutritive value of forage crops. *Adv. Agron.*, **21**, 1–108

Schneider B. H. & Flatt W. P. (1975) *The Evaluation of Feeds Through Digestibility Experiments*. The University of Georgia Press, Athens USA

Van Es A. J. H. (1975) Feed evaluation for dairy cows. *Livestk Prod. Sci.*, **2**, 95–107

Van Soest P. J. (1976) Laboratory methods for evaluating the energy value of feeding stuffs. In Swan H. & Lewis D. (eds), *Feed Energy Sources for Livestock*, 83–94. Butterworth, London

Chapter 4

Grazing management

4.1 GRAZING MANAGEMENT

Good grazing management should provide a supply of nutritious
herbage over the growing season at low cost, avoid physical waste
of herbage, and inefficient utilization by the animal, and maintain
the productive capacity of the sward. The needs of both the animal
and the pasture must be considered, and severe adverse effects on
either avoided. There is no universal system of grazing management
and a wide range can be found in practice (Section 4.12). However,
depending on the physical and economic circumstances, a range of
optimal practices can be recommended. The principles and practices of grazing management are outlined in the following sections.
Throughout Britain and other temperate regions, for all but the
most hardy stock, grazing is practicable only for a portion of the
year, ranging from about five months in the extreme North of Scotland to about nine months in South West England. Grazing cannot,
therefore, be considered in isolation. Provision must be made also
for feeding the stock in the winter period. The conservation of grass
is dealt with in Chapter 5.

4.2 POTENTIAL PRODUCTION FROM GRAZING

The potential production from grazing depends on the quantity and
quality of the herbage, on the numbers and potential productivity of
the animals and on the efficiency of utilization of the pasture. Factors affecting the quantity of pasture are discussed in Chapter 2 and
those affecting feeding value in Chapter 3. Some data are summarized in Table 4.1. The potential yield of dry matter ranges from
2000 to 25000 kg per ha and the quality in terms of metabolizable
energy from 6 to 13 MJ per kg DM. The higher qualities also have

TABLE 4.1 Approximate levels of performance attainable from grass diets of varying ME concentration. Based on ME requirements and assumptions on appetite of MAFF (1975) Bulletin No. 33.

	Energy concentration		
DOMD (%)*	62	68	75
MJ ME kg^{-1} DM	10	11	12
	Daily milk yield kg (no change in live weight)		
Dairy cows			
Jersey	9	12	15
Ayrshire	17	21	24
Friesian	22	27	31
	Daily gain kg		
Beef cattle			
200 kg W	0·75	0·90	1·00
300 kg W	0·75	1·00	1·25
400 kg W	0·75	1·00	1·25
500 kg W	0·75	1·00	1·25
	Daily gain g		
Lambs			
20 kg W	200	250	300
40 kg W	300	350	400

* Approximate conversion from ME (see Table 3.9).

high intake characteristics, and as Table 4.1 indicates milk yields of 30 kg and daily gains of 1·25 kg from cattle and 400 g from sheep are attainable on pastures. If 15 000 kg DM per ha containing 11 MJ ME per kg DM were utilized with 90% efficiency, and if the livestock attained on average two-thirds of maximal production this would yield 150 GJ of metabolizable energy, about 20 000 kg milk or from 1100–1600 kg live weight gain per hectare. At present, yields of half these figures are regarded as highly satisfactory. Detailed targets for a range of conditions are given in Chapter 7.

4.3 GRAZING BEHAVIOUR

This section refers both to the way in which the animal harvests grass from the sward and to the normal daily pattern of events when ruminants are grazing.

Grazing may occupy from six to eleven hours per day, normally in two major periods, one before dusk and one after dawn, with shorter periods during the day, and at night, if the nights are long. In the tropics, animals may graze for longer times in the cooler hours of darkness. The provision of supplementary concentrated feed will normally reduce the total grazing time.

During a grazing period cattle move slowly over the pasture and take successive bites by drawing grass into the mouth with the tongue and then, with the grass firmly held between the tongue and the lower incisors, pull or tear it from the sward, often with a jerking movement. The normal rate of eating is from 40 to 70 bites per minute. Sheep follow a similar pattern but because of their smaller mouthparts they 'nibble' the grass, achieve a somewhat higher frequency of biting and may bite rather than tear the chosen grass by cutting it between the lower incisors and the dental pad of the upper jaw. This method may also be used by calves. The grazing animal moves only slowly through a uniform sward, whereas in a sparse or more variable sward it may take several steps between bites. The herbage grazed is swallowed and accumulates in the rumen. After a grazing period the animal rests and normally also ruminates, regurgitating the herbage, chewing it, mixing it with saliva and swallowing again. Rumination may occur while the animal is standing or lying. The time spent in ruminating depends on the fibrousness of the grass consumed, but normally ranges from five to nine hours, the longer times with more fibrous material. Normally, grazing time increases with the difficulty of harvesting the grass whether it is sparse or long but of low quality, while ruminating time increases as the quality of the grass eaten decreases.

Animals walking to and from pasture and seeking grazing may travel from two to six kilometres per day. Faeces are deposited ten to twelve times per day, with milk cows about half on the night pasture, 10–15% at or going to and from milking, and the remainder on day pasture. The animals normally urinate four to six times per day and drink water two to four times per day depending on the moisture content of the herbage (Maclusky 1959).

Grazing animals select their food using the senses of touch, sight and smell (Arnold 1970). They tend to select the more leafy portion of a sward and may also choose immature seed heads partly because these are both more accessible. Sheep and calves with smaller mouthparts are more selective than larger ruminants. Grazing animals tend to avoid pasture fouled by, or near to, faeces of their own species. Whether they can do so depends on the abundance of pasture.

The 'palatability' of pasture is difficult to assess and indeed is regarded as an unacceptable term by some research workers. However, green succulent material and material with a high content of sugars is usually preferred, while dead, mature or fungus-infected material is usually rejected. Early work on grazing behaviour was reviewed by Waite (1963), and Arnold & Dudzinski (1978) have summarized more recent work.

4.4   THE MEASUREMENT OF HERBAGE INTAKE

The quantities of grass consumed by grazing cattle and sheep can be estimated by direct or indirect methods. For the direct method the mass of herbage per unit area is assessed before and after a grazing period by cutting or measuring a sufficient number of samples and the amount consumed is estimated by difference. If the grazing period exceeds one day, some allowance should be made for growth of grass. Recent work on this is summarized by Walters & Evans (1979). Direct methods normally estimate the intake of groups of animals although they may be used with individual animals in separate paddocks.

Indirect methods depend on assessing the daily output of faeces from each animal or group of animals and estimating the digestibility of the feed consumed. Faeces can be collected from sheep fitted with suitable harnesses and collecting bags, although the possibility that grazing behaviour is affected cannot be discounted, but faeces collection is difficult with cattle. The alternative is to feed or dose the animal with known quantities of a non-toxic, indigestible, easily dispersible chemical (chromium sesquioxide, Cr_2O_3, is commonly used) for a period of seven or more days so that it is uniformly distributed through the digestive tract, and then while continuing to administer Cr_2O_3, to collect representative samples of faeces from the dung pats or directly from the animals over a subsequent period of four to six days. From the quantity of marker supplied and its concentration in the faeces, the daily faecal output can be estimated.

Digestibility of the ingested feed and the consumption of digestible nutrients can then be estimated. Since the range of herbage digestibilities is now well known (e.g. MAFF 1976), an appropriate figure may be chosen. Hand plucking may be attempted to simulate selection by the grazing animal, or in restricted conditions surgically modified animals with fistulae in the oesophagus may be used to select samples. These animals may, however, not be representative of the group nor may the sampling periods represent wholly the feed consumed. The *in vitro* digestibility of the samples is then estimated (Section 3.7.4). Other methods applicable to normal intact animals estimate digestibility from a constituent of the faeces. For this purpose it is desirable that a local relationship is calculated for the particular conditions and animals. These methods are described in detail by the Grassland Research Institute (1961) and Mannetje (1978). A simple example of a faecal index is:

$$OMD = 0.4 + 0.01 \text{ (g N kg}^{-1} \text{ faeces OM)}$$

e.g. if the N concentration in faeces organic matter is 30 g kg^{-1}

$$OMD = 0.4 + 0.01 \text{ (30)} = 0.7 \text{ (or 70\%)}.$$

The use of nitrogen as an indicator of digestibility has been criticized since a large proportion of faecal nitrogen is of microbial origin. The fibrous constituents of the feed, or naturally occurring chromogens have also been used as faecal indicators. The accurate estimation of intake by indirect methods remains difficult and subject to error. The coefficient of variation of a single estimate is usually 10–15% and there is also the possibility of bias. Comparisons within experiments are, therefore, more reliable than between experiments.

When animals receive feeds in addition to grazing, the total intake of nutrients can be estimated if the quantity of faeces attributable to the supplementary feed is calculated from its content of indigestible organic matter. The remaining digestible nutrients derived from grass can be estimated by one of the methods described. If a faecal index is used to estimate digestibility, it should be based on control animals which do not receive the supplement but graze on the same pasture. This method does not account for possible associative effects of the supplement on the digestibility of the pasture and may overestimate intake on high quality pasture and underestimate it on low quality pasture but the biases are unlikely to be large.

4.5 THE EFFECT OF THE PASTURE ON THE ANIMAL

The pasture affects the animal as a source of feed, of parasites (see Section 4.9) and of minerals (see Section 4.10).

4.5.1 *Factors affecting the intake of herbage*

Herbage intake by grazing animals is affected by factors associated with the animal and those associated with the sward.

4.5.2 *Animal factors*

Intake of grazing animals is closely associated with their metabolic weight ($W^{0.75}$), their production expressed as milk yield or change in liveweight and, for lactating animals, the stage of lactation.

Many equations take the form:

intake = a. metabolic weight + b. milk yield + c. live weight change.

Two examples are (see also Section 4.5.4):

$$DOMI = 0.046 \ W^{0.73} + 0.3 \ FCM + 0.56 \ LWG, \ RSD \pm 1.8 \ lb$$

(Corbett *et al.* 1961)   (4.1)

$$DOMI = 0.098 \ W^{0.73} + 0.2 \ FCM + 0.76 \ LWG, \ RSD \pm 2.15 \ lb$$

(Holmes & Jones 1965)   (4.2)

where $DOMI$ = daily intake of digestible organic matter, $W^{0.73}$ = weight (W lb) to the 0.73 power, LWG = daily gain in weight.

N.B. Conversion to kilograms should be made only after DOMI have been calculated. The power 0.73 is appreciably different from 0.75 which is now adopted as the standard estimate of metabolic weight.

For beef cattle a similar equation with two components may be calculated, for example:

$$DOMI = 0.055 \ W^{0.75} + 1.56 \ LWG \ (RSD \pm 1.1) \ (Wanyoike \ 1979).$$

(In this example all figures are calculated as kg.)

Curran & Holmes (1970) discussed the difficulties of interpreting such prediction equations.

Selection. As shown in Table 3.1, grazing animals tend to select a diet higher in digestibility than the cut sward.

4.5.3 The sward factors

The major sward factors which influence herbage intake are (a) quantity of herbage and (b) quality of herbage.

The quantity of herbage may be expressed as herbage allowance but this is affected both by the density and by the stage of development of the sward which also affects the quality.

Stobbs reviewed earlier studies on grazing behaviour and developed equipment to record intake, grazing time and bite size (Stobbs 1970). He examined the influence of sward structure and density (Stobbs 1973a and b) on bite size and found that with Jersey cows, bite size fell from 0·33 to 0·15 g OM with advancing maturity of pasture, and increased from 0·13 to 0·39 g OM on swards of similar botanical composition but increasing in density. Dense leafy and sparse stemmy swards developed from the same species by the use of growth substances gave bite sizes from 0·52 g on dense swards to 0·4 g on stemmy swards. Bite sizes are smaller with calves and sheep.

Intake of herbage is proportional to grazing time and rate of grazing, which, in turn depends on rate of biting and bite size. Since the maximum bites per day seldom exceed 36 000 (600 minutes × 60 bites per minute), Stobbs suggested that for a 400 g animal an average bite size less than 0·3 g OM could limit intake. That the animal can modify its grazing time in response to the ease of grazing was shown by Hancock (1950), but the extent to which this may be done is not yet known. Stobbs' work indicates the limits to this variation, shows that maximal intakes occur only when animals can graze dense leafy swards and that stemmy swards may limit intake even when herbage allowance is high.

Hodgson (1975) reviewed the factors affecting herbage intake and showed a curvilinear relationship between intake and herbage allowance (see Figure 3.12) but its precise shape varies depending on the density and quality of the sward and the type of animal grazing. Intake generally increases linearly with digestibility over the range of values of herbage consumed from 50 to 75 D value.

Since digestibility falls as herbage mass increases, herbage allowance and digestibility are interrelated. Moreover some reduction in

intake per animal may be necessary to achieve maximal production
per hectare (4.7).

4.5.4   The effort of grazing

Grazing animals expend energy, additional to their normal maintenance requirements, both in walking in search of food (and with
milk cows to and from milking) and in the act of grazing.

The effort of walking on the level has been estimated at 2 to
2·5 J per kg W per metre (Agricultural Research Council 1965)
with an additional 28 J per kg W per metre for climbing. A cow of
500 kg W would, therefore, require 1·0 MJ of ME per kilometre
travelled with additional 1·4 MJ per 100 m climbed, possibly 3 to 7
MJ per day, a small proportion of the total requirement of 100 to
200 MJ per day.

Graham (1964), with sheep in calorimeters, estimated that the
maintenance requirement might be elevated by up to 50% in
difficult grazing conditions. Langlands *et al.* (1963) estimated that
for sheep the maintenance requirement on grazing was elevated on
average by 25% and Van Es (1974) considered that with cows the
overall increase in energy expenditure due to grazing was about
12%. Observations based on intake measurements on cows have
yielded varying results. For example from equations (4.1) and (4.2)
in section 4.5.2, for a cow of 500 kg W yielding 20 kg of fat corrected
milk and gaining 0·5 kg per d the estimated DOM intakes would be
9·8 kg and 11·8 kg respectively. The latter and similar equations
have been taken to indicate a greater requirement on grazing but
the differences may be due to experimental bias. It is probable that
except in very difficult grazing conditions a 25% increase in maintenance allowance is an appropriate allowance for grazing effort. In
estimating stocking rates, see Table 7.3, it has been assumed that the
indoor standards which include an overall safety margin of 5%
(MAFF 1975) apply, but some allowance has been made also for
inefficiency of grazing which may compensate.

4.6   THE EFFECT OF THE ANIMAL ON THE PASTURE

The grazing animal can influence the botanical composition of the
pasture, cause treading and poaching and also distribute fertility.

4.6.1 Botanical changes

Frequency and severity of grazing can influence the botanical composition of the pasture. Frequent, close grazing encourages prostrate species and in British conditions results in a dense sward of perennial ryegrass and white clover. In contrast, infrequent and lax grazing, or cutting, results in a less dense sward and encourages tall and stemmy plants such as cocksfoot.

With rotational grazing management, frequency of grazing is largely dictated by the length of the rotation cycle. On continuous stocking, frequency increases as herbage allowance declines.

4.6.2 Treading and poaching

Grazing animals exert pressure on the sward estimated to be about 0·1 megapascals (M Pa) (approximately 1 kg per cm^2) for sheep and 0·2–0·3 M Pa for cows. These figures compare with 0·2 M Pa for man and 0·1–0·2 for tractor tyres (Patto et al. 1978). Where this pressure is applied at normal stocking rates and in favourable conditions treading occurs and the soil is gradually compacted until its bearing capacity equals the pressure exerted. Compaction is more severe when the soil is wet. The effect of treading depends on the stocking rate, the soil type and rainfall (Edmond 1970). Pasture species vary in resistance to treading. Perennial ryegrass is most resistant and Yorkshire fog least. Treading may be beneficial by reducing the proportion of less desirable grasses, e.g. *Holcus* and *Poa* spp., but in wet conditions, particularly on soils of high plasticity, treading may break the surface of the sward, cause poaching, impairment of the drainage and seriously reduce the production of the sward (Patto et al. 1978).

4.6.3 Dung and urine

The daily production of faeces from grazing stock varies with the factors affecting herbage intake (4.5.1) and ranges from about 2·5 to 3·5 kg DM for dairy cows, 1·2 to 2·0 kg for young cattle and 0·3 to 0·6 kg DM for sheep. Adult cattle faeces may cover 0·5 to 1·5 m^2 per day with proportionately smaller areas for smaller animals. For a similar weight of faeces, distribution is more widespread and uniform for smaller stock, particularly sheep, because of smaller individual defaecations.

The total quantity of faeces deposited per year on pastures depends on the numbers of stock carried and may be as much as 3000 kg DM per ha (1000 cow grazing days at 3 kg per day). The content of fertilizer nutrient in faeces is also variable depending on the composition of the diet and the type of animal. Typical values are from 20 to 40 g N, 5 to 11 g P and 4 to 14 g K per kg dry matter. These eventually contribute to the fertility of the soil but because of their uneven distribution and the low availability of the nitrogen (about 25% in the first year) Petersen *et al.* (1956) considered that dung was of little immediate fertilizer value.

Grazing which had provided 750 cow grazing days per ha would, at average values, receive some 67 kg N, 18 kg P and 20 kg K per ha. The rates of application on areas covered by faeces would be about 900, 240 and 270 kg per ha of N, P and K respectively. Grass surrounding dung pats is often rejected. Marsh & Campling (1970) concluded that the degree of rejection depended on stocking rate, and Yiakoumettis & Holmes (1971) in grazing trials with young beef cattle recorded that the area rejected was reduced from 42% to 29% as stocking rate was increased from 6·4 to 10·3 cattle per ha. Attempts to distribute faeces by mechanical treatment have not yielded worthwhile results. Harrowing tends to smear faeces over the grass and reduce acceptability.

As with dung, the quantities of urine deposited on pastures and the composition of the urine are extremely variable. Individual urinations may be from 1·5 to 3·5 litres in volume for cows and about 150 ml for sheep so that 6 to 25 l per day may be voided by cows. The urine may contain 6 to 15 g N and 6 to 16 g K per litre. The content of P is negligible. The areas covered are larger than for dung, from 1 to 4 m^2 for cows. For 750 cow grazing days per ha therefore, at average values, about 100 kg each of N and K would be deposited as urine, and the areas actually affected would receive plant nutrients at a rate of about 550 kg per ha. The plant nutrients in urine are readily available. Urine, therefore, immediately contributes to pasture growth and it does not cause rejection of pasture. The effect of urine patches on newly sown leys on infertile soils is dramatic. Sears (1950) and Wheeler (1958) showed that full return of sheep faeces and urine increased herbage yield by 20 to 40% compared with similar areas which were grazed by sheep but received neither dung nor urine. The major effect was attributable to urine. Occasionally in dry conditions or on heavily fertilized swards, urine 'burn' or scorching of the pasture by concentrated urine may occur, but it is seldom severe. Wolton (1979) reviewed the effects of excreta on pastures.

4.6.4   *The application of slurry to grazing*

In addition to the normal deposition of faeces and urine on pasture by grazing animals, slurries from housed cattle, pigs or poultry are often applied to grassland. Preferably they should be applied to arable land or to grass to be cut for conservation. When applied to pasture, at least five weeks should be allowed before grazing.

Slurries vary widely in composition and in uniformity of application. The range in composition is from 2 to 10 g N per litre, 0·6 to 4 g P per litre and 0·6 to 7·0 g K per litre. Compared with nitrogen fertilizer the effectiveness was, for cattle slurries 26%, pig 38% and poultry 100%. Slurries applied at 30 t per ha caused no difficulties but at higher rates of 60 to 90 t per ha animal grazing was impaired for several weeks and there was considerable accumulation of potassium in the upper layers of the soil (Collins 1979).

4.7   STOCKING RATE AND GRAZING PRESSURE

Full production from pastures is gained only when the needs of the animal and the productive capacity of the pasture are in balance. Stocking rate which affects intake and animal performance has, therefore, a major influence on pasture utilization.

Stocking rate is normally expressed as number of animals per hectare for a given time period. Since animals vary in size and in nutrient requirements a more precise measure is the weight, or for comparing animals of different sizes, the metabolic weight ($W^{0·75}$) per hectare. With growing animals allowance should be made for growth over the season. However, at its crudest, stocking rate merely measures the robustness of the fences. It is common and preferable to express stocking rate as animals or animal weight per hectare, although the reciprocal, hectares per animal is used, especially in extensive hill or range conditions.

Stocking density expresses stocking rate at a point of time.

Grazing pressure refers to the number of animals of a specified class (or to the weight, or metabolic weight, of animal) per unit mass of herbage. A more useful measure is the reciprocal, *herbage allowance*, the weight of herbage (dry matter or organic matter) present per unit of animal weight (or $W^{0.75}$). Herbage allowance is most precisely defined with daily allocations of pasture. Some examples of these measures are given in Table 4.2. As stocking rate increases the grazing pressure rises accordingly, the herbage allowance falls, competition between animals increases, the opportunity for the animals to select from the pasture is reduced, there is a reduction in intake and progressively the animal is prevented from satisfying its nutrient requirements. An inadequate herbage allowance is the most common reason for low production per animal from pasture.

The influence of herbage allowance in the short term and of stocking rate in the long term have been examined in many investigations. When herbage allowance is high animal production is maximal and as the allowance declines production per animal declines. Over the normal range production per animal declines linearly with increasing stocking rate. In consequence, production per unit area rises to a peak and then declines. Jones & Sandland (1974) reviewed the subject and showed that with beef cattle and sheep, live weight gain per hectare is maximal at a stocking rate half that which gives zero live weight gain (Figure 4.1). The situation is more complex with milk and wool production, when the animal may draw on the body reserves and continue to produce at a level higher than is justified by its current nutrition (Figure 4.2). Journet & Demarquilly (1979) found that, on average, an increase of one cow per hectare reduced milk yield per cow by 10% but increased yield per hectare by 20%. Recorded data from a number of experiments are given in Table 4.3. The provision of supplementary feed in effect reduces the stocking rate. A major concern in grazing management is the satisfactory combination of high production per animal with high production per hectare.

4.8   Efficiency of grazing

The herbage harvested by cutting either for one growth or for the whole season may be compared with that harvested by grazing. Direct comparisons with rotational methods of grazing are feasible, since the quantities of herbage present before and after grazing can

TABLE 4.2. An illustration of terms relating to grazing management.
Example 1. Dairy cows on excellent pasture with 450 kg N per ha (c.f. Table 7.3 and Appendices to Chapter 7).

Time periods	Herbage accumulation (kg ha^{-1})	Average herbage mass d^{-1} (kg)	Stocking rate (animals ha^{-1})	Stocking density in 28 daily paddocks (animals ha^{-1})	Herbage allowance (kg d^{-1})	Grazing pressure (animals per 100 kg DM)	Live weight per animal (kg)	Live weight (kg ha^{-1})
Mid-April–mid-June	7060	118	8·3	232	14·2	7·1	520	3660
Mid-June–mid-August	4030	67	4·9	137	13·7	7·3	550	4015
Mid-August–mid-October	3310	55	4·2	118	13·1	7·6	580	4408
	14 400		5·8					

Example 2. Beef cattle growing from 200–360 kg in 180 days on average pasture with clover (see Table 7.3).

Time periods	Herbage accumulation (kg ha^{-1})	Average herbage mass d^{-1} (kg)	Stocking rate (animals ha^{-1})	Stocking density in 4 paddocks (animals ha^{-1})	Herbage allowance (kg d^{-1})	Grazing pressure (animals per 100 kg DM)	Live weight per animal (kg)	Live weight (kg ha^{-1})
April–May	3900	65	8	32	8·1	12·3	230	2829
June–July	2250	38	4·4	17·6	8·5	11·7	290	3393
Aug–Sept	1850	31	3·6	14·4	8·6	11·6	335	4118
	8000		5·3					

If mean herbage intakes were 13·5 for cows and 6·3 kg for beef cattle, average efficiency of grazing would be 85% and 75%.
If grazing pressures were expressed per kg $W^{0.75}$ the value for mid-April to mid-June would be 7.05×108.8 (i.e. $520^{0.75}$) = 767 kg$^{0.75}$ and 12.3×59.1 ($230^{0.75}$) = 727 kg$^{0.75}$ for dairy cows and beef cattle respectively.

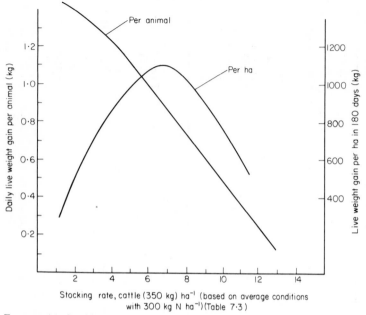

FIGURE 4.1. Stocking rate and live weight gain per animal and per ha. (Example.)

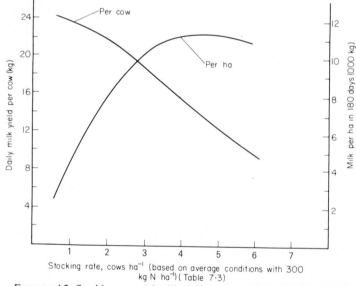

FIGURE 4.2. Stocking rate and milk yield per cow and per ha. (Example.)

TABLE 4.3 The effect of stocking rate on yield per animal and per hectare.

Reference	Animals (ha^{-1})	Production per animal (kg)	Production per hectare (kg)	Comments
Dairy cows		*Milk*		
McMeekan & Walshe 1963	2·44 / 2·96	4282 / 3929	10 352 / 11 646	New Zealand, 12 months, 2 years
Gordon 1973				N. Ireland, 22 weeks, 3 years, 150 kg conc. per cow
400 kg N ha^{-1}	4·94 / 7·41	2542 / 2139	12 527 / 15 815	
700 kg N ha^{-1}	4·94 / 7·41	2455 / 2297	12 099 / 16 977	
Beef cattle		*Live weight*		
Conway 1963	2·47 / 4·32 / 6·18	198 / 182 / 119	489 / 786 / 735	Ireland
Horton & Holmes 1974				England, 24 weeks
50 kg N ha^{-1}	5·0 / 6·7	154 / 132	771 / 885	
504 kg N ha^{-1}	7·6 / 9·2 / 10·9	154 / — / 124	1171 / 1208 / 1348	
Sheep				
Conway 1962				Ireland
Ewes with twin lambs	7·5 / 15·0 / 22·5	23·3 / 18·9 / 14·7	350 / 567 / 662	
MacLeod 1975				England, 12 months, 4 years
Ewes with lambs				
113 kg N ha^{-1}	11·1 / 13·3 / 15·6	52·2 / 52·7 / 52·7	580 / 701 / 822	
226 kg N ha^{-1}	13·3 / 15·6 / 17·8	54·4 / 53·0 / 50·2	724 / 829 / 894	

Note that the data refer to different periods of time.

TABLE 4.4 The efficiency of grazing for a single grazing.

	Herbage cut to ground level	Herbage cut to 5 cm above ground level
(a) Herbage mass before grazing kg DM ha^{-1}	2500	1800
(b) Herbage mass after grazing kg DM ha^{-1}	1000	300
(c) Herbage consumed kg DM ha^{-1}	1500	1500
(d) Apparent efficiency (%) $\left(\dfrac{c}{a} \times 100\right)$	60	83

be estimated, but comparisons with continuous methods of stocking are more difficult. For a single harvest the calculation of efficiency depends on the base line. An example is shown in Table 4.4. More important is the comparison over the whole season because herbage inefficiently utilized at one grazing may be consumed later together with subsequent regrowths. The following relationship is based on Leaver (1976).

$$\text{Total utilization of herbage DM (\%)} = \frac{\text{herbage consumed}}{\text{herbage accumulation}}$$

$$= \frac{I_1 + I_2 \cdots I_n}{A - B - C - D + G} \times \frac{100}{1}$$

Where I_n = herbage DM intake in grazing number n, A = herbage mass at the beginning of the period, B = herbage mass at the end of the period, C = herbage consumed by non-agricultural fauna, D = the sum of losses by decay in n grazings, and G = the sum of gross herbage accumulation in periods 1–n.

The same principles apply to the utilization of continuously stocked pastures where herbage accumulation, consumption and decay occur also, although not at regular intervals on the pasture as a whole.

Efficiency of grazing ranges from under 50% to over 90%.

4.9   PASTURES AND PARASITES

The helminth diseases. Parasitic worms cause a wide range of disease conditions described in detail by Soulsby (1965) and discussed in relation to grazing by Michel (1976).

The parasitic worms all have complex life cycles. Generally eggs are passed into the alimentary tract and thence to the pastures and animal houses. With some parasites, another animal, the alternate host, is essential. Eventually an infective organism is ingested by an animal of the original host species. An example is the cycle for a trichostrongyloid infection outlined by Michel (1976).

Parasitic adult worms → eggs → larvated eggs → first stage larvae → second stage larvae → third stage larvae in faeces → third stage larvae on herbage → larvae ingested by the host → parasitic third stage larvae → early fourth stage larvae → late fourth stage larvae → immature fifth stage larvae → adult worms.

The numbers of eggs shed and larvae hatched are enormous, but their survival depends on climatic conditions, and desiccation in dry conditions or inactivation by low temperature may severely reduce numbers. The life cycle in Figure 4.3 from Michel & Ollerenshaw (1963) shows many points where losses occur, so that only a small proportion of the organisms are likely to survive. However, so many ova are shed that the probability of some infection is very high.

An understanding of the biology of the parasites enables management and control methods to be applied. The likelihood of parasitic survival is reduced by hygiene in buildings, desiccation on pastures, removal of host animals, destruction within or outwith the host by chemicals, and elimination or at least a reduction in the population of alternate hosts. The major parasites are referred to briefly.

4.9.1   *Liver fluke—Fasciola hepatica*

This can cause ill-thrift and death in sheep and cattle and may also render sheep more susceptible to clostridial diseases. It can also infect rabbits which may become a source of infection for farm animals. The complicated life history of fluke requires the snail *Limnaea truncatula* as an intermediate host. The snail in turn requires moist conditions and temperatures exceeding 10°C for its

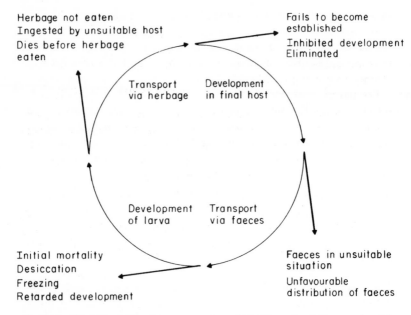

Herbage not eaten
Ingested by unsuitable host
Dies before herbage
eaten

Fails to become
established
Inhibited development
Eliminated

Transport
via herbage

Development
in final host

Development
of larva

Transport
via faeces

Initial mortality
Desiccation
Freezing
Retarded development

Faeces in unsuitable
situation
Unfavourable
distribution of faeces

FIGURE 4.3. A diagrammatic representation of the life cycle of *Dictyocaulus viviparus*. (From Michel & Ollerenshaw 1963.)

survival. The life cycle of the snail takes about one year but there can be two fluke cycles a year in favourable conditions. Control depends both on treatment of infected animals and on elimination of the snail. Rafoxanide may be administered to infected animals alone or with thiabendazole. In addition, control of conditions favourable to the fluke can be increased by draining or fencing off wet areas and applying molluscicides such as copper sulphate (at 30 kg per ha). Elimination of the snail is almost impossible, but application of molluscicides in March or April to kill an overwintering infection, and in August to reduce infection if the early summer has been wet have been recommended. Official warnings of fluke risk based on climatic conditions are now issued.

4.9.2 *Parasitic bronchitis—Dictyocaulus viviparus—Husk*

This results in a distressing bronchitis normally in calves but occasionally in adult cattle. Infection is normally of 50 to 60 days duration. It may be fatal but if the animal survives it acquires an active immunity to the disease. This has led to the development of a vaccine containing a suspension of irradiated larvae. This can be given to calves, six weeks and two weeks before turnout to grass. Immunity may not be complete or permanent for all cattle in a group and the possibility of infection in adult cattle exposed to severe challenge remains. A particular risk to be avoided is the amalgamation of groups of calves. If an older group is turned out in spring and joined later in the season by younger cattle, the latter may be infected and suffer a severe attack. Similarly, calves which had grazed infected pastures in autumn could infect autumn- and winter-born calves if they were all turned out together in the following year. Complete elimination of the parasite is almost impossible. The use of clean pastures for calves and the avoidance of the practices referred to above should, however, reduce the risks (see p. 246).

4.9.3   *Parasitic gastro-enteritis—Gut worms*

Many organisms contribute to these diseases which result in scouring and impaired performance and may render the stock more susceptible to other infections. Infestation is seldom responsible for death but it can reduce growth rate of sheep and cattle and retard development. The main roundworms are *Haemonchus contortus* and several species of *Ostertagia* and *Trichstrongylus*. In addition, *Nematodirus battus* and *N. filicollis* cause nematodiarisis in lambs.

The life cycle of the round worms other than *Nematodirus* can be completed in a few days but may take as long as six months. Worm eggs in the faeces hatch, the larvae pass through several stages and become infective and, provided temperatures exceed 10°C, then move on the film of moisture on grass leaves. Larvae consumed infect the grazing animal and the cycle is repeated. With *Nematodirus* spp. there is an annual cycle and outbreaks normally occur between May and July.

Animals develop a tolerance of round worms. The presence of adult stock mixed with younger stock may be beneficial because the concentration of susceptible animals on the pasture is reduced and the adult stock may consume some of the infected herbage without suffering harm. Control is aided if susceptible animals can be turned on to clean pastures, but it is commonly reinforced by the use of anthelminthics. These should be administered to ewes in the spring to combat the 'spring rise' of larvae embedded in the gut wall which may develop following the stress of lambing, to young cattle before turnout in spring and again in July after which they should move to clean pasture, and to lambs at weaning when they should move to clean pasture. Anthelminthic treatment of dairy cows at calving may be beneficial.

Confirmation of infection is usually based on worm egg counts but failure to detect worm eggs does not guarantee worm freedom. For all classes of stock and particularly for sheep where *Nematodirus* infection occurs, repeated grazing from year to year of the same field by the same class of stock should be avoided. Grazing by different classes of stock in successive years, the interpolation of cutting for conservation or, in extreme cases, ploughing and cropping the land may all be used to control severe worm infestations.

4.9.4. *Tapeworms*

Tapeworms of the genera *Moniezia*, *Multiceps*, *Echinococcus* and *Taenia* may all establish in grazing animals and impair production. These infections are generally of localized incidence. Clean grazing combined with specific dosing are the control measures.

Apart from worms, protozoans such as *Coccidia* may infect grazing animals. *Coccidia* are commonly found in faeces samples but when dense stocking coincides with favourable weather conditions, they may cause heavy losses in lambs and lowered production in milk cows.

4.9.5 *Ecto-parasites*

Ticks and flies affect grazing animals. The most important tick, *Ixodes ricinus* occurs mainly on upland moors and hill pastures which provide a relatively moist environment for the free-living tick. The main incidence is in the spring months and again in late summer. The tick is more important as a vector of the virus diseases such as louping ill, tick-borne fever and pyaemia and of red water than because it sucks blood from its host. Regular dipping or spraying with benzene hexachloride or an organophosphorus preparation is the method of control.

Fly pests include the sheep maggot fly *Lucillia sericata*, the sheep nostril fly *Oestrus ovis*, the warble fly *Hypoderma bovis* and the head fly *Hydrotaea irritans*. Maggots in sheep cause severe disturbance, pain and in neglected cases, death. Sheep should be sprayed or dipped to reduce the risk of fly strike, and regular inspection by the shepherd, especially in hot humid weather conditions is essential. The sheep nostril fly is of more limited incidence. It causes discomfort and disturbance and is difficult to control.

The warble fly disturbs cattle in hot summer weather when eggs are laid in the cattle. Larvae on hatching penetrate the skin and migrate in the body. The hides of infected animals are seriously damaged by the breathing holes of the mature larvae which appear in the following spring. The warble fly is controlled by application of organophosphorus dressings to the back of the susceptible animal in November or by applications in spring. An eradication campaign to eliminate warble fly began in Britain in 1978. Head flies have been associated with the incidence of summer mastitis in cattle. Persistent insecticide sprays may reduce the incidence of all fly pests.

4.10   PASTURES AND MINERALS

Grazing animals derive some of their mineral supply from the pasture and the soil which they normally ingest with pasture (Healy, 1973). Minerals also may be provided in supplements included in concentrate feed or supplied as mineral licks or by injection. The mineral composition of pasture is influenced by the soil, the fertilizer treatment and the species and stage of growth of the pasture constituents (Chapter 3). Soil ingestion depends on the severity of defoliation and weather conditions. While faeces normally contain 10 to 20% of ash or mineral matter, close grazing in wet conditions can result in faeces containing 40% of ash, which implies a daily ingestion of over 1·5 kg of soil by adult cattle or 300 g of soil by an adult sheep. Healy (1973) showed that soil ingestion may considerably increase the daily retention of minerals such as Mg and Ca. It probably also contributes trace minerals. Where a need is established the provision of the required minerals as supplements may be justified. Mineral licks for free choice selection generally contain 40 to 50% of common salt to which the other necessary salts are added. The nutrient minerals in grassland were reviewed by Whitehead (1966). Mineral deficiencies are treated by Underwood (1966, 1971) and Blood & Henderson (1974) and the relevance of mineral supply to metabolic diseases in farm animals is discussed by Payne (1977). Mineral deficiency diseases generally affect the herd or flock as a whole although only the animals under greatest physiological stress may show overt symptoms.

4.10.1   Calcium

Frank calcium deficiency occurs only rarely, but the metabolic or production disease, hypocalcaemia is common as 'milk fever' in dairy cattle and as 'lambing sickness' in ewes. It is of seasonal incidence and occurs in cows often in the winter and spring months. It is not due to a deficiency of calcium in the diet but to the inability of the cow or ewe to mobilize calcium from the skeleton in response to the increased demands of lactation. The serum calcium falls rapidly from a normal value of 10 mg per 100 ml to about 5 mg per 100 ml. Treatment is relatively easy by injection subcutaneously or, in extreme cases and under veterinary supervision, intravenously, of about 450 ml of a 20% calcium borogluconate solution. Prevention is more difficult but the provision of low calcium diets before calving may prepare the cow to mobilize skeletal calcium. Unfortunately such diets can include only small proportions of forage especially from leguminous crops. Soils of high Ca content may result in herbage with a high Ca : P ratio inducing P deficiency in livestock.

4.10.2   Phosphorus

In rare conditions in Britain phosphorus deficiency may limit productivity of pasture and result in grass with low P concentration (P < 20 mg per kg). In these conditions, especially on soils high in Ca content, the ratio of Ca : P in the diet may exceed 2 : 1 and reduce availability of P to the animal, which can impair performance and fertility. Phosphorus can be provided in mineral supplements.

4.10.3   Magnesium

Hypomagnesaemia, 'grass staggers' or 'grass tetany' is attributable to low concentration (< 20 mg per kg DM) or low availability of magnesium in the diet, resulting in low blood magnesium (1 mg per

100 ml compared with a normal of 2·5 mg per 100 ml). It occurs most commonly in animals under nutritional stress, such as milking cows or ewes on spring pasture and undernourished suckler cows in late winter. It is rare in growing stock. The concentration of Mg in herbage is generally lowest in spring growth. Affected animals become nervous and excitable and these subclinical signs should be noted by an observant stockman. In severe cases the animal walks in a stiff or staggering manner and, under stress it may collapse, 'pedalling' with its forelegs and grinding its teeth. Urgent treatment is then necessary by subcutaneous injection of 400 ml of a 25% solution of Mg SO_4. The incidence of severe hypomagnesaemic tetany averages 2% per year in cows and it is responsible for many deaths. Short-term prevention is attained by daily administration by dusting on the pasture or provision within a small quantity of concentrates, of 60 g MgO for adult cows or 8 g MgO for lactating ewes. Alternatively, magnesium acetate solution may be added to the drinking water. A daily supply of Mg in deficient conditions is vital. Omission even for one day can result in severe losses since the labile reserve of magnesium in the blood and soft tissues is rapidly exhausted. Slow release 'bullets' containing magnesium introduced via the oesophagus to the rumen or reticulorumen can provide a regular supply of magnesium, although they are occasionally regurgitated. In the longer term, efforts may be made to raise the Mg content of pastures by the application of magnesian limestone on acid soils. Paterson & Crichton (1960) and 't Hart (1956) have associated an increased incidence of hypomagnesaemic tetany with the application of potassium or ammonium fertilizers in the spring months. Potassium fertilizers, if required, should be applied later in the season.

4.10.4 Minor elements

Sodium. Deficiencies of sodium may occur, and in soils of low exchange capacity receiving high applications of potassium fertilizer, low sodium contents have been recorded. Lucerne usually has a low sodium content. Sodium chloride is usually the major constituent of salt blocks or salt licks.

Iodine. Deficiencies in iodine occur in some regions, particularly in diets composed mainly of *Brassica* crops. They may result in thyroid deficiency and goitre. Iodine supplies are often below estimated requirement (Table 3.10) and iodized salt licks or oral dosing of potassium iodide may be necessary. Iodized licks are considered unnecessary where there is no known iodine deficiency (Underwood 1966).

4.10.5   Trace elements

Copper. Of the trace minerals, copper provides an example of complex relationships. Frank deficiency of copper may occur when the pasture contains less than 5 ppm of Cu. This is rare and 'conditioned' copper deficiency resulting from other elements especially molybdenum (Mo), is much more widespread, for example high contents of Mo or of Mo plus inorganic sulphate in the herbage may limit the utilization of copper by the animal. A range of conditions may occur and local knowledge is desirable to deal with them. Underwood (1971) discusses this subject in detail.

Copper deficiency may result in many manifestations of ill thrift. In cattle, scouring, anaemia, bone deformation and impaired pigmentation may occur. In sheep, impaired growth of wool and neonatal ataxia, or sway-back in lambs, are associated with copper deficiency.

Application of 7 kg of $CuSo_4$ per ha incorporated in superphosphate, has given adequate protection for three to four years where there was a simple deficiency. But such treatment is less effective in calcareous soils or when there is a conditioned deficiency. Salt licks may include 5 to 10 g of $CuSo_4$ per kg but the provision of salt licks *ad libitum* is a hazard to sheep since they are also subject to copper poisoning.

In difficult conditions, e.g. the teart pastures of South West England, regular administration of Cu to the animal is essential, and subcutaneous or intramuscular injections of slowly absorbed copper complexes are used. Since supplementary concentrate feeds usually provide additional copper, the likelihood of sway-back is greater in mild winters when it is not considered necessary to provide concentrates to ewes wintering on pasture.

Cobalt. In contrast to copper, cobalt (Co) deficiency is fairly straightforward. A variety of geological formations in many parts of the world give rise to herbage containing less than 0·1 ppm of Co. Dependence entirely on such diets impairs the ruminant's ability to form vitamin B_{12} and results in failure of appetite and mild or eventually extreme emaciation and listlessness, described as pine. Inclusion of cobalt salts in fertilizers at 0·5 kg $CoSo_4$ per hectare is sufficient for several years. Again this is less effective on calcareous soils. The provision of salt licks containing 10 g Co per kg may control the disease, or oral drenching at weekly or monthly intervals may be adopted. Cobalt bullets administered to the animals remain in the rumen or reticulum and slowly release the mineral, providing an alternative to drenching.

Selenium. Another complex mineral situation is found with selenium. Selenium has been responsible in some areas, not in the UK, for toxic conditions, but when the content is inadequate, less than 0·1 mg per kg selenium in the dry matter, deficiency interrelated with vitamin E may occur in cattle and sheep, causing ill-thrift including 'white muscle disease', or muscular dystrophy. Treatment is possible by oral dosing, subcutaneous injections as sodium selenite or by oral dosing with 'bullets'. As with Cu the situation is complex and local knowledge is desirable (Underwood 1971).

4.10.6 *Ionic balance*

In considering the mineral nutrition of farm animals, the concept of ionic balance is useful. Minerals are absorbed in plants and supplied to animals in varying proportions depending on their relative concentrations so that in the plant

$$\frac{Mg + Ca + K + Na + NH_4}{P + S + Cl} \text{ all expressed as milliequivalents} = \text{constant.}$$

Bosch (1954) referred to 'alkali-alkalinity' and other mineral ratios. As an example, the likelihood of hypomagnesaemia can be predicted if the following ratios exceed the values shown (Wolton 1960).

$$\text{Minerals as g per kg} \frac{K}{Ca + Mg} \ngtr 2·2$$

$$\text{Minerals as milli-equivalents} \frac{K \times 100}{K + Ca + Mg} \ngtr 70.$$

The adverse effect of liming on the availability of some trace minerals is also attributable to changes in ionic balance.

4.10.7 *Mineral deficiencies*

Mineral deficiency diseases can seriously reduce the productivity of grazing stock. Although they rarely cause major difficulty on British farms, it is necessary, on the basis of local experience, to anticipate and prevent the occurrence of hypomagnesaemia and copper, cobalt or selenium deficiency. When animals fail to thrive it is wise to consider parasitic infection and mineral deficiencies as possible causes.

4.11 DIGESTIVE AND PHYSIOLOGICAL DISTURBANCES

4.11.1 *Bloat*

Grazing animals are occasionally subject to digestive disturbances. Bloat refers to the swelling of the rumen by entrapped gas which may cause discomfort, inappetence and, in extreme cases, death. It may occur on grass pastures or brassica forage crops but it is most common on leguminous crops such as lucerne, red clover or on white clover-dominant grass swards. Gas accumulates in the rumen possibly because of foaming agents consumed in the green feed. It normally occurs on grazed feeds and is rare with forage feeding. The incidence is localized and difficult to predict. It is more likely to occur on some farms with certain breeds or strains of livestock and is more common with cattle than with sheep. When it is expected, provisions of some fibrous feed reduces the risk, cutting and wilting the pasture is usually an effective but expensive way of protection, and the spraying of anti-foaming agents on the affected pastures has been used. The administration of vegetable oil or poloxalene in a proprietary product may control bloat.

4.11.2 *Scouring*

Normally the ruminant produces faeces with a moisture content of 85–90% but ingestion of low fibre high moisture herbage, or indeed of concentrated feeds may result in loose, watery faeces containing over 90% of moisture. If this continues, it may result in dehydration and loss of Na and K from the body. Nutritional scour is generally cured by the provision of more fibrous feed in the diet. If it is not, worm infestation or other disease should be suspected.

4.11.3 *Oestrogenic substances in pasture*

The presence of oestrogens has been observed in some pasture legumes especially in red clover (*Trifolium pratense*). The isoflavone, formononetin and some coumestans have been identified as responsible. Their concentration depends on season and on the species and variety. The effects may be observed in increased udder development in heifers and in the extension of teat length in sheep. The presence of oestrogens may impair the fertility of sheep but cattle appear to be less affected.

4.12 GRAZING PRACTICES

Grazing practices vary widely in the degree of control which they provide, their requirements for capital and labour and their influence on animal performance and on pasture utilization.

The suitability of a grazing practice depends both on the pattern of pasture supply and on the needs of the animal. Whereas with a spring-calving herd of milk cows the nutrient demands of the stock coincide fairly closely with the supply of herbage, a milking herd with level milk production or successive batches of finishing beef animals require a more uniform supply of herbage. Figure 4.4 gives some examples of pasture growth and animal requirements.

Many of the experimental comparisons of grazing systems in recent years were reviewed by Journet & Demarquilly (1979). Although there has recently been a return by the majority of farmers to simple grazing systems, the development of more complex systems coupled with the increased use of nitrogenous fertilizer in the 1950s and 1960s are directly responsible for the current appreciation of the potential productivity of grassland. These studies of grazing systems have emphasized the overriding importance of stocking rate and have indicated that the choice of grazing system should be affected more by ease of management than by any major differences in productivity between the systems. In comparing grazing practices, attention should be paid to simplicity and convenience of operation and to their effect in maintaining the productivity of the pastures.

The major distinction is between continuous and rotational methods. These methods have different effects on the swards. Continuous stocking tends to encourage the development of a dense

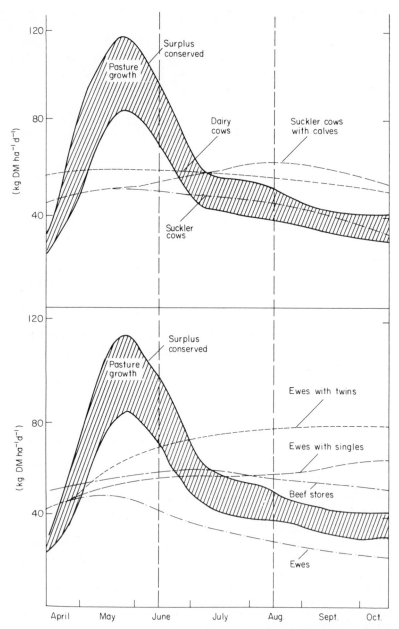

FIGURE 4.4 Grazing requirements in relation to pasture growth.

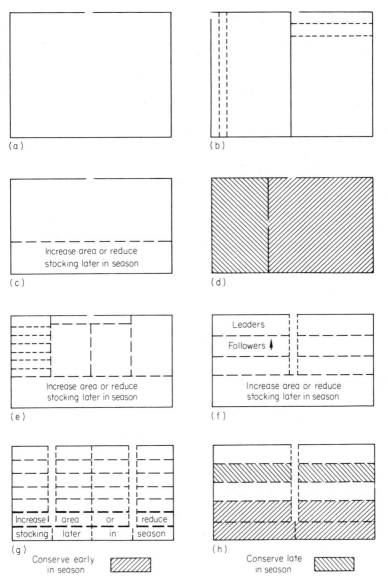

FIGURE 4.5. Outline of grazing systems. (a) continuous stocking; (b) strip grazing (alternative methods); (c) intensive continuous stocking; (d) integrated grazing and conservation; (e) rigid rotational grazing; (f) leader and follower rotational grazing; (g) daily rotational paddocks; (h) flexible rotational paddocks.

Permanent fence ———, temporary fence – – – –, movable electric fence - - - - -.

sward with little bare ground and may encourage the maintenance of clover in the sward. In contrast, rotational methods, especially with long grazing cycles tend to develop a more open sward which may be as, or more productive, but may be more sensitive to damage from poaching and less suitable for the maintenance of white clover. The main grazing systems are summarized in Figure 4.5.

4.12.1 Continuous stocking

This occurs when a group of stock have access to one area of pasture for the whole grazing season. It exists in its pure form only in extensive conditions where the stocking rate in relation to pasture production is low. There are, therefore, periods when grass growth exceeds the needs of the animals, herbage becomes mature, dies and dilutes the available feed. Conventional hill grazing systems may approach continuous stocking. If the overall herbage allowance is high, grassland is underutilized, coarse grasses dominate, shrubs or trees may establish and the nutritive value of the pasture deteriorates. If the overall herbage allowance is low, pasture is severely grazed, poaching or erosion may occur and the stock are undernourished and may be heavily parasitized.

4.12.2 Intensive continuous stocking

The simplicity of continuous stocking, which makes few demands on fencing, water supplies or labour and allows the stock some choice in the selection of feed and shelter, coupled with the realization that stocking rate is the dominant factor affecting grazing output, has led to the widespread adoption of intensive continuous stocking both with sheep and with cattle. The stock are allowed access to an area of pasture for the early part of the season with numbers so adjusted that grass production and utilization are in balance. To allow for the lower rate of production of grass towards the end of the year, stock requirements are then reduced by the sale of fat stock, and the removal to other pastures of dry cows or ewes, or of weaned calves or lambs. Alternatively, the area available may be expanded by the inclusion of regrowths from areas previously cut for silage or hay, or by the inclusion of pasture sown in the spring which becomes productive in mid-season. The seasonal distribution of herbage over the season may be modified also by fertilizer practices. These intensive, continuous stocking methods are widely practised for cattle, dairy cows and sheep.

4.12.3 *Integrated grazing and conservation*

This is also referred to as the '1, 2, 3' or 'full graze' system. It combines some advantages of continuous stocking with some of rotational grazing. An area of pasture is allotted for a group of stock and subdivided in two in a ratio between 33 : 67 and 40 : 60 by the grouping of existing fields or by dividing one large field. At the beginning of the grazing season the larger area may be grazed for one to two weeks (see turnout of stock 4.13.1). During the period of maximal herbage growth (mid-April to mid-June) the smaller area is grazed and the larger area allowed to grow for five to seven weeks and then cut for silage. During the middle of the growing season (mid-June to mid-August) the larger area is grazed while the smaller area, including any residues left when grazing ceased, is fertilized, allowed to grow for five to seven weeks and then cut for silage. After mid-August the stock have access to the whole area. The area available increases in the ratio 1 : 2 : 3, hence the name. This method is simple to operate, requires few fences and few water supplies. It allows the stock considerable freedom of choice and if surplus grass accumulates it can be cut and conserved. It also allows each area of the pasture to grow vigorously and possibly build up root reserves before it is cut for conservation, and the fact that each area is free from stock for a period of five to seven weeks helps to reduce the incidence of parasitic worms. This method is particularly suitable for young, growing cattle and can also be adopted for milking cows and suckler cows. It is less commonly used for sheep but the principle could be adapted, with the lambs weaned on to the regrowths.

Fertilizer may be applied in continuous stocking systems. It is preferable to mark off three or four similar areas within each pasture and during the grazing phase to apply the appropriate fertilizer to each subdivision in sequence, at intervals of a week so that the whole area receives fertilizer once in three or four weeks.

Continuous stocking methods allow the animal freedom of choice and are simple to operate. However, they are subject to variations in herbage growth associated with weather variations. If they are to be successful, it is essential that the stockman should regularly assess the progress of the animals both by inspection and by comparing the milk yields or growth rates with appropriate targets.

4.12.4   *Rotational grazing*

A greater degree of management control is provided by rotational methods of grazing which may also facilitate greater grass production, although it is now accepted that the benefits are of the order 5–10% (McMeekan & Walshe 1963) and not 30–50% as was claimed earlier.

In rotational grazing the pasture area is divided into a number of similar-sized paddocks and the stock are moved in a regular sequence around the paddocks. Certain definitions apply.

Rotation or grazing cycle—the total number of days elapsing from the beginning of one grazing period in a particular area until the beginning of the next.

Grazing period—the number of days within a cycle that each paddock is occupied by grazing animals.

Rest period—the number of days within a cycle when there are no stock in the paddock (referred to as spelling in Australia and New Zealand).

Hence the rotation or grazing cycle = grazing period + rest period.

e.g. rotation cycle = 28 days = 4 grazing + 24 rest.

$$\text{Number of paddocks} = \frac{\text{Rotation cycle}}{\text{Grazing period}} \quad \text{e.g.} \quad \frac{28}{4} = 7$$

$$\text{or} \qquad 1 + \left[\frac{\text{Rest period}}{\text{Grazing period}}\right] \quad \text{e.g.} \quad 1 + \left[\frac{24}{4}\right] = 7$$

Many variations within the rotation grazing principle are possible. Experience has shown that the grazing cycle in British conditions should be within 20 to 30 days, but the farmer may vary the length of the cycle and the rest period from time to time over the season, he may vary the number of paddocks, he may subdivide paddocks depending on grass growth, and he may arrange that a sequence of stock with varying nutrient demands occupy the paddocks. Rotational grazing systems may be classified as follows.

4.12.5   Rigid rotational grazing

Here the stock spend a similar time in each paddock of similar size and move according to a predetermined timetable, irrespective of the degree of defoliation of the sward. A degree of understocking may occur in the early part of the season, but the stocking rate is so chosen that overall utilization of the pasture will be high. A typical situation, sometimes referred to as the Wye College system includes four paddocks each grazed for one week and rested for three. For dairy cows it is preferable that each paddock is divided by a temporary electric fence to give a fresh allocation on each day of the week. The area allowed should be larger than one seventh of the area on day 1 and less on day 7, to allow adequate room for cow movement on day 1 and to avoid undergrazing on day 7. Similarly, seven paddocks may be each occupied for four days. Rigid rotational grazing is simple to operate and at appropriate stocking rates can achieve high performance with minimal management effort. To avoid excessive growth and deterioration of pasture quality the grazing should be so arranged that the first cycle is completed before ear emergence. Subsequent tillering of leafy material then enhances the quality of any stemmy residue so that overall pasture quality is maintained. In seasons of unusual growth or on weedy pastures this system may produce unsightly pastures but normally they have been restored to good condition by grazing alone by the end of the third grazing cycle. An additional area for grazing or a reduction of stock numbers is usually required later in the season.

4.12.6   Flexible rotational grazing

Adjustment to the variation in pasture growth rate is possible by varying the number of days within a paddock, depending on the quantity of grass present, and/or conserving some of the paddocks. This may be practised on inspection or it may be included in a basic plan, subject to modification according to the exigencies of the season. An example of the latter approach particularly suitable for milk cows is the allocation of eleven paddocks with the intention that four or five of these would be conserved in May. Each of the six or seven grazed paddocks would be occupied for four days in the first two cycles and thereafter paddocks may be added, and some others may be conserved to maintain grazing cycles within 22–33 days, with each grazing paddock occupied for 2–3 days. In such flexible systems it is most important that in the first half of the season the cycle remains within 21 to 28 days. Attempts to achieve apparently efficient utilization of the first paddocks to be grazed may result in the later paddocks reaching too advanced a stage of growth. It is also vital that conservation of surplus paddocks is so arranged that a continuous supply of fresh grass for grazing is maintained. While the provision of fresh regrowths following conservation cuts is beneficial, a comparison of rigid rotational grazing with the provision of a succession of regrowths revealed only a small and insignificant difference in yield per cow (Holmes *et al.* 1972). Unless the manager can exercise close control, rigid rotational systems or 1 : 2 : 3 systems are more efficient in maintaining stocking rate than more flexible systems.

Paddock grazing describes either rigid or flexible rotational grazing with a large number of paddocks (21–30) where normally stock occupy each paddock for only one day.

Strip grazing describes the fresh allocation of pasture daily by moving an electric fence. It is best organized within a cycle of rotational paddocks, but may be employed in one field, for early bite, autumn saved pasture and in times of pasture scarcity. In these circumstances a back fence should be provided so that the crop is not re-grazed too soon.

4.12.7   *Leader and follower rotational grazing*

Within the rotational pattern successive groups of stock of differing nutrient requirements may rotate. More than two groups complicate the operation and may restrict the recovery period. For ewes with lambs, two age groups of young beef cattle or of growing heifers the practice is useful. The animals which need the highest quality diet should be the leaders. With sheep and lambs *forward creep grazing* is the descriptive term. An eight paddock, 24-day cycle is preferred, lambs are encouraged to creep ahead through specially constructed gaps in the fences where they choose a high quality diet and are possibly less exposed to worm larvae. As the grass consumption of the lambs increases, the ewes receive a less digestible diet which coincides with their declining lactation. With dairy heifers, cycling the calves of six to twelve months age ahead of the

18- to 24-month-old cattle gave better growth rates than grazing of the two groups together and reduced the incidence of worms (Leaver 1970). Leader-follower systems are complex to operate but are valuable with lambs and young cattle. The additional complication of leader-follower grazing of milk cows is probably not justified. In any leader-follower system, care should be taken that the followers are not penalized and the pasture is not overgrazed.

4.12.8 *The length of the rotation cycle*

Cutting experiments have shown that the yield of DOM is likely to increase with increasing length of rotation cycle over the range 21 to 42 days (Anslow 1967), but grazing studies on temperate pastures have failed to reveal any major effect of length of grazing cycle. With milk cows, Marsh *et al.* (1971) detected no difference in performance between a four week and a five week cycle, and comparison of 15 and 30 day cycles (McFeely *et al.* 1975) also resulted in no significant differences. However, when Escuder *et al.* (1971) compared two, four and six week cycles with beef cattle they found there was no significant difference between four and six week cycles but that a two week cycle with one week grazed and one week rested was harmful to the pasture and severely depressed output. The failure of any experiment to reveal any advantage from grazing cycles longer than four weeks is the basis of the current recommendation that they should normally fall within the limits of 20 to 30 days. Voisin (1959) laid great stress on the importance of the rest period and on the avoidance of grazing of the regrowth within one occupation of a paddock. Ideally, rotational paddocks should not be occupied for more than four days at one grazing, although where the electric fence was used to subdivide a paddock daily for up to seven days cows did not return to the earlier strips to any serious extent.

4.12.9 *Other grazing methods*

Control of time of access. Cattle normally graze from six to eleven hours of each day but the grazing pattern over the 24 hours can be affected by changing the time of providing fresh pasture from evening (which is preferred) to morning or by housing the cattle overnight. The efficiency of grazing might be increased, and waste from treading reduced by limiting the time for grazing, but since cattle indoors normally spend at least five hours eating it is unlikely that they can successfully gain a full diet from grazing in less than six hours.

Rationed grazing. When herbage is scarce, as may occur in spring or in drought conditions, rationing of grazing can be achieved with movable electric fences, preferably within a rotational paddock system. Where alternative forage supplies are available, such as silage or a forage crop of maize, lucerne or grass at a more advanced stage of growth, a combination of grazing with indoor feeding may be suitable. Indeed a recent survey showed that over 40% of Dutch dairy farmers with more than 70 cows housed their cattle at night, offered them silage and severely rationed their spring grazing.

It is possible to restrict pasture supply and provide supplementary concentrated feed to maintain a normal level of animal production. Holmes & Curran (1967) reported that where pasture was restricted to half the normal allowance and cereal concentrates were provided at 0·3 kg per kg, normal milk yield was maintained. Similar practices may be adopted for beef animals. Although they are not normally economic in the long term, they may be useful to overcome temporary shortages.

Forage feeding (*zero grazing or mechanical grazing*). Because grazing is inefficient, the cutting and carrying of green herbage to stock has been claimed to increase output per hectare. These claims are not well substantiated (Holmes & Allanson 1967) but forage feeding is useful with very large herds of cows on dissected farms where access is difficult, and with the larger tropical forage grasses. Difficulties from the technical point of view include the maintenance of herbage quality, the conflict between the ease of handling of long herbage and its lower nutritive value, and the provision of an adequate supply of herbage, without waste and reduction of choice by the animals. Other drawbacks include the initial cost of and maintenance of the machinery in working conditions seven days per week and the disposal of the slurry produced by the housed cattle. Provision must also be made to deal with surpluses at periods of maximal growth of grass.

Storage feeding. In theory the ultimate method in grass and forage utilization is storage feeding where each parcel of herbage is cut and conserved at the optimal stage of growth, stored in silos and then used as required throughout the year. This is technically feasible but it makes heavy demands on agronomic skill and on capital for harvesting machinery, storage and feeding facilities although it avoids costs of fencing and water supplies. It is applicable only to large-scale, intensive units in favourable economic conditions and is not practised in the United Kingdom.

Deferred grazing. This term refers to range or upland pastures where in order to provide a reserve of 'standing hay', to restore the pasture, or allow stock to be concentrated on another area, an area of pasture is rested for several months. On tropical ranges a regular two-year cycle might be operated in two grazing blocks with one of the blocks being rested for up to six months in each alternate wet season.

4.13 ASPECTS OF GRAZING MANAGEMENT

4.13.1 *The transition to pasture*

Although there is little experimental evidence on this subject, when housed stock start grazing in spring it is considered to be preferable that they have access to the pasture before it has grown a large mass of herbage, or that their time of access is restricted for some days, so that the diet is changed gradually rather than abruptly. Ideally, animals should be turned out first to a well-drained, sheltered permanent pasture or one due to be ploughed, so that they can dissipate excitement without damaging the sward. Dairy cows might then be allowed strip grazing on forage rye, Italian ryegrass or other early ley. In wet weather more lax grazing may be necessary to avoid poaching. Dairy cows normally return to the shed at night for some time, where they should continue to receive hay or silage while concentrated feeds are reduced. Indeed this transition can take weeks, with advantage. Young cattle or in-wintered sheep are preferably turned on pasture 4 to 6 cm in height so that the grass 'grows to the stock'. Fodder should be offered in the field and concentrates may be discontinued or, for calves, gradually reduced and then eliminated within two to three weeks. The milk yield of dairy cows generally increases on turnout to pasture. If the increase exceeds 10%, they have been underfed. If milk yield declines, the herd has been fed too liberally in winter. Cattle usually lose body weight on turnout because of a reduction in gut contents (Balch & Line 1957).

The same principles apply to the return of stock to winter housing, in that a gradual change to the winter diet should be achieved by offering conserved forages and possibly concentrates in the field or the shed for some weeks before the stock are housed.

4.13.2   Extending the grazing season

Early bite. Early grazing can be obtained from autumn sown forage rye, Italian ryegrass or early cultivars of perennial ryegrass, preferably on sheltered, well-drained sites. The pastures should be rested from January and receive fertilizer nitrogen about four weeks before grazing is expected to begin. They are usually strip grazed.

Autumn saved pasture, foggage, winter grazing. Fields with free draining soils and a sheltered aspect are also preferred for autumn grazing. A perennial ryegrass ley or permanent pasture may be used but pastures dominant in tall fescue (*Festuca elatior*) or cocksfoot (*Dactylis glomerata*) are particularly suitable. These should be rested from late August, fertilized and allowed to grow until November and strip grazed. Cocksfoot has been grown in 50 cm drills to facilitate winter grazing but this is not now practised.

4.13.3   Trimming, harrowing and rolling of pastures

If pastures are weed infested or have been allowed to become stemmy due to understocking, it may be desirable to trim them mechanically to prevent the seeding of weeds and of grasses and, by eliminating apical dominance, to encourage the grasses to tiller. However, well-established and well-managed pastures, stocked at an appropriate rate should not become weed infested or stemmy. The need to trim pastures is an indication of understocking and is likely to result in loss of production since much of the trimmed material will decay, although the regrowth will be improved. Trimming if required should be to 5 cm from ground level—stock will eat some of the trimmings.

Harrowing is seldom beneficial in high quality pastures, but it may be necessary to spread mole hills and level poached areas. It is also practised in spring on old, matted pastures to aerate and open the sward.

Rolling is normally done when grassland is to be cut, in order to reduce damage to machinery and contamination of herbage with soil.

4.13.4   *Coping with shortages*

Summer rainfall is variable and unreliable. In the event of drought and a prolonged reduction in the rate of growth of pasture the following tactics may be adopted.

(a)   Give priority to the classes of stock which would suffer most and restrict the grazing of less important stock.

(b)   Reduce the number of stock by sale (seldom economic in practice).

(c)   Provide supplementary feed as hay, silage, forage crops, brewers grains, concentrated feeds or liquid feeds with straw.

Cows in early lactation, calves and lambs, and cattle in the later stages of finishing or in advanced pregnancy deserve the best nutrition. Ewes and heifers about to be mated also must be maintained in good body condition. Dairy cows in mid-lactation, heifers in mid-pregnancy, young cattle 6 to 15 months old and ewes at the end of lactation, can withstand a month of reduced feed availability. Growing stock will compensate when pasture growth resumes and milking stock will also recover milk yield. The quality of supplementary feeding should depend on the overall nutritional needs of the stock. If it can be provided from home-grown forage or by-products such as brewers grains, it will be more economical than from purchased compound feeds although concentrates are more convenient.

4.14   FENCES

The separation of fields by walls, banks, hedges or fences is normal and their subdivision by temporary fences is common. Only where all the feed is carried to housed stock, where the stock are tethered

or where a shepherd controls their movements is fencing unnecessary. Permanent divisions provided they do not enclose areas too
small for modern machinery, are valuable. Their maintenance in
good repair is important (MAFF 1970). Permanent fences, of
wooden post and rail, post and wire or post and wire netting are
commonly used as permanent field divisions and are described by
MAFF (1969).

The advent of the electric fence in the 1940s greatly simplified the
provision of fencing and reduced its cost. The electric fence provides, through a unit powered from mains electricity, batteries or by
wind or solar generators, an electric pulse of high voltage. This is
carried in the fence wire which may be plain wire 1·5 to 2 mm
diameter, woven wire 1·5 to 2 mm diameter or stranded nylon including a metal strand. Stranded nylon netting is also available. The
animal or man touching the wire completes the circuit to earth and
receives a shock. These fences can provide field divisions and subdivisions for paddocks at low cost. Moreover with light posts and
strainers they provide an easily movable fence which may be used
for 'strip' grazing. The electric fence is described in some detail in
MAFF Bulletin No. 147 (MAFF 1976).

It is essential that animals are trained to respect electric fences.
When calves are turned out they should be in small enclosures not
more than 0·5 ha. If a single electric wire is used, it should be made
clearly visible by hanging string or other visible markers on the wire.
Occasionally recalcitrant animals are present which may need
special treatment such as a light metal chain around the neck with a
dangling end as an additional contact, or in extreme cases they may
need to be removed from the group.

4.15   PRACTICAL GRAZING MANAGEMENT

In general, the more expensive the land or the more productive the
stock the more intensive or controlled should be the grazing system.
The extent to which fertilizer use is justifiable also depends on the
response to nitrogen, the efficiency of grazing and the type of livestock used as well as prices. It is likely to be more worthwhile with
dairy cows or growing cattle than with beef sucklers or a sheep
flock. It should be stressed that different systems including extensive
and intensive management, may be quite appropriate for different

classes of stock on the same farm. Moreover some groups of stock at less critical stages of life may follow no clear-cut system, and depending on the exigencies of the weather and the farming system, may move from one pasture to another over the grazing season. However, haphazard grazing management, like cropping without a rotational plan, increases the need for management decisions and the risk of poor performance and should be avoided. (Approximate stocking rates for each class of stock are given in Table 7.3.)

4.16   DAIRY COWS

Dairy cows receiving from 500 to 1500 kg of concentrated feed per year are normally stocked at two to three cows per ha over the whole year, with grazing stocking rates of three to five over the grazing season and peak stocking rates of five to eight cows per ha. The grazing area is usually expanded later in the grazing season with silage regrowths, maiden seeds or specially grown forage crops. The preferred methods include continuous stocking, rotational paddock grazing and integrated grazing and conservation. A survey (MAFF 1980a) showed that 73% of dairy herds adopted controlled grazing (paddock or strip grazing). Dairy cows are the most efficient of the grazing animals as feed converters and in economic terms they justify intensive pasture management and fertilizer application. Applications of 300 to 500 kg N per ha over the grazing season may be justifiable (Gordon 1974a) (Chapter 6 refers to input-output relationships). Routine application of 50 to 80 kg N per ha at four week intervals may be made or daily rates of application may be varied from 1·5 to 3 kg N per ha over the season. In rotational grazing fertilizer should be applied to each paddock immediately after grazing since delay can reduce herbage yields. With continuous stocking fertilizer can be applied, preferably to successive blocks of pasture at weekly intervals, referred to as 'Follow-N'. Applying fertilizer to the whole area at intervals of four weeks increases the risk of loss of fertilizer by leaching following heavy rain or by volatilization and might also, in wet conditions, produce a flush of grass too high in nitrogen content and temporarily unacceptable to stock. The need for mineral fertilizers must be considered but recycling of mineral nutrients occurs especially on intensively grazed dairy pastures. Potassium should not be applied in spring since this increases the risk of hypomagnesaemia tetany. Phosphorus should preferably be included in the seed bed but if more is required it may be applied at at any suitable time over the season. Fertilizer application is simplified if parallel lines at intervals equal to the width of the fertilizer spreader are marked on the field by herbicide or a marker plant. If a rigid rotational system or a continuous stocking system is adopted, no decisions on movement of cows are required. With continuous stocking, however, it is now considered that if the average height of the sward measured by ruler falls below 7 cm, performance will be impaired and in rotational paddock systems pastures should not be grazed below 7·5 to 9·5 cm (Baker 1978).

Cattle should move to a fresh paddock in the afternoon. With strip grazing, a fresh strip should be allotted each day preferably after the afternoon milking, since cows will eat the major proportion of their feed between turnout and dusk and the risk of bloat is slightly less since pasture is more likely to be dry. Moving the electric fence twice a day may not increase productivity and increases bloat risk. Combined grazing systems are feasible. A convenient night paddock might be continuously stocked while more distant pastures are grazed in rotation during the days.

Herds of cows up to 100 in number may graze as a group. With larger herds stress and delay at milking will be reduced if the herd is divided into groups of up to 100 cows and each group is grazed and milked separately.

Access tracks and water supplies must be adequate for large numbers. Tracks should be not less than six metres wide and water supplies should be capable of providing 50 litres per cow per day, much of it consumed at or after milking (Castle & Watkins 1979).

Attempts to deal mechanically with fouling of pastures by dung have failed and it is now accepted that occasional resting and cutting of the sward for conservation is the most practical method. As pastures become older, faeces and urine are more uniformly distributed, the population of natural fauna, of earthworms and insects increases, and these break down and distribute the animal faeces and the problem of fouling is reduced.

Some flexibility in grazing management should be retained. Particularly in rotational or strip grazed systems extreme conditions of rainfall or storm may result in poaching and severe damage to the pasture or exposure of the animals. The manager must be prepared to modify the system temporarily to avoid such difficulties without relaxing the overall stocking rate.

The feeding of concentrate supplements to cows on pasture is common although most surveys and experiments have shown that the practice is usually uneconomic (Leaver *et al.* 1968, MAFF 1980). This is mainly because the net increase in nutrient intake from concentrates is small when grass of high digestibility is readily available (Chapter 3). Supplements may be necessary to provide mineral supplements to each cow and they may increase the carrying capacity on small farms but the provision of additional protein and energy is seldom justified except as a buffer to temporary shortages. Even if it is judged desirable to supplement high yielding cows, care is needed to prevent waste of concentrates for other cows in the herd.

Application of the stocking rates suggested in Table 7.3 can support milk cows for 150 to 200 days per year, and result in milk yields per hectare ranging from 6000 kg in poor conditions to 16 000 kg in good conditions. Even if concentrates were fed over the grazing season at 0·2 kg per kg milk, a high figure, the effective yields after allowing for the area needed to grow the concentrates would be 4600 to 9000 kg per ha of grass.

4.17 SUCKLER COWS

Suckler cows graze over a wide range from good lowland pastures where overall stocking rates of one to two cows per ha and grazing stocking rates of two to four cows per ha are possible, to extensive hill or range conditions where stocking rates may not reach one cow per ha. In good conditions some grass conservation may be possible but less intensive methods of grazing management are usually adopted. Hence, although an integrated grazing and conservation method or rotational paddocks may be used, the majority of beef cattle are on continuous stocking or intensive continuous stocking systems.

Liberal fertilizer use is seldom justifiable and dependence on natural sources of fertility is normal.

Forward creep grazing can be practised but is rare. Autumn-born calves may be weaned at seven to nine months and placed on the better pasture, while the cows in mid-pregnancy remain on the poorer pastures. It is important of course that the cows are well nourished in late pregnancy. Hypomagnesaemia is a common problem with suckler cows.

4.18   CALVES

Calves deserve special attention. Suckled calves stay with their dams and learn to graze with them, otherwise calves in Britain are generally raised indoors until about three months of age and about 100 kg weight. Provided that parasitic problems have been avoided, or anticipated by the appropriate dosing or vaccination (Section 4.9) calves then grow well on pasture. Pastures for calves should be clean and worm-free, dense and of high feeding value. They should preferably be recently sown or used previously for conservation or for sheep. Where, as is common for convenience, calves are grazed near the farm buildings, if at all possible, these paddocks should be occupied by calves once in two years and conserved in alternate years followed by adult stock or sheep grazing. Calves have a particularly selective habit of grazing and leave the pasture very patchy, so that an integrated cutting and conservation system where the residues are cut and removed is particularly suitable. A leader and follower system may be adopted where calves precede older cattle, or indeed (but seldom in practice) dairy cows, in a rotational grazing cycle. Particular care is needed with calves as they change from indoor feeding to pasture and they should continue to receive hay and concentrated feed (say 1 kg per head per d) for the first few weeks.

4.19   DAIRY HEIFERS

Dairy heifers should be raised to the appropriate size and weight at target calving age, normally two to two and a half years. Calving at two years demands fairly rapid growth throughout life and target live weight gains on pasture are 0·7 to 0·8 kg per day. Where calving at two and a half years is acceptable it is probable that similar overall live weight gains will be expected in summer to compensate for slower winter growth. Intensive heifer rearing on a rotational grazing system with leaders and followers has been satisfactory. The younger heifers lead and the older in-calf heifers follow. Care must be taken that the growth rate of the latter is maintained. Heifers in-calf should preferably be grazed on land which is free from steep banks which might cause injury, and should graze in airy sites, free from flies and less likely to result in summer mastitis infection. Intensive dairy farmers may find it worthwhile to transfer or 'agist' heifers to outlying rented pastures or hill grazings for the summer period although summer growth rates will then be lower.

Stocking rates and fertilizer rates on low land are similar to those suggested for beef cattle.

4.20 BEEF CATTLE

The grazing of growing, finishing cattle has been studied intensively in recent years (Kilkenny *et al.* 1978). Overall stocking rates for the whole year may range from two to five cattle per ha depending on the size of the cattle, the natural conditions and the level of fertilizer applied. Peak stocking rates early in the season may reach 15 cattle of 200 kg W per hectare or ten cattle of 350 kg W. It is difficult to provide conditions which favour continued growth of young beef cattle throughout the season and a reduction in stocking rate through sale of cattle or expansion of the area is essential. Even in favourable conditions it is unusual to maintain the high growth rates (1·25 kg per head per d) which can occur in the early part of the season and normally daily gains of 1·0 kg in mid-season and 0·75 kg in late summer are acceptable.

Rotational paddock systems or integrated grazing and conservation systems are preferred. With longer leys and large groups of cattle rotational paddock systems with a cycle of 24 to 32 days are convenient. Care should be taken that especially later in the season cattle are moved to a fresh paddock before intake is severely limited. Where the paddock layout permits it, a leader follower system with the finishing cattle leading may be adopted but this is not common.

On arable farms with short leys where the costs of fencing would be spread over two to three years, or for small groups of cattle, where paddock size would be too small for machinery to operate efficiently, the integrated system (1, 2, 3) is convenient and indeed it is preferred in many circumstances. The majority of beef pastures receive relatively little fertilizer but provided the stocking rates are adjusted in accordance with fertilizer level responses to 450 kg N per ha have been recorded (Holmes 1974, Marsh 1975). The targets shown in Table 7.3 should maintain cattle over a period of 180 to 200 days and yield from 500 to 1700 kg live weight gain per hectare.

Many beef cattle are purchased in the spring as stores and continuously stocked with a progressive reduction of stocking rate by the sale of finished cattle.

4.21 SHEEP

Where sheep are grazed as a separate enterprise, overall stocking rates range in the lowlands from 10 to 16 ewes per hectare with higher rates in the summer months. It is much more common for sheep than cattle to graze all the year round and the need for conserved feed is less since even where sheep are housed this is seldom for more than three months.

Sheep normally graze on shorter pastures than cattle and are better adapted to do so. Continuous stocking methods are, therefore, preferred. When intensive stocking is adopted it is convenient to wean the lambs and turn them on the regrowth from the conserved area to provide clean high quality pasture for the lambs, while the ewes can be dried off and then build up body reserves on the area which they grazed earlier in the season.

If a rotational forward creep grazing method is adopted, the sheep may be stocked at 12 to 18 ewes per hectare depending on the level of fertility of the pasture area. Eight paddocks are usually preferred with a rotation cycle of 24 days. Fertilizer applications to sheep pastures seldom exceed 200 kg N per ha.

On mixed sheep and cattle farms it is common for the cattle to be housed during four to six months of the winter, and normal for the breeding flock of ewes to graze the cattle pastures in sequence during late autumn and winter until February. Not only does this provide clean sheep grazing but it is also valuable in closely grazing the cow pastures and reducing the risk of winter kill. Indeed to maintain pasture condition some dairy farmers buy store lambs to finish, or let winter grazing to sheep farmers. It is vital that sheep should be off the cow pastures by the end of February.

4.22 MIXED GRAZING

Sheep and cattle may graze together in the same field or in sequence. It is claimed that mixed grazing ensures better utilization of the pastures, reduces, by dilution, the risk of parasitism and ensures that the nutrient requirements of the animals coincide more closely with grass growth. A major benefit of mixed grazing in practice is due to the higher overall stocking rate which is commonly a result. Sheep select a diet of higher quality than cattle on mixed grazing and lambs have grown better when grazed with cattle. The subject was reviewed by Nolan & Connolly (1977).

4.23 HILL GRAZING

On hill and upland grazings the same principles apply as on the lowland. Pasture growth depends on climatic conditions and natural fertility, and the animal's ability to select an adequate diet depends on the quality of the pasture and on the competition between animals. However, because of the greater extremes in weather on the hills and the tendency until recently to stock at a rate which would support animals throughout the winter with little supplementary feed, underutilization of the summer growth was common and was responsible for the low productivity of many hill grazings. Underutilization could establish an undesirable sequence of events. Because of understocking in June much of the hill pasture matures, decays and dilutes the remaining leafy growths so that the quality of the pasture is depressed. Sheep are therefore unable to attain good body condition at mating, ovulation and implantation are impaired, the ewes are undernourished through the winter, produce a weak lamb and cannot provide enough milk for it. In consequence many hill flocks wean 60 to 90 lambs per 100 ewes and the weight of the lambs at the autumn sales is low.

The Hill Farming Research Organisation (1979) identified these problems and has developed a programme to attain and maintain a higher pasture quality on the hills and provide better nutrition to the ewes and their lambs at the most critical points of their life.

The essentials of this programme are:

(1) The improvement of selected areas of pasture which are accessible and well drained, by fencing, liming and possibly the sowing of white clover seed and fertilizer.

(2) Identification of the critical periods in the annual cycle of the hill ewe, when a good plane of nutrition is particularly important. These include before and at mating and before and after lambing.

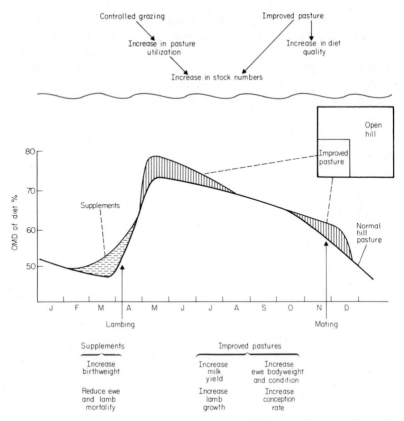

FIGURE 4.6. Improved utilization of hill pasture. (After Cunningham and Russel 1979.)

TABLE 4.5 The increase in production following improvements on a hill grazing of 283 ha. (HFRO Seventh Report 1977, Tables 1 and 12, pp. 74 and 92.)

	1969	1972	1976
Total breeding sheep	398	528	620
Lambs weaned per 100 ewes	85	105	109
Weight of lamb weaned per ewe mated (kg)	19·6	26·6	28·9
Gross margin per ewe at 1975/76 prices (£)	9·24	13·42	15·88

(3)   Co-ordinating the use of the improved pasture with the critical periods in the ewe's life cycle so that the improved pasture contributes to the improved nutrition of the sheep, resulting in better conception rates, higher lambing percentages and better growth rate of lambs. This procedure is summarized in Figure 4.6 and some results from a successful hill farm are given in Table 4.5.

These methods have permitted a gradual increase in stocking rate and an improvement in the overall utilization and quality of the hill pastures. Winter stocking rates have been improved by the introduction of supplementary feeding to augment the feed supply and improve the utilization of the low quality winter pasture. The accumulation of mature grass due to understocking in summer may be combated also by the adoption of mixed grazing either with spring calving suckler cows or with young stock such as growing heifers agisted from the lowlands.

FURTHER READING

ALLEN D. & KILKENNY B. (1980) *Planned beef production.* Granada Publishing Co., St. Albans.

CASTLE M. E. & WATKINS P. (1979) *Modern milk production.* Faber, London

COOPER M. MCG. & MORRIS D. W. (1973) *Grass Farming.* Farming Press, Ipswich

CUNNINGHAM J. M. M. & RUSSEL A. J. F. (1979) The technical development of sheep production from hill land in Great Britain. *Livestk Prod. Sci.,* **6**, 379–85

HILL FARMING RESEARCH ORGANISATION (1979) *Science and Hill Farming. HFRO 1954–1979.* The Hill Farming Research Organisation, Edinburgh

HODGSON J. & JACKSON D. K. (eds) (1975) *Pasture utilization by the grazing animal.* Occasional Symposium No. 8. British Grassland Society, Hurley

KILKENNY J. B., HOLMES W., BAKER R. D., WALSH A. & SHAW P. G. (1978) Grazing management. *Beef Production Handbook No. 4.* Meat and Livestock Commission, Milton Keynes

LEAVER J. D. (ed.) (1982) *Herbage Intake Handbook.* British Grassland Society, Hurley.

OWEN J. B. (1976) *Sheep Production.* Bailliere Tindall, London

PRINS W. H. & ARNOLD G. H. (eds) (1980) *The role of nitrogen in intensive grassland production.* Centre for Agricultural Publishing and Documentation. Wageningen, Netherlands.

SPEDDING C. R. W. (1971) *Grassland Ecology.* Clarendon Press, Oxford

WILKINSON J. M. & TAYLER J. C. (1973) *Beef Production from Grassland.* Butterworth, London

WORDEN A. M., SELLERS K. C. & TRIBE D. E. (eds) (1963) *Animal Health, Production and Pasture.* Longman, London

Chapter 5

The conservation of grass

5.1 INTRODUCTION

Production from cattle and sheep during winter is based largely on forage conserved from the grass crop. Grass conservation is not of course the only way of overcoming the winter feeding problem, and arable by-products, arable crops specifically grown for stock, home-grown grain and purchased compound feeds can also be used with advantage in many situations.

TABLE 5.1. Estimated production of silage and hay in the UK and artificially dried forage in England and Wales (thousand tonnes) (MAFF 1981).

Year	Grass silage	Hay	Artificially dried forage
1960	5580	6935	85
1965	6830	7313	84
1970	9010	7990	82
1975	16 780	6880	160
1980	27 750	7000	N.A.

However, large quantities of hay and silage are made in the UK (Table 5.1). There has been a steady increase in the amount of silage made relative to hay. This has been more marked in some areas, for example, on the basis of equal dry weights, in 1978 silage represented about 42% of the total herbage conserved as hay and silage in the UK, but 61% for Northern Ireland. This difference may reflect both the difficulty in making hay and the higher proportion of cattle enterprises in N. Ireland. Artificially dried forages form only a small proportion of the total conserved.

5.2 PRINCIPLES OF CONSERVATION

Foodstuffs can be preserved in several ways. The moisture content can be reduced to a level which will prevent the growth of bacteria and fungi as in haymaking and artificial dehydration. Substances can be added which inhibit bacterial growth, or an acid medium may be created which has a similar effect. These, in conjunction with airtight storage, form the basis of silage-making. Finally, the product can be kept at a low temperature. Freezing has been used in preserving grass for experimental purposes and vegetables, but it is too costly for farm use.

The main objectives in conserving grass are to make a product which closely resembles the original herbage in feeding value, has suffered minimal losses and is acceptable to the animal. It is, unfortunately, true that much conserved forage is of poor quality, partly as a consequence of the original herbage having a low feeding value and also as a result of the use of inappropriate or inefficient methods (Jackson *et al.* 1974, McDougall & Jackson 1977). Although low quality forage will suffice to feed stock of low productivity, for example suckler beef cows, this is no reason for accepting a badly made product. For milk production and winter finishing of beef cattle, a product with a high feeding value is generally required.

It is also important that nutrient losses are controlled at all stages of the process including losses in the field, during storage and when the forage is being given to the animals. The relative importance of these sources of loss will depend on the conservation technique, but clearly nutrient losses represent a waste of resources and increased costs of production and it is desirable to conserve as much of the original material as possible.

5.3 THE CROP

5.3.1 *Crop quality*

The growth and management of the crop and the nutritive value of herbage is discussed in Chapters 2 and 3 and it is necessary only to relate this information to crop conservation because the technique employed can modify or limit herbage production and feeding value of the product.

The feeding value of any conserved product is largely dependent on that of the original herbage and a high digestibility product can only be obtained from a crop with a high digestibility. It follows that stage of maturity at time of cutting, the grass species or cultivar, the proportion of legumes present and the amount of nitrogen fertilizer applied to the crop will all influence the nutritive value of hay, silage and artificially dried forage.

5.3.2   Method of conservation

Artificially dried forage, barn-dried hay and silage can be produced efficiently from young, leafy herbage. However, immature herbage has a high moisture content and swaths formed by this type of herbage will tend to be too dense for normal hay making, impeding air flow and restricting the drying process. In addition, field-cured hay and, to a lesser extent, barn-dried hay, are dependent on weather conditions, which tend to be more favourable in early summer than late spring. For these reasons herbage for field curing is normally cut at a later stage of growth than other conserved products and, in consequence, is usually of lower feeding value.

The possibility of increasing herbage production by the use of nitrogen fertilizer also is limited with field-cured hay both because heavy crops are difficult to make into hay and because the interval between cuts is long and the optimum amount of nitrogen cannot be readily applied.

5.3.3   Frequency of cutting

The digestibility of grass crops falls as yield increases (Table 5.2). The greatest increase in dry matter yield occurs at cutting frequencies of less than four weeks, but appreciable differences may also be obtained at greater defoliation intervals. Dry matter digestibility is reduced to an increasingly greater extent as cutting interval increases and, consequently, there is little or no difference in digestible dry matter yield with infrequent cutting. Similarly with the primary cut of grass, the increments in yield decrease with later cutting, digestibility is reduced consistently after ear emergence and the yield of digestible herbage increases to only a small extent at later stages of maturity (Table 5.2 and Figures 3.6 and 3.7).

When a forage is being offered *ad libitum*, as is common with

TABLE 5.2. (a) The effect of cutting frequency on the yield and digestibility of grass.

Cutting interval (weeks)	Annual dry matter yield (kg ha^{-1})	Dry matter digestibility (%)	Digestible dry matter yield, (kg ha^{-1})
4	12690	73·8	9350
6	13360	71·1	9530
8	14050	67·0	9420

(b) Effect of date of cutting on the yield and digestibility of primary growth of grass.

Date of cutting	Dry matter yield (kg ha^{-1})	DOMD (%)	Yield of DOM (kg ha^{-1})
23 April	2140	76·4	1630
1 May	2920	76·3	2230
8 May	3780	74·0	2800
19 May	5170	67·9	3510
29 May	5600	63·0	3530
11 June	6160	59·3	3650

50 % ear emergence 17 May. DOM ≃ 93 % of DDM
(After Chestnutt *et al.* 1977, and Minson *et al.* 1960.)

silage, a certain quantity is required to carry the animals through the winter period. Animals will consume greater quantities of a high digestibility material, but concentrate feeding can be reduced with a conserved product of high digestibility. The problem, therefore, is how to achieve the best compromise between yield and quality, except with artificially dried forage where the main consideration is the production of a high quality feed. Available information is conflicting, the best solution depends on the circumstance of the particular farm and the ratio of feed costs to value of animal product. However, an early first cut followed by cutting intervals of about six weeks will produce grass silage of high digestibility, capable of contributing significantly to the production of milk and beef and without a marked reduction in herbage yield (Table 5.3). These results were obtained in Northern Ireland. It is possible that in areas subject to summer drought a large first cut is more important, as herbage growth thereafter might be affected by low soil moisture contents. Nevertheless, early harvesting of the primary cut maintains the vigour of the sward and allows application of nitrogen fertilizer at a time when soil moisture may be adequate to allow absorption and influence the succeeding growth.

TABLE 5.3. The effect of frequency of cutting on the digestibility of silage and animal performance.

Cutting interval (weeks)	D value (*in vivo*)	Silage and concentrates[1] Milk yield (kg d⁻¹)	Silage only[2] Live weight gain (kg d⁻¹)
5	70–71	29·0	0·77
7	68	28·2	0·73
9	58–59	26·3	0·50

[1]Gordon (1979)
[2]McIlmoyle (1978)

5.3.4 *Height of cutting*

It is possible to vary the height of cutting but, in spite of arguments in favour of leaving a long stubble (Donald & Black 1958), yield of dry matter and digestible dry matter is not increased by cutting at heights greater than 2·5 cm above ground level in the UK (Table 5.4). Cutting very close to ground level can retard the recovery of the sward and can result in soil contamination of silage which can have an adverse effect on fermentation and on voluntary intake by animals. When the crop is to be partially or wholly dried in the field a cutting height about 5 cm above ground level will assist the drying process as there will be freer circulation of air through the swath.

TABLE 5.4. The effect of height of cutting on the annual yield of herbage. (After Harrington & Binnie 1971.)

Height of cutting (cm)	Yield of dry matter (kg ha⁻¹)	Yield of digestible dry matter (kg ha⁻¹)
2·5	11 530	8206
7·6	11 640	8043
12·7	11 040	7401

5.3.5 *Sward composition*

Sward composition tends to deteriorate more rapidly under a cutting regime than under grazing. Infrequent defoliation, particularly in association with heavy applications of nitrogen, increases the proportion of bare ground (Bartholomew & Chestnutt 1977) and is likely to facilitate the ingress of less desirable species in the sward.

Frequent defoliation is preferable if the maintenance of a sward is important. Recovery of a sward may also be retarded by wilting or drying herbage in a swath or by damage or soil compaction caused by harvesting equipment.

The crop may also influence the conservation technique. The soluble carbohydrate content of the herbage has an important bearing on the method of making silage. This can be affected by either the use of nitrogen fertilizer or by choice of plant type, legumes having particularly low water-soluble carbohydrate contents.

5.4   Cutting the crop

A crop of silage or artificially dried forage may be cut direct with a forage harvester. However, for hay and for wilting before ensilage or artificial drying the crop is cut first and collected later. A pre-cut crop can then be harvested more rapidly than with direct cutting.

Irrespective of the cutting system, ground preparation is vital. Stones and flints on the soil surface can damage cutter blades and forage harvesters and an uneven surface can lead to soil contamination. Heavy rolling when soil conditions are suitable can do much to reduce these difficulties.

The crop should be cut as rapidly as possible once it has reached the desired stage of growth. Machinery should be capable of a high rate of work, with a low maintenance requirement and with little risk of breakdown. Additionally, it should leave an open swath to allow aeration or one which is suitable for conditioning.

At the present time a high proportion of conserved forage, especially for silage, is cut with drum, disc or horizontal rotary mowers. These mowers have low maintenance requirements, are capable of a high work rate and are unlikely to block even in laid or very heavy crops. Reciprocating mowers, which were formerly used, had a lower power requirement but were difficult to maintain in good working order and were subject to frequent blocking except in relatively light, standing crops. The 'double-knife' form of this mower does not block to the same extent as the 'single-knife' type, but is even more difficult to maintain. Rotary mowers bruise the herbage to some extent as it is in contact with the blades more than once during cutting, but reciprocating-blade mowers do not have a similar action. However, for rapid drying some form of additional conditioning is necessary in both cases and, for the best results, this should take place at cutting or as soon as possible thereafter. The flail mower will both cut and condition the crop by bruising the herbage and this accelerates the rate of drying. This type of mower has a low maintenance requirement, but its disadvantages include a relatively high power requirement and a low rate of cutting. Unless it is operated carefully, it produces small herbage particles which are difficult to pick up, thus increasing field losses.

5.5   SILAGE

The changes taking place in silage result mainly from the action of plant enzymes, bacterial fermentation and, under aerobic conditions, from bacterial, fungal and yeast growth.

5.5.1   *Plant respiration*

Plant respiration can continue for some time after ensiling when oxygen is present in the mass and, even under anaerobic conditions, plant enzyme action can continue. More important, however, is aerobic respiration which involves the action of enzymes on the carbohydrate fraction of herbage and which results in the production of water, carbon dioxide and heat. If sufficient oxygen is present, the result of gaseous movement rather than entrapped oxygen which is rapidly exhausted, two major effects ensue. The first is that carbohydrate supply is reduced and this may restrict the quantity of lactic acid formed in the silage. Secondly, the heat produced raises the temperature of the silage and, if this rises above 40°C, the digestibility of crude protein can be reduced markedly. It is essential, therefore, to control the gaseous exchange which leads to the presence of oxygen in the silage mass.

5.5.2   *Fermentation*

Coinciding with and following plant respiration, bacterial fermentation occurs and a major aim in silage making is to control this bacterial action. Silage which has undergone an undesirable fermentation is characterized by a relatively high butyric acid content and an extensive degree of proteolysis and has a reduced digestibility, low intake characteristics and may increase the incidence of metabolic upsets in animals to which it is offered. Inhibition of the growth of clostridia, which are largely involved in an undesirable fermentation, is essential for the production of well-made silage. In many types of silage there is a negative correlation between lactic acid content and the contents of butyric acid and ammonia nitrogen, and a positive correlation between pH value and the latter

TABLE 5.5. An example of acid and ammonia contents of unwilted silage in relation to pH value.

pH	Lactic acid	Butyric acid	NH_3N
		(as % of dry matter)	
3·9	11·0	0	1·4
4·1	11·8	0	2·2
4·5	6·3	1·6	2·7
5·2	0·3	3·8	5·1
5·7	0·1	5·8	9·8

two substances (Table 5.5). A notable exception is wilted silage where preservation appears to be the result of osmotic pressure rather than a reliance on acidity. Silage made from wilted herbage can have a relatively high pH value and a low content of lactic acid but contains little or no butyric acid and a small amount of ammonia nitrogen. In general, however, with unwilted silage a rapid increase in acidity is required to prevent an undesirable fermentation and a critical level of acidity must be attained to achieve this objective. However, the buffering capacity of herbage can vary widely, for example clover has twice the capacity of ryegrass, and it also increases markedly during ensilage. Wilting the herbage before ensiling reduces the buffering capacity (Playne & McDonald 1966).

The importance of the development of sufficient acidity has given rise to the concept of 'stable' and 'unstable' silages. A stable silage is sufficiently acid to prevent deterioration of the silage over a long period of time. On the other hand, an unstable silage will, in the initial stages, have had increased acidity (lactic acid will have been formed), but not sufficiently to control clostridial growth, and subsequently there will be a progressive deterioration in the fermentation quality of the silage. This deterioration occurs because clostridia utilize lactic acid as a substrate (Table 5.6).

TABLE 5.6. Data illustrating the development of stable and unstable silages. (After Langston *et al.* 1958.)

Days after ensiling	Stable silage		Unstable silage	
	pH	Lactic acid (% of dry matter)	pH	Lactic acid (% of dry matter)
5	3·9	6·9	4·3	2·9
8	4·0	7·1	4·6	3·7
12	3·9	6·4	4·7	2·9
27	3·9	8·1	4·9	2·2
34	3·9	7·7	5·2	1·6
62	4·0	8·3	5·2	0·5

If the silage is untreated, two essential requirements for a desirable fermentation are sufficient inoculum of lactobacilli and an adequate supply of soluble carbohydrate (the substrate required for a lactic acid fermentation) in the plant tissue. There can be considerable variation in the numbers of lactobacilli present on herbage and, in some cases, there may not be enough to ensure a rapid formation of lactic acid. To remedy this, attempts have been made to develop a suitable inoculant, but although laboratory studies have provided encouraging results, experimental results have given little evidence that inoculants are effective on the farm scale.

Soluble carbohydrate content of the herbage is important in two respects. If the silage is untreated, the carbohydrate content must provide sufficient substrate for the production of enough lactic acid to preserve the silage. Alternatively, any deficiency should be known so that an appropriate treatment can be applied. Attempts are being made to provide an analytical service for this purpose, but information is already available on several factors which influence the soluble carbohydrate content of herbage.

The type of crop is a major consideration, some crops having an inherently low and others a high carbohydrate content. Maize and mature cereal crops always contain a sufficiently high carbohydrate content to ensure a desirable fermentation in silage. The grass crop may or may not have an adequate carbohydrate content depending on a number of factors. One of these is that there can be marked variations between grasses (Table 5.7), for example cocksfoot (*Dactylis* spp.) will usually have a lower carbohydrate content than ryegrass (*Lolium* spp.), but it has been demonstrated that this trait can be improved by breeding within a species. The legumes rarely, if

TABLE 5.7. The soluble carbohydrate content of primary growth of grasses and legumes (%). (After ap Griffiths 1963 and Davies *et al.* 1966.)

| | Date of cutting | | | |
	10 April	10 May	28 May	22 June
Grasses				
S.24 perennial ryegrass	18·1	25·4	28·5	22·6
S.48 timothy	18·4	19·0	24·0	15·9
S.215 meadow fescue	15·1	20·7	24·5	16·8
S.170 tall fescue	14·9	18·0	22·0	19·7
S.37 cocksfoot	10·5	15·9	22·1	17·4
	4 May	1 June	29 June	
Legumes				
White clover	8·1	10·7	13·1	
Red clover	8·5	9·8	10·3	
Lucerne	7·2	6·6	8·0	

ever, contain sufficient carbohydrate for a satisfactory fermentation although the difference in content between the legumes and grasses is not always as great as shown in Table 5.7. The non-structural carbohydrates of clover and lucerne also differ from those in grasses, as sucrose and starch rather than fructosan form the reserve material.

There is an apparent difference in carbohydrate content of grasses caused by stage of growth and season, but this may be confounded with the effect of climate. The data in Table 5.7 indicate that carbohydrate content increases until just after ear emergence and then declines. Generally, carbohydrate content is higher in May–June than later in the year (Aldrich & Dent, 1963) and it has been suggested that this may be due to the low leaf/stem ratio following ear emergence and a higher ratio during the later vegetative phase, but the same general trend in content has been found for flowering and non-flowering ryegrass. The marked variations in carbohydrate content in monthly cuts suggest that climate has an effect (Aldrich & Dent 1963) and both light and temperature have been shown to influence carbohydrate content (Deinum 1966). Diurnal variations also occur, carbohydrate content of grasses increasing between 0600 and 1800 h, but in lucerne increasing from 0600 to 1200 h and levelling off thereafter (Holt & Hilst 1969).

Fertilizer nitrogen increases the nitrogen content of the herbage but decreases the carbohydrate content (Nowakowski 1962). Immature grass will also tend to have lower contents of carbohydrate than more mature grass, and herbage cut early in the day has a lower content. However, nitrogen is essential for high yields, leafy grass will produce silage with a high digestibility and in practice silage cannot be made only at selected periods of the day. Carbohydrate deficiency should therefore be remedied by an appropriate treatment rather than by attempting to modify management to increase carbohydrate content of the grass.

Plant respiration after ensiling reduces the amount of available carbohydrate and the extent of the enzymic action is indicated by a rise in temperature in the silage mass (McDonald *et al.* 1966). Respiration should therefore be controlled by efficient sealing of the silage overnight when the silage is being made and on completion to conserve the maximum amount of carbohydrate for fermentation and reduce nutrient losses. Chopping or lacerating the herbage before ensiling will make the carbohydrate content of cells more readily available as a substrate for bacteria and will promote rapid formation of the lactic acid (Murdoch *et al.* 1955). Neither of these techniques will guarantee a desirable fermentation, but they will be of some assistance.

5.5.3   Nutrient losses

Crop losses can occur during harvesting and filling the silo, but these can be minimized by good design and efficient operation of equipment. A further possible source of nutrient loss (arising from mechanical losses and continued plant respiration) occurs if the herbage is wilted before ensiling. Respiration losses are greater when the herbage has a low dry matter content and when ambient temperatures are high. They are also increased under poor weather conditions (Honig 1979). However, loss of dry matter appears to be negligible for wilting periods shorter than 24 hours (Nash 1959).

Losses during storage are caused by plant respiration and fermentation (gaseous losses), effluent and surface waste. An indication of the range of these losses is given in Table 5.8. Some gaseous losses are unavoidable, but they are increased when respiration is uncontrolled and when an undesirable fermentation occurs. Effluent losses, in terms of dry matter, are not large, but the dry matter is composed of soluble constituents which have a high feeding value.

TABLE 5.8. The range of dry matter losses in silage (%).

Gaseous (respiration and fermentation)	5–10
Effluent	0–7
Waste	0–50
Secondary deterioration (after silo is opened)	0–15

The effluent may contain a substantial proportion of a silage additive and can cause severe pollution of drains and water courses. The amount of effluent produced is largely dependent on the dry matter content of the herbage ensiled but pressure on the silage and some additives may also affect the volume. Unless the silage is wilted, however, some effluent losses must be accepted. Surface waste is caused by aerobic conditions and this allows the proliferation of putrefactive bacteria and fungi. The conditions are similar to those required for making compost and the results are similar with the formation of inedible waste or mouldy silage which will be rejected by animals. Waste can be eliminated by sealing the silage efficiently. However, with inefficient sealing, or in some cases no sealing, dry matter losses can be very high, the visible waste being only a fraction of the true loss.

Further loss may occur after the silo has been opened. It is now evident that substantial losses can occur as a result of secondary deterioration of the silage caused by air entering the silage after it has been disturbed. Deterioration is accentuated by high ambient temperatures, high dry matter contents in the silage, poorly compacted silage or in a well-preserved silage with a low lactic acid content. In grass silage secondary deterioration appears to be caused initially by the growth of yeast followed by bacterial action. It has been suggested that losses of dry matter in the order of 10–15% can take place in a 10-day period after exposure (Honig & Woolford 1979). Therefore, when the silo is being emptied by mechanical means the silage should be disturbed as little as possible and the silage face exposed for as short a time as is feasible. Block cutters are, therefore, preferred to fore-loader forks.

5.5.4   Harvesting

There are three main types of forage harvester, the flail, double-chop (combining flail cutting with a fly-wheel chopping mechanism) and precision-chop. The precision-chop harvester can cut direct or pick up herbage from a swath, the herbage being cut into short lengths by either a fly-wheel or a cylinder chopper. There is also the choice between trailed and self-propelled models. All harvesters chop the grass to some extent, but the variability in chop length is least with the precision-chop harvester and increases markedly with the double-chop and to an even greater extent with the flail harvester.

The choice of harvester is partly dependent on factors associated with particle size. Voluntary intake may be increased when silage has a smaller particle size, particularly with self-feeding where the animals have less difficulty in removing the silage, but the major advantages are in handling the herbage and the silage. Indeed, only silage harvested with a precision-chop harvester is suitable for tower silos and for self-unloading trailers or forage boxes. Herbage in short lengths packs better into trailers and by significantly increasing the amount carried in the trailers reduces transport time. Precision-chopped material is also more easily consolidated in the silo, an important asset when wilted herbage is being ensiled in a clamp silo. Precision-chop harvesters are relatively expensive. Harvesters with a chopping mechanism are more vulnerable to damage from metal objects or stones picked up with the herbage, but the risk can be reduced or eliminated by good ground preparation and some form of metal detector on the harvester. In contrast, flail harvesters are generally robust machines, have a low maintenance requirement, and are relatively cheap. However, the low maintenance needs may be deceptive as the flails may receive inadequate attention, becoming blunt and chipped with the result that cutting is uneven and less laceration takes place.

Although silage is now normally picked up by a forage harvester, a baler can be used. Conventional small bales are difficult to handle but the recently introduced 'big baler' provides a convenient method of storing small batches of grass. The bales must be sealed within a plastic envelope and mechanical handling is essential.

There are many possible combinations in harvesting systems, ranging from the one-man 'team' (one man harvesting, transporting and filling the silo) to the large four- or five-man team (one cutting the crop, one harvesting, one filling the silo and the others transporting). Other things being equal, the larger the team the greater the amount of herbage ensiled in a given time. However, team size is clearly dependent on the availability of men and equipment and a small team may give an adequate output where distances from field to silo are small and the amount of silage to be made is limited. Distance from field to silo is usually the main determinant of team size as, with a given number of men, there is a marked reduction in output as distance increases (MAFF 1977b).

Speed of filling the crop into the silo is important. Herbage digestibility declines with time, particularly with the primary cut, and while harvesting the grass crop should begin on an appropriate date it is equally important that the period of harvesting should be as short as possible, otherwise there will be an inevitable decrease in feeding value. This problem, however, can be lessened by the use of a range of varieties with different dates of ear emergence (Chapters 2 and 3). Rapid filling of the silo reduces the risk of overheated silage and lack of uniformity which can create problems when self-feeding silage. Finally, as with any farm operation, the shorter the period devoted to silage making, the more time can be given to other important activities on the farm. It is essential, therefore, that the preparation of machinery, to avoid delays due to breakdowns and maintenance, and efficient organization of the harvesting system should be major considerations. Distance from field to silo is of importance and it is essential to keep the harvester in continual operation, bearing in mind that trailer changeover is where much time can be lost. Equally, the organization and technique of filling the silo can have a marked effect on output as this is often where bottlenecks occur.

The method of filling depends on the type of silo, a blower being required for the tower and bunker silo and usually some form of buckrake for the clamp silo. For the latter a front-mounted buckrake is preferable and some type of 'push-off' mechanism is an advantage in placing the loads.

Uniform filling of the silos is important particularly in a tower silo because there will be increased stress on the structure if herbage builds up on one side, and difficulties can also be encountered in mechanical unloading. With clamp silos uniform filling assists consolidation and sufficient herbage must be placed close to the silo walls, otherwise spoilage will occur.

All silos should be filled as rapidly as possible to reduce surface spoilage and variation in silage quality. Efficient consolidation of the silage by tractor rolling also reduces overheating and waste (Lancaster & McNaughton 1961). Spoilage can be controlled by an air-tight seal or by the use of plastic sheeting on clamp silos. To be fully effective, this should be used at the end of each day and, for longer breaks in filling, put on immediately filling ceases (Henderson & McDonald 1975). It is essential that airtight conditions are obtained and considerable care should be taken to seal the edges effectively and to make sure that the sheet is not damaged. If warm air cannot escape from the silo, air will not enter and respiration will be reduced.

Where the silo has a larger capacity than is required by a particular batch of silage, there is merit in the case of a clamp silo in reducing the exposed surface as much as possible. This can be achieved by filling the silo in a series of wedges rather than utilizing the whole floor space.

5.5.5   Silos

The type of silo will depend largely on the system adopted for feeding the stock and the choice of silo will influence methods of harvesting the crop, transporting the herbage and filling and emptying the silo. It is, therefore, part of an integrated system. The capacity of the silo, or silos, will be determined by the amount of forage required to feed the animals but, if possible, it is better to avoid the use of very large clamp silos as they can give rise to a variable product and may also increase the risk of secondary deterioration when a wide silage face is left exposed. Other considerations are effluent collection and disposal, when the herbage is ensiled unwilted, safe working conditions and cost.

Care must be taken in siting the silo. Generally, with forage harvester systems, the silo should be sited close to where the animals are housed. There should be easy access to the silo with a sufficiently large area of concrete for convenient and rapid unloading and filling operations. A concrete area is necessary to avoid soil contamination of herbage. The site should, if at all possible, allow for extension, but it is equally important that the area over which the animals move, as in self-feeding, should be restricted to a minimum to avoid the need for excessive cleaning.

There are several types of silo ranging from those which are basically heaps of silage in the shape of a clamp or stack to the sophisticated airtight tower silo. With unwalled silos it is difficult to control surface waste, and working conditions can be unsafe when they are being built. Wastage can be restricted, however, by the use of a plastic sheet covering. A variation of this is a complete enclosure of the silage with sheeting followed by evacuation of air, the 'vacuum silage' process (Lancaster 1968). This method can prevent waste and ensure low nutrient losses providing that the plastic sheet remains intact during the storage period but, as the silage is usually not as dense as when made by conventional methods, it is more subject to deterioration after opening.

In the UK the three main silo types are the walled clamp, the bunker and the tower silo, the most common being the clamp silo.

Normally the clamp silo will have three walls which should be airtight, and preferably sloping. They should also be sufficiently strong to sustain the lateral pressure from the silage and the weight of any tractor which is working on the silage. There is now a recommended safety standard (MAFF 1978b). For safety and prevention of waste the walls should always be higher than the surface of the silage at the time of filling the silo, because unless the silage is packed tightly against airtight walls wastage will occur.

The preferred height of finished silage depends on the method of feeding the animals. For self-feeding with cattle the maximum height is about 2 m, but when the silo is emptied mechanically greater settled depths of silage can be used with a consequent better utilization of the silo.

Protection from rain is important, the acidity being reduced when rain enters silage. This can be accomplished with plastic sheeting, which also provides an airtight seal, or with a permanent roof over the silo. A roof will protect the silage at all times, as will plastic sheeting if the silo is covered when the silo is being filled and care is taken in stripping the sheet when the silo is being emptied, but if this is not done the silage is vulnerable during filling and emptying operations. Roofing a silo is a costly extra and, for new silos, may not be justifiable.

A bunker is rectangular with four walls and the finished height normally exceeds 2 m. It is intermediate in other characteristics between the clamp and the tower.

The tower silo is usually constructed of steel sheet or concrete staves. The steel silo can be airtight and losses due to aerobic spoilage can be eliminated. Even with the non-airtight types, control of surface waste is easier because of the relatively small surface which is exposed. The tower is the only type of silo which lends itself to complete automatic feeding, but this involves considerable cost in equipment. Also, because of filling and emptying requirements, pre-wilting of the herbage and the use of a precision-chop harvester are necessary.

TABLE 5.9. Sources of dry matter loss in tower and bunker silos (%). (After Gordon *et al.* 1959.)

	Wilted silage (tower silo)	Unwilted silage (tower silo)	Unwilted silage (bunker silo)
Dry matter (%)	30·2	26·4	23·7
Source of loss			
Spoilage	0	0	1·5
Effluent	1·6	7·4	2·8
Gaseous	8·8	10·2	8·1
Total loss	10·4	17·6	12·4

Harvesting and feeding equipment costs may be higher with tower silos, but the silo cost is not much different from a roofed, walled clamp silo. Silage of equally good feeding value can be made in both types of silo. The other main consideration is the loss of nutrients. It is suggested that losses, particularly those associated with waste, are lower in the tower silo than in the clamp silo, because the less well the silage is protected from aerobic conditions the greater the losses. However, nutrient loss can be similar for a tower and clamp silo provided that the clamp silage has been sealed well with plastic sheeting (Table 5.9). The advantages of the tower silo lie in it being easier to attain a good seal and in simpler handling of the silage from the silo to the stock. The advent of mechanical unloaders for silage made in clamp silos has eroded the latter advantage.

5.5.6   *Silage with a desirable fermentation*

When a crop has a high soluble carbohydrate content, a satisfactory fermentation will normally occur in silage without any treatment being given. However, some crops, such as legumes, will usually be deficient in carbohydrate, and grass crops, unless at a mature stage

TABLE 5.10. Quality, intake and live weight gain from silages made with and without an additive. (After Collins *et al.* 1977.)

	Untreated	With formic acid $(1.7\ l\ t^{-1})$
pH	4·8	4·2
Dry matter digestibility (%)	70·7	73·5
Intake of silage dry matter (kg d^{-1})	6·3	8·7
Live weight gain (kg d^{-1})	0·47	0·88

of growth, may or may not contain sufficient carbohydrate to ensure a good fermentation. When the carbohydrate content of grass is not known, an assessment can be made from the factors known to influence carbohydrate content. In some cases a treatment will be applied as an insurance against a poor fermentation, with no guarantee that the treatment was required. The inferiority of the product from a silage with a poor fermentation will, however, be so marked that it is a good policy where doubt exists to apply a treatment. An extreme example is shown in Table 5.10. Normally an additive improves intake by 8–12% and daily live weight gain by 10–15%.

When the crop is deficient in carbohydrate, several approaches are possible. Additives applied at ensiling can supply soluble carbohydrate (e.g. molasses), partially acidify the mass (e.g. formic acid) or inhibit bacterial growth (e.g. formaldehyde). An alternative is to pre-wilt the herbage before it is ensiled.

The characteristics of wilted silage differ from those in unwilted silage. Wilted silage may have a relatively high pH value, usually has a low lactic acid content, but proteolysis is restricted and it has a high soluble carbohydrate content (Table 5.11). This

TABLE 5.11. The composition of wilted and unwilted silages (% of dry matter). (After McDonald *et al.* 1968.)

	Unwilted	Wilted	Wilted	Wilted
Dry matter (%)	15·9	28·4	34·1	47·6
Soluble carbohydrate	1·7	9·3	10·6	20·3
Non-protein N	2·0	1·9	1·2	1·1
pH	3·7	4·2	4·2	4·9
Lactic acid	12·1	5·5	5·5	0·9
Butyric acid	Nil	Nil	Nil	Nil

may be due to increased osmotic pressure in wilted silage (Wieringa 1960) or to the reduced buffering capacity of this type of silage (McDonald & Whittenbury 1967).

Additives. The choice of an additive depends on its effectiveness, availability, cost and ease of application. Application of the additive should not interfere with the speed of harvesting the crop and the method of application must be safe for the operator. It must also ensure a uniform mixing of herbage and additive, otherwise the effectiveness of the additive is considerably reduced. For this reason an additive is normally applied as a liquid by an applicator on a forage harvester, and is delivered in a steady stream to the incoming herbage. Further mixing occurs between this stage and filling the silo. It is also essential that the additive is applied at the correct rate; too low a rate may be ineffective and too high wasteful.

Many possible additives could be used to improve silage fermentation but, because they are not readily available or there are difficulties associated with their use, only a few need be discussed. The recent widespread use of silage additives in the UK is largely due to the introduction of applicators and additives which can be used conveniently with them. At one time molasses was the main additive, but it suffered from severe disadvantages. A relatively large quantity (4·0–10·0 l per t), usually diluted by at least an equal quantity of water, was applied by watering can, a laborious task which could not ensure uniform distribution. Although some applicators were designed, the quantity required even of undiluted molasses interferred with harvesting operations.

Formic acid, at the rate of about 2·5 l per t herbage, partially acidifies the silage (to below pH 5·0) and, with the subsequent formation of lactic acid, normally ensures good preservation of grass and legumes. Formic acid has been known to be an effective additive for a considerable time, but a suitable applicator only became available in the late 1960s and only since then has it been widely used.

An additive based on a mixture of formaldehyde and sulphuric acid is also available (Pike 1972). Both of these substances have been shown to be effective additives when used alone. Sulphuric acid was used in association with hydrochloric acid in the additive formulated by Virtanen in the 1930s and formaldehyde is a well-known sterilizing agent. Much interest has been shown in formaldehyde as an alternative to acids following observations that voluntary intake of acid silage may be reduced and that protein breakdown in the rumen is diminished when silage is treated with formaldehyde (Wilkins *et al.* 1974). However, while silages with low organic acid content can be produced by formaldehyde treatment, it may affect rumen function and may also reduce intake. Moreover, the silage is also vulnerable to secondary deterioration. There has been a renewed interest in dilute sulphuric acid as an additive, the objective being to partly acidify the silage in contrast to complete acidification in the Virtanen process. Preliminary results suggest that this treatment is as effective as formic acid.

The above-mentioned additives are liquids, but solid materials have also been used, two examples being sodium metabisulphite and calcium formate. Only the latter is of current interest and a product containing calcium formate and sodium nitrite is available in both solid and liquid forms.

All these additives, and many more, are effective, but there may be some inconsistency in comparative results.

So far, consideration has been given only to additives which influence the fermentation of silage. Secondary deterioration of silage may take place after the silo has been opened and techniques which restrict bacterial growth tend to make silage more susceptible to deterioration. Propionic acid and other long-chain fatty acids are effective in controlling secondary deterioration (Honig & Woolford 1979) but are expensive.

Wilted silage. Silage made from wilted herbage will be well-preserved when the dry matter content of the silage is about 30% or greater, little or no effluent will be produced and losses during storage are low partly because of the reduced effluent loss (McDonald *et al.* 1968). The voluntary intake of wilted silage will normally be higher than that of unwilted silage from similar herbage (Moore *et al.* 1960). However, wilting herbage complicates harvesting, particularly in either excellent or poor weather conditions, there can be increased loss of nutrients in the field, physical damage being more important than wet weather or slow drying (Gordon *et al.* 1969) and it is more difficult to control heating in the silage and losses due to wastage both during and after storage. Under adverse conditions, regrowth of the sward may be restricted where wilting is practised and the importance of the increased voluntary intake of wilted silage is also being questioned (Section 5.8.3). Wilting should not be confused with pre-cutting as, where facilities permit, this increases the speed of harvesting the crop.

It would seem, therefore, that wilting only has the advantages of reducing effluent production (and consequent losses) and eliminating the need to use an additive when a treatment is required. In the case of tower silos, high dry matter above 30% is essential to avoid the production of effluent, and for the operation of mechanical unloaders. Where weather conditions are favourable there may be good reasons for practising wilting, but in an adverse climate additives may be the preferred choice.

5.5.7   Feeding methods

Silage can be presented to animals on a self-feed basis or by mechanical methods. In general, it is too heavy and bulky to give by hand.

For self-feeding, the silage depth should not exceed 2 m and it must be uniform, otherwise the animals will be selective. Access to the silage face must be controlled by an electrified or physical barrier to prevent waste. The length of face required depends on time of access. With 24-hour access about 15–18 cm per animal is sufficient, but with limited access when all animals feed at one time about 75 cm per animal is required. While self-feeding has a minimal labour requirement, silos and yards must be arranged so that the area between them is as small as possible to minimize time spent in cleaning.

Although self-feeding has low labour and equipment demands, mechanical removal of silage from clamp silos is being more widely practised, since suitable equipment is now available and because of the difficulty in planning a suitable self-feeding layout for large numbers of animals. Additionally, silage removed mechanically from the silo is usually eaten in greater quantities than with self-feeding or, alternatively, when necessary, restriction of the amount of silage on offer is more easily accomplished by mechanical methods. However, to minimize secondary deterioration of the silage, silos should be designed so that large areas of the face are not left exposed for long periods of time and there should be as little disturbance of the silage face as possible.

Tower silos are usually equipped with either top or bottom unloaders which may be controlled automatically. After unloading the silage is either transported by conveyor or by a forage box (MAFF 1977b).

5.6   HAY

In haymaking the objective is to reduce the moisture content of the forage to 25% or less so that fungal and bacterial growth is suppressed. In extreme cases spontaneous combustion caused by the proliferation of thermophilic bacteria can occur when hay is stored with a high moisture content, especially in the loose form. Another risk is the production of mouldy and overheated hay which results in low intakes or possible rejection of the forage, increased nutrient losses, decreased feeding value and is a hazard to human health as the cause of 'farmer's lung' and allergies.

The overriding consideration is the weather at the time hay is being made. Under dry conditions with low humidity haymaking presents little problem, except possibly leaf shattering, because leaves dry more quickly than other parts of the plant. However, even in the most favoured areas of the British Isles the number of periods without rain is limited and the length of these periods restricted. There are on average 2·0–2·5 periods of 3 days or more of fine weather in May–August in the south of England and the mean length of these periods is 6–8 days (MAFF 1963). Conditions are less favourable in the north and west of the UK and also, even in the absence of rain, these regions will normally have a higher atmospheric humidity. These data indicate that there are limitations on the choice of time when hay can be made and that the best use must be made of each occasion, with full use of weather forecasting services. With the possible exception of barn-dried hay this, associated with the fact that mature herbage is preferred, since it produces a swath with better ventilation characteristics, is the main reason why the feeding value of hay is normally lower than that of silage.

Crops at the haymaking stage may contain some 20–25 tonnes water per hectare, a quantity which can be removed by transpiration from plants in one day during the months May–July. However, in practice, at least three days are normally required to achieve this in haymaking under good weather conditions because of limitations in the loss of water from the cut herbage from the swath.

In cut herbage, water loss causes the closure of stomata, in some conditions as early as one hour after cutting, and thereafter moisture must pass through the cuticle which is less permeable. Damaging the cuticle, possibly by mechanical methods, increases the loss of moisture. The rate of drying diminishes as the drying process continues, the removal of water being more difficult at low moisture contents because of an increase in osmotic pressure in the plant cells. Leaves also dry at a more rapid rate than stem by a factor of 10–15 and about 30% of the water in stems is lost through the leaf.

Variations also occur in the rate of loss of moisture between different grasses and it may be possible to select for this trait in breeding programmes.

When herbage is cut for hay a swath of varying depth and density will be produced and drying is more rapid on the surface of the swath. Poor circulation of air through the swath is a further contributor, as humidity in the lower layers inhibits moisture loss, an effect which is more apparent in the early stages of the drying process. This is accentuated by the structure and depth of the swath, immature herbage producing a dense swath and a heavy crop a swath of greater depth. Immature herbage also has a higher moisture content and will, therefore, require a longer drying period.

In practice, therefore, the objective is to create swath conditions conducive to rapid drying of the herbage, thus reducing the nutrient losses caused by plant respiration and the risk of leaching of nutrients by rain. However, physical losses caused largely by leaf fragmentation can result from movement of the swath with a consequent marked reduction in feeding value of the product. These losses are accentuated by some forms of swath conditioning, by mechanical treatment in the later stages of drying and by increased swath movement following rain. The data in Table 5.12 illustrate

TABLE 5.12. Losses of dry matter and digestible crude protein in haymaking. (After Watson & Nash 1960.)

	Loss of dry matter (%)	Loss of digestible crude protein (%)
No rain—no mechanical loss	8·7	16·5
No rain—mechanical losses	14·7	22·3
Rain	23·7	34·7
1–2 showers of rain (1–20 mm)	18·9	22·9
5–6 showers of rain (12–63 mm)	27·1	38·3

effects of mechanical treatment and rain on nutrient losses, showing the marked effect on digestible crude protein losses caused by loss of leaf and the adverse effect of increased frequency of rainfall.

The conclusion is that severe mechanical treatment should be applied only before the leaf becomes brittle and that the period when the hay is exposed to the elements should be reduced as much as possible. For the latter, possibilities include accelerating the rate of drying and protecting the hay before drying is complete. With field-curing of hay the former is the only option, with the additional possibility of using a preservative if the hay is baled with a high moisture content.

In addition to an accelerated drying rate the field-curing phase can be curtailed by several methods. In the past curing was completed in small ricks in the field, this being modified subsequently by the use of tripods which enhanced ventilation. While drying on fences is still practised on the Continent, tripods are now seldom used in the British Isles largely because of labour requirements and handling problems. However, barn-drying of hay, involving artificial drying of hay with moisture contents of less than 55%, allows the production of high digestibility hay without incurring high nutrient losses.

Losses can occur during storage and the extent of these losses depends almost completely on the moisture content of the hay, nutrient losses increasing markedly as the moisture content increases. The adverse effect of high moisture contents in the hay is increased by greater bale densities.

5.6.1   Conditioning

A major objective in haymaking is to reduce the period when the crop is at risk. Moreover, prolonged drying in the field will also reduce the yield of the regrowth. Only the flail mower or, to a much lesser extent, drum and rotary mowers will increase drying rate and other methods, such as bruising the crop, turning or tedding must also be used. Normally these techniques are complementary rather than exclusive, as severe treatment of the crop, such as crimping, can be practised only in the early stages of the drying process and must be followed by treatments of less severity.

An additional objective of any treatment is to produce hay which has dried uniformly. Moist patches in hay are subject to moulding and deterioration which may spread to adjacent areas, and a uniform product is desirable in all forms of haymaking including barn drying. It follows that all conditioning operations should not only be designed to increase drying rate, but also to ensure uniform drying. Any technique which causes the swath to be uneven in thickness or 'ropes' the swath should be avoided, since this usually results in uneven drying and is difficult to remedy once it has occurred.

Before considering mechanical methods of increasing the dry matter content of the crop it should be noted that moisture content can be reduced by heat or steam treatment (Philipsen 1971), but the cost of the machines is high and they do not appear to be a viable proposition at the present time. Desiccants, such as formic acid and diquat, have also been used for this purpose (Klinner & Shepperson 1975), but results have been variable and they are less effective in poor weather conditions. Both forms of treatment suffer from the disadvantage that, at best, the crop is only partially dried and further drying in the swath is required to reach a sufficiently low moisture content for the hay to be stored safely.

Conditioning by machines usually results in increased nutrient losses. An example being the flail mower which, by reducing particle size, can give rise to high losses (Murdoch & Bare 1960), and to a varying extent all conditioning treatments tend to increase losses. Therefore, in good weather conditions the most gentle treatment of the swath is indicated, but weather is not predictable or guaranteed, and in the UK conditioning of the swath must be accepted to avoid the risk of even greater losses of nutrients than those incurred by conditioning.

Many conditioning machines are available and it is only possible to discuss the type of action without mentioning specific equipment. Some machines are designed to fulfil more than one function, for example cutting and conditioning or tedding and side-raking. In some cases the multi-purpose machine may not be the most efficient at the individual operations.

Turning is the simplest and most widely used technique in haymaking both for making and wind-rowing hay. The objectives of turning are to invert the swath, increase aeration and transfer the hay to relatively dry ground. The reasons for this are that there is a drying gradient in the swath and inversion of the swath will expose relatively undried parts to the atmosphere, aeration of the swath will be increased by swath movement and a swath in contact with damp soil will inevitably have humid conditions underneath. While turning is useful in these respects and will normally be employed in conjunction with other techniques, it alone will not increase drying rate to the same extent as other methods of conditioning.

Tedding. A swath of hay will become more dense as the herbage settles thus impeding air flow. For rapid drying it is essential that circulation of air should take place and tedding will assist in this, either as the sole treatment or as an adjunct to other forms of conditioning.

The effect of tedding on drying rate has been known for many years, with the results of Cashmore & Denham (1938) and others showing that there is a marked increase in drying rate when the swath is tedded and that frequent tedding is more effective than a single operation. Additionally, tedding can also improve the uniformity of drying provided that the operation of the machine does not create lumpiness in the swath.

Conditioners which bruise the herbage are normally used only in the early stages of the drying process and subsequent treatment is achieved by means of a tedder or turner. While tedding may be applied frequently and initially with some severity, it is essential that more gentle treatment is given when the leaves become brittle (at about 50% moisture content) otherwise loss of nutrients will occur. At this stage the turner or a 'back-action' tedder are the indicated equipment.

It is essential that the tedder is designed to deposit the hay gently, this usually being achieved by baffle plates on the machine, otherwise the objective of allowing maximum air circulation through the swath will not be achieved.

Bruising or laceration. The stems of herbage will dry more slowly than the leaves and bruising of the plants will reduce this differential drying and increase the drying rate. Bruising or laceration of the herbage results from the use of a flail mower, crimper, roller crusher or, more recently, with combined mower-conditioners involving the use of either metal or plastic mechanisms (Klinner & Hale 1979).

TABLE 5.13. The effect of some forms of conditioning on drying rate. (After Murdoch & Bare 1963.)

Conditioner	Experiment 1 Moisture content (%) 30 h after cutting	Experiment 2 Moisture content (%) 50 h after cutting
Tedder	34	44
Roller crusher × 1	25	36
Roller crusher × 2	21	32
Crimper × 1	—	33
Crimper × 2	—	27
Flail harvester	20	27

The drying rates which can be achieved by these techniques are substantially greater than those obtained by tedding, and a further improvement occurs when the hay is treated twice by certain machines (Table 5.13). The reduction in time required to reach the moisture content required for safe storage will thus be reduced and the risk of the hay being damaged through poor weather conditions will be lessened. However, this form of conditioning will produce material which will absorb moisture from rain or dew to a greater extent than with less severe treatment, but nutrient losses do not appear to be increased when this occurs in the early stages of the drying process (Murdoch & Bare 1963). In spite of this the loss of nutrients is generally higher when the herbage is bruised as compared with hay which has only been tedded, particularly when a flail mower is used, although the adverse effect can be reduced by slowing rotor speed (Shepperson & Grundey 1962). These increased losses seem to result because the baler does not pick up the smaller particles of hay. This has led to the interest in mechanisms with less severe action (Klinner & Shepperson 1975).

Timing of conditioning. Conditioning is most effective in increasing drying rate when it takes place at, or close to, the time when the crop is cut (Murdoch & Bare 1963) and the number of operations can be reduced by combining mowing and conditioning. Conditioning at this time may, however, make the hay more vulnerable to damage by rain, but the advantage in rapid drying will normally outweigh this disadvantage. In addition, the hay will be less susceptible to mechanical damage in the early drying stages and it is preferable that any severe treatment should be applied at this time.

5.6.2 Barn-drying

Hay which has been barn-dried will normally have a higher feeding value than swath-cured hay. In one series of experiments the mean organic matter digestibilities were 69% and 64% respectively (Shepperson 1960), but the range extended from digestibility being about the same for the two types of hay to a 12 percentage unit difference in poor weather conditions. The difference in loss of dry matter is also dependent on weather conditions, but is normally higher with swath-cured than with barn-dried hay. For example, the mean dry matter losses for swath-cured and barn-dried hay were 28·3% and 15·0% respectively in a review by Carter (1960). The difference is mainly due to the barn-dried hay being baled at moisture contents of up to 50%, which reduces the time the crop is at risk in the field and leaf fragmentation, the difference being greater under adverse weather conditions. Although it has distinct advantages over field-curing, barn-drying of hay has not been widely accepted in the UK due to the additional capital required, the difficulty in conserving large quantities at any one time and, even with the use of bale-handling equipment, the requirement for hand-loading of the drier.

Several forms of radial drying are used in Europe, these being circular stacks of loose or chopped hay which are ventilated from a central duct. In the UK, however, the most common methods are tunnel, batch or storage drying of baled hay. Storage driers provide facilities for both drying and storing the hay, thus avoiding double-handling, but have the disadvantage that drying ducts are needed in each section of the barn. Batch drying refers to a suitably enclosed, roofed area which is used only for drying, the hay being stored elsewhere. Tunnel drying may be done either in the field or under a roof, the bales being built in the shape of a clamp around a portable plenum chamber—this again involves double-handling.

The moisture content at which the hay is baled depends on whether or not heat is used in the drying process. Where heat is used the hay may be baled at up to 55% moisture content, but without heat the maximum moisture content is about 35%. In all systems, it is essential that the air passes through the bales and this requires an adequate air flow, a suitable plenum chamber, bales of uniform density, and stacking of the bales so that they are bonded (Culpin 1962), to prevent air from flowing between the bales and the walls of the drier.

5.6.3   *Preservatives*

The techniques mentioned above have the objective of reducing the
moisture content of hay to 25% or less, when it can be stored
without any subsequent deterioration. If stored at higher moisture
contents, there is progressive deterioration due to fungal and bacterial activity. The temperature in the bales will rise, nutrient losses
will increase and the digestibility of the hay will decrease (Table
5.14). The higher temperatures will also reduce the digestibility of
crude protein in the hay (Miller *et al.* 1967). Additionally, mouldy
hay can give rise to mycotoxins and allergies which can create
health problems in humans and animals (Nash & Easson 1972).

TABLE 5.14. The effect of moisture content at storage on losses
and digestibility of hay. (After Nash & Easson 1977.)

| | Moisture content (%) | | |
	45	35	27
Maximum temperature (°C)	65	55	45
Dry matter loss (%)	17·6	13·9	7·4
In vitro DOMD (%)	56·5	58·7	60·8

It may be difficult to achieve the desired safe moisture content in
field-cured hay and this, along with the possibility of creating a
system of storing hay at high moisture contents, has lead to an
interest in the use of preservatives. A number of possible fungicides
have been investigated and, of these, propionic acid or its salts,
anhydrous ammonia and the hydroxides (ammonium or sodium)
appear to have potential value. Propionic acid has been more
widely tested than the other substances and it appears that rates of
addition of 1–2·5% of the acid for hays ranging from 30–50% moisture content would be required (Nash & Easson 1978). At the
appropriate rate of addition, temperature rise in the bales is controlled, losses of dry matter decreased and digestibility increased.
Ammonium propionate appears to be the most effective of the salts,
but is somewhat less so than propionic acid. A major difficulty in
the use of these substances is method of application. It is important
that the preservative is applied uniformly to the hay (partly due to

differences in swath density) and adjusting rate of application to cope with variations in moisture content of the hay is difficult.

Anhydrous ammonia is also an effective preservative, except that there may be deterioration of the hay when it is exposed to the atmosphere for long periods. Apart from having to enclose the hay in plastic sheeting for application, ammonia has the advantage of being evenly distributed through the hay and also increasing its nitrogen content. Hydroxide treatment of hay has an additional advantage that, if preservation is adequate, there will also be some increase in the digestibility of the hay (Tetlow *et al.* 1978).

5.6.4   Baling

The standard bale ($26 \times 46 \times 90$ cm) weighing 15–20 kg has been the normal method of handling hay for many years. On the small farm it is a relatively convenient method of handling hay but, while bale-handling techniques are available, the conventional bale has to be manhandled into store and at feeding. For larger scale enterprises the 'big-bale' has become popular because it can be fully mechanized.

Hay should have a moisture content of 20–25% when baled without the use of a preservative. At higher moisture contents, the bales should have a lower density, but precise rules are difficult to formulate. Weather conditions may allow baled hay to be left in the field to lose moisture; the type of crop, moisture content and setting of the baler will influence bale density. The only certain method of ensuring that hay is fit for storage is to bale at the correct moisture content.

Normally the standard bale is rectangular, but 'big-bales' weighing up to 500 kg may be either rectangular or cylindrical ('round'). 'Round' bales are relatively impervious to rain and may be left outside with little deterioration occurring, but they do not allow moisture loss to the same extent as rectangular bales and moisture content at baling is more critical. On the other hand, large rectangular bales are susceptible to penetration by rain if unprotected and this results in high losses. 'Big-bales' also present some difficulty in barn-drying. The only reliable way of barn-drying round bales is in a single layer, but rectangular bales can be dried satisfactorily provided that their moisture content does not exceed 30%.

5.7 Artificially dried forage

5.7.1 *Green crop drying, or grass drying*

Green crop drying was introduced into Britain in the 1930s and was practised fairly widely until about 1950. There followed a period of recession, but interest was renewed in the mid-1960s because of the introduction of more efficient driers and improved field equipment resulting in a reduction in labour and drying costs. However, the dramatic rise in the cost of oil has had an adverse effect on drying costs, and dehydration of forage for ruminant feed can only survive if there are marked economies in drying costs or an alternative, cheaper source of fuel is employed. To this end the moisture content of herbage can be reduced by wilting or mechanical de-watering and interest is again being shown in solid fuel.

There are two types of modern driers, conveyor driers which operate at relatively low temperatures (150–250°C), and high temperature (600–1000°C), rotary-drum driers. Both operate only with precision-chopped herbage. Low-temperature driers have a low output caused largely by the time taken to dry the forage (a range of at least 30–60 minutes), while herbage is dried in only 2–3 minutes in a high-temperature drier. Output of dried product is dependent largely on the initial moisture content of the crop and drier capacity, but can be 5–6 tonnes per hour or more, with about 25–30 tonnes water per hour being evaporated.

Dehydration is the most efficient conservation process, nutrient losses are low (in the order of 3–10% of dry matter) and, with efficient drying the product has a similar feeding value to that of the original herbage because the rapid removal of water from the herbage causes an immediate cessation of plant respiration. However, some loss of fine particles may occur after drying. As the moisture content of the dried product is controllable and low, there is little possibility of fungal or bacterial growth. Dehydration is a reliable process; a consistent product can be produced irrespective of weather conditions and immature grass or legumes can be conserved efficiently.

Dehydration has always been a relatively high-cost method of conservation. The drier and field machinery are expensive and drying costs are high. It is, therefore, necessary to have a high output of dried forage over a long season to spread capital cost, and

TABLE 5.15. The effect of moisture content of herbage on oil consumption in crop drying. (After Manby & Shepperson 1975.)

Herbage moisture content (%)	Oil consumption ($l\ t^{-1}$ dried grass)
85	367
80	279
75	212
70	168

a high quality product is essential to justify the high production cost. This requires a high degree of management skill to ensure that a continuous supply of suitable herbage is available for drying.

Drying costs are highly correlated with the initial moisture content of the crop. Oil consumption decreases dramatically with decreasing moisture content (Table 5.15) thus reducing cost of production. These data indicate that dehydration will be more costly in the wetter regions of the country as the initial moisture content of the crop is normally higher than in drier areas, and wilting herbage before drying is also more difficult. They also show that costs may be lessened by reducing the moisture content of the herbage through wilting or de-watering.

5.7.2 Wilting

Even a small degree of field drying will reduce oil consumption and increase output from the drier. With longer wilting periods, particularly when the crop has been conditioned, substantial economies can be obtained. However, nutrient losses may be incurred during wilting, which increase with the length of the wilting period. It is, moreover, more difficult to ensure a continuous flow of uniformly wilted herbage to the drier and marked variations in moisture content may lead to some of the product being overheated. Uniform drying in the swath is essential and treatment of the crop must have this objective in addition to obtaining rapid drying.

5.7.3 Mechanical de-watering

Interest in protein extraction from crops and the introduction of suitable presses have provided another method of reducing the moisture content of herbage. Jones (1976) suggested that there are three extraction stages. The first is de-watering where the objective is to remove the maximum amount of water with a minimum loss of dry matter to the juice. Wilting the crop reduces the proportion of protein which can be lost. The second is partial extraction, based on the argument that forages may contain protein in excess of requirements, the aim being to provide a more nutritionally balanced food rather than extracting the maximum amount of protein. Finally there is exhaustive extraction where the high protein juice is the primary product. Of these three, de-watering appears to be the appropriate method to be used in conjunction with green crop drying.

TABLE 5.16. The effect of de-watering (pressing) on the feeding value of herbage. (After Connell & Houseman 1976.)

	Grass		Lucerne	
	Before pressing	After pressing	Before pressing	After pressing
Moisture content (%)	83	74	80	72
Crude protein (% of DM)	18	15	20	16
In vitro DOMD (%)	68	66	58	56

Some values for the change in feeding value are given in Table 5.16 for grass and lucerne before and after pressing when the objective was to limit protein extraction. It is suggested that fractionation reduced the crude content by about four percentage units, with a smaller reduction when the forage had a higher dry matter content, and that digestible organic matter in the dry matter may be reduced by up to five percentage units. Fractionation of the herbage results in fuel economy and a higher output from the drier, but this must be balanced against the cost of producing and utilizing the extracted juice, and the juice must be used effectively because of its valuable nutrient content.

5.7.4   *Factors affecting feeding value*

Potentially the product from artificial drying will suffer only a low nutrient loss and is not markedly different in feeding value from the original herbage, although the metabolizable energy content of dried grass may be 4% lower than that of the grass from which it was made (Ekern *et al.* 1965). However, several management factors may change this situation. A reduction in feeding value can result from wilting the crop. This depends on the length of the wilting period, weather conditions and the extent of physical losses.

It is also common practice for herbage to be kept for varying periods at the drier before being dried. Under these conditions plant respiration will continue and the temperature in the herbage will rise. Short storage periods are unlikely to have a marked effect on feeding value, but after 12 hours (or possibly less) digestible organic matter and digestible crude protein contents are depressed consistently (Marsh 1976).

TABLE 5.17. The effect of drier exit temperature on the digestibility of dried grass. (After Marsh 1976.)

Exit temperature (°C)	Organic matter digestibility (%)	Crude protein digestibility (%)
77	69·3	64·8
99	69·0	64·2
119	68·0	60·4
145	59·9	36·0
166	44·0	11·1

If there is an excessive reduction of herbage moisture content in the drier, overheating will occur. Particles which are dry should be removed from the drier, particularly with high-temperature driers. Over-drying also reduces the efficiency of the drier. It will, also, have a marked effect on feeding value as shown by the effect of the related parameter, exit temperature of the drier (Table 5.17). There is a marked reduction in protein digestibility with overheating, although some denaturing of the protein may be acceptable because it reduces the loss of nitrogen as ammonia in the rumen (see Chapter 3).

The effect of processing on feeding value is discussed in Section 5.8.4.

5.8   CONSERVED FORAGES FOR ANIMAL FEEDING

5.8.1   *Evaluation*

Conserved forages vary in feeding value and it is necessary to have some method of assessment so that potential production can be estimated and the quantity of supplementary feed assessed. Assessment may be based on chemical analysis and advisory services are available to the farmer for this, the results usually being accompanied by recommendations on the level of supplementary feeding (see Chapter 3).

A cruder form of assessment is to judge the forage by sensory means and it has been shown that this method can give a useful estimate of feeding value (Troelson *et al.* 1968). Judgement is based on texture, smell and colour and, for silage, a squeeze test for dry matter content. The digestibility of the crop can be assessed by the proportion of leaf to stem present in the hay or silage. A bleached hay is one which has been badly weathered, a silage which has a dull, olive-green colour usually has undergone an undesirable fermentation and a brown colour in both products indicates over-heating. A stale smell is indicative of mouldy hay, and badly fermented silage has a characteristic, clinging odour. All these sensory evaluations show that the product has a reduced feeding value. Where an estimate of silage dry matter content is required a rough guide can be obtained by squeezing some silage by hand. When liquid is expressed easily the dry matter content is less than about 18% and no moisture can be expressed when the content is 25% or more. Further details are given in MAFF Bulletin 37 (MAFF 1977b).

5.8.2   *Hay*

Although it is possible to make hay of high quality, field-cured hay is a variable product, usually of relatively low feeding value, as a result of weathering and the late stage of growth at which the crop is cut. It is normally low in both energy and protein and as such can only be regarded as a maintenance feed, often being inadequate to achieve this modest objective.

On the other hand, barn-dried hay has the potential to maintain the animal and contribute substantially to production. This potential is largely dependent on the hay being made from a crop which has a high digestibility. It is expressed fully when the hay is offered *ad libitum* (Table 5.18).

Normally hay is offered to animals in restricted quantities and, to a large extent, factors affecting voluntary food intake are unimportant. However, they are critical when hay is offered *ad libitum* or when given in large quantities. Intake of hay rises with increasing

TABLE 5.18. Intake and live weight gain of cattle offered barn-dried hay or silage made from the same crop. (After McCarrick 1966.)

	Dry matter intake $(kg\ d^{-1})$	Live weight gain $(kg\ d^{-1})$
Early cut		
Barn-dried hay	7·69	0·77
Silage	6·50	0·75
Late cut		
Barn-dried hay	7·41	0·44
Silage	5·69	0·35

digestibility (Blaxter *et al.* 1961) and the effect of other factors may also be influenced by digestibility of the hay. Milling or grinding hay increases intake, but the response is greater with hays of low digestibility (Minson 1963). On the other hand chopping hay, even to fairly short lengths (2·5 cm), has no effect on intake (Murdoch 1965). Supplementing hay with concentrates reduces intake of the forage and this effect increases consistently with greater hay digestibility (Blaxter *et al.* 1961) (see Chapter 3).

The major disadvantage of hay is, however, its low digestibility caused by the poor quality of the original herbage and by the large nutrient losses which may take place in the field and during storage. Where the objective is to base animal production on grass products, the choice must lie between adopting another conservation method, usually ensilage, or using a technique which allows grass with a high digestibility to be made efficiently into hay. At the present time, and particularly in the wetter areas of the UK, the only method of haymaking which satisfies this requirement is barn drying, which has not been widely adopted. Nevertheless, hay will continue to be made for sale, where convenience in handling is important, for example on hill farms, and when only small areas of herbage are available for conservation. In these circumstances it is likely that hay will continue to have a relatively low feeding value and that any improvement will be the result of better field methods and through the use of preservatives.

5.8.3 Silage

The chemical composition of silage is greatly different from that of the herbage from which it is made because of the various enzymic actions taking place during the ensilage process. The nitrogen content is mainly in the form of non-protein nitrogen, soluble carbohydrate content is low and the silage contains appreciable quantities of lactic and volatile fatty acids. However, many of these components are produced in the rumen and they can be utilized by the ruminant, but these changes in composition affect voluntary food intake and may also influence the utilization of nutrients by the animal. Nevertheless, silage can make a significant contribution to production. Substantial live weight gains in beef cattle can be supported by unsupplemented silage (see Table 5.10) and a considerable part of the nutrient requirements for milk production can be obtained from silage (Table 5.19). Animal production from

TABLE 5.19. The influence of silage quality and concentrate allowance on intake and milk yield. (After Gordon & Murdoch 1978.)

	Medium quality silage			High quality silage
Dry matter digestibility of silage (%) (*in vivo*)		70·0		72·9
Dry matter intake (kg d^{-1})				
Silage	9·2	9·6	10·0	11·5
Concentrate	6·4	4·9	3·3	3·3
Milk yield (kg d^{-1})	25·0	22·3	21·0	22·7

silage is, however, dependent on the digestibility of the original herbage, the efficiency of the ensilage process and intake of silage. Some indication of the effect of these factors is shown by the data in Tables 5.10 and 5.19. Silage is of value in the diet of ewes and lambs, but has to be of high quality for this purpose. It has been suggested that young animals do not grow well when given silage rather than hay. Some recent data, however, indicate that the live weight gain of calves was similar when they were offered silage or hay as a basal forage, the lower intake of silage being compensated by its higher digestibility. The low dry matter intake of silage was particularly marked when the calves were less than 6 weeks of age, but this did not reduce the live weight at 12 weeks of age compared with those receiving hay. While there was no marked production advantage in giving calves silage, the need to make or buy hay is obviated.

Supplementation. It is often necessary to supplement silage to obtain optimal animal production and both quantity and composition of concentrates affect silage intake. Intake is reduced progressively as the quantity of the supplement is increased (Campling & Murdoch 1966) and with decreasing protein content in the concentrate. Good quality silage normally has a relatively high crude protein content and feeding standards suggest that it is only necessary to use a low protein concentrate and, while protein supplementation would be expected to increase the intake of poor quality hay, a response with silage is unexpected. However not only is silage intake increased, but milk production is usually increased by giving concentrates with a higher protein content, a response which is not wholly accounted for by the increased intake (Gordon & McMurray 1979). The response may be related to type of silage and may be greater with high-digestibility, wilted silage.

While supplementation of silage is often necessary, the pursuit of maximum production may be self-defeating. As with all forages, silage intake is reduced by increasing supplementation with concentrates and, although replacement of silage dry matter by concentrates is seldom complete, the incremental value of concentrates is reduced. This is particularly important when residual, as well as direct effects, of supplementation are considered.

Voluntary intake. Silage is normally offered *ad libitum* to animals and factors affecting intake are, therefore, of importance. Voluntary intake usually increases with increasing silage digestibility, but other factors such as dry matter content of the silage may interfere with this relationship (Trimberger *et al.* 1955). However, intake of unwilted silage is always lower than with a dried forage of comparable digestibility (McCarrick 1966), thus limiting potential production. Several explanations have been suggested. Intake is reduced when the silage has undergone an unsatisfactory fermentation as indicated by a high ammonia nitrogen content and may also be limited by high acidity in the silage, the former having the greater adverse effect. In addition, retention time in the gut is greater for silage than for hay and this indicates that there is a possibility of physical restriction of intake.

For high silage intakes, the first essential is to produce silage which has been preserved satisfactorily and has a low ammonia nitrogen content. Further increases in intake may be obtained by

several means and these include wilting the herbage prior to ensiling. Generally the intake of wilted silage is markedly higher than
that of unwilted silage (Marsh 1979), but in the experiments
reviewed there was some inconsistency in production response. This
has been emphasized further by the lack of response in milk production (Gordon 1979) and carcase gain in beef cattle (Collins *et al.*
1977) to wilted silage, although intake was greater for this type of
silage. It may be that the production response depends on whether
wilted silage is compared with a well-preserved, unwilted silage or
not. The value of wilted silage, therefore, rests on any saving from
not using an additive, the elimination of effluent and advantages in
harvesting the herbage.

The free acid content of silage can be partially neutralized, for
example by applying sodium carbonate before the silage is given to
the animals, or it may be reduced by the use of additives at a higher
rate than normal. Formaldehyde has been used for this purpose and
increases in intake have been obtained in a few cases, but high rates
of application resulted in a severe depression of silage intake
(Wilkins *et al.* 1974).

The possibility of physical restriction of intake has aroused interest in the effect of particle size. Intake is increased by short particle
length (1–2 cm), the response being greater with sheep than with
cattle. Length of chop may also influence silage fermentation, but it
has been shown that chopping silage just prior to feeding also increases intake, although to a lesser extent. Response in production
to increased intake is small but consistent (Marsh 1978).

Particle size also has an associated effect with feeding methods,
production being higher when self-fed silage has a short chop length
(Comerford 1979). Intake is normally higher when silage is offered
in troughs than with self-feeding. Physical restriction on intake may
also be shown in the effect of time of access to silage. There is an
increase in silage intake of up to 30% when access time is increased
from 5 hours to 24 hours, although total feeding time is not increased to the same extent. Increasing time of access to hay being
offered *ad libitum* has a much smaller effect than with silage.

If the objective is to achieve maximal production from silage,
intake can be increased by ensuring satisfactory preservation of the
silage, allowing 24 hour access, limiting supplementation to the
minimum required level and reducing the chop length of silage,

bearing in mind that the last mentioned will usually slow down harvesting operations.

5.8.4 Artificially dried forage

Dried forage is normally processed into small packages, as long material is difficult to handle without incurring physical losses. Wafers (about 55 mm diameter) and cobs (about 15 mm diameter) are formed from unmilled material, whereas pellets are made from the milled product, the choice of packaging depending on how the product will be used. Particle size in cobs is reduced to some extent by processing through a die and milling before pelleting produces uniformly small particles. As particle size is reduced there is a progressive reduction in digestibility, particularly that of crude fibre (Table 5.20). However, digestible organic matter intake is increased by reduction in particle size. In addition, while energy lost in faeces is greater with milled, dried forage, the energy lost in heat production and in methane formed in the rumen is lower than with unmilled material and the net energy value is similar for both products (Table 5.21). There is, therefore, little difference in animal produc-

TABLE 5.20. The effect of processing of dried grass on digestibility and intake by sheep. (After Marsh & Murdoch 1975.)

	Chopped	Cobs	Milled and pelleted
OMD (%)	64·2	57·2	51·1
Crude fibre digestibility (%)	63·8	51·3	38·4
Intake of dry matter (kg d^{-1})	0·92	1·22	1·56

TABLE 5.21. The effect of processing on energy losses and net energy of artificially dried grass. (After Blaxter & Graham 1956.)

	Chopped	Milled and pelleted
Energy loss in		
Faeces (%)	26·8	34·8
Heat (%)	28·8	21·2
Methane (%)	7·6	5·9
Urine (%)	5·2	4·9
Digestible energy (MJ kg^{-1} DM)	16·1	12·0
Net energy (MJ kg^{-1} DM)	5·8	6·1

tion when the same quantity of milled and unmilled dried forage is given to animals. When offered *ad libitum*, production is normally higher with milled, pelleted forage as it is consumed in greater quantities than the unmilled product, the response increasing with decreasing forage digestibility (Minson 1963). It is important that some long fibrous feed, at least 0·5% of live weight, be offered to maintain rumen function. The physical quality of the processed product also influences intake—unstable or high-density pellets reduce intake (Tayler 1970).

Production from artificially dried grass given alone can be high (McCarrick 1967), but on economic grounds it should be regarded as a concentrate supplement to grass or other conserved products as these supply basal nutrients at a lower unit cost. As such, dried forage must, therefore, be compared with cereals or compound concentrates.

It has been suggested that dried forage as a supplement may complement silage or grass better than conventional concentrates (Tayler & Aston 1973) and it appears that silage intake is greater when supplemented with dried grass than with barley (Castle & Watson 1975). However, when dried forage is compared with a concentrate of similar protein content the response in silage intake is less consistent, some results showing an increase and others not (McIlmoyle & Murdoch 1977a, 1977b). When introduced as a proportion of the concentrate supplement, there is generally an increase in silage intake up to about 50% inclusion rate (Tayler & Aston 1973). Digestible organic matter content is normally lower for dried forage than for concentrates and higher total intake merely compensates for this, but higher milk yields have resulted when dried grass is compared with barley (Castle & Watson 1975), and similar results have been obtained when grass was supplemented with dried forage (Gordon 1975).

The quality of hay and, to a lesser extent, silage, is affected by season, but artificial dehydration is not affected except by variations in initial moisture content of the crop. Although there are marked differences in the crude protein and soluble carbohydrate content of dried grass made in spring and autumn, milk production was similar for both (Gordon 1974b).

Processed dried grass can contribute significantly to milk and meat production. It appears to be most suitable as a proportion of the concentrate diet or when it replaces barley as a supplement.

When it is the only supplement or is a high proportion of the concentrate, production is normally lower than with normal concentrates.

FURTHER READING

MAFF (Ministry of Agriculture, Fisheries and Food) (1977) Silage. *Bulletin* No. 37. HMSO, London

McDONALD P. & WHITTENBURY R. (1973) The ensilage process. In Butler G. W. & Bailey R. W. (eds), *Chemistry and Biochemistry of Herbage*, Vol. 3, Ch. 28, 33–60. Academic Press, London

NASH M. J. (1978) *Crop conservation and storage.* Pergamon Press, Oxford

RAYMOND W. F. SHEPPERSON G. & WALTHAM R. (1978) *Forage conservation and feeding.* Farming Press, Ipswich

ROOK J. A. F. (ed) (1982) *Silage for milk production.* NIRD–HRI Technical Bulletin No. 2. The Hannah Research Institute, Ayr. (In preparation.)

SPEDDING C. R. W. & DIEKMAHNS E. C. (1972) Grasses and legumes in British agriculture. *C.A.B. Bulletin No. 49*

THOMAS C. (ed) (1980) *Forage conservation in the 80's.* Occasional Symposium No 11. British Grassland Society, Hurley.

WATSON S. J. & NASH M. J. (1960) *Conservation of grass and forage crops.* Oliver and Boyd, Edinburgh

Chapter 6

Economic aspects of grass production and utilization

6.1 THE BASIC ECONOMIC PRINCIPLES

Assuming it has already been decided to have the particular live-stock enterprise on the farm, and how many to keep, there are two economic problems (Barnard & Nix 1979):
(1) The optimal level of target yield, or performance, and thus the level of inputs;
(2) The optimal feed mix, i.e. the least-cost combination of the different feeds, at any given level of target yield, or performance.

In practice, (1) is usually decided before (2), but in theory (2) should come before (1).

6.1.1 *The optimal input/yield level*

The two relevant principles here are the *law of diminishing returns* and the *marginal principle* (marginal revenue (MR) = marginal costs (MC)), both of which are illustrated in Figure 6.1. The former law states that when one or more variable inputs, e.g. a particular feed, or the optimal combination of feeds at each particular level of yield or performance, are added to one or more fixed inputs (such as a cow of a particular quality and yield potential), the extra production from each additional unit of input (i.e. the marginal product) will gradually decline. The marginal principle states that the most profitable level of yield will occur where the MC (i.e. the cost of the last unit input of feed) just equals the MR. Where the price of the product is constant (at a particular point in time), as with milk of a given quality, the MR equals the marginal product (i.e. extra milk obtained) multiplied by its price. While this principle is usually illustrated per animal, it is equally relevant per hectare.

Instead of *diminishing returns*, i.e. extra output from additional units of input, one may think in terms of *increasing costs*, i.e. extra

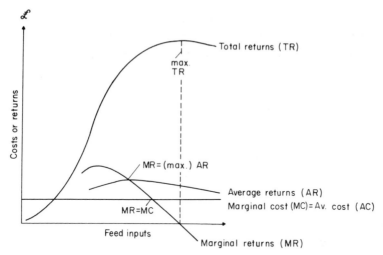

FIGURE 6.1. Law of diminishing returns and optimal feed input (MR = MC).

input, e.g. feed, to obtain successive equal additions to output, e.g. milk yield.

6.1.2   *The optimal feed mix*

The main relevant economic principle here is *the principle of substitution*. This is applied to factor–factor relationships in order to find the optimum combination of variable resources, the 'least cost outlay', to produce a given output. The rate of substitution, i.e. the rate at which factor X substitutes for factor Y, is the amount of Y which is replaced by one additional unit of X without affecting production. The marginal rate of substitution may be constant throughout the range of possible substitutions, but it is often diminishing. The optimal combination is where the marginal rate of substitution equals the price ratio of the two factors (or feeds), i.e. where

$$\frac{\Delta \text{ Quantity of feed Y}}{\Delta \text{ Quantity of feed X}} = \frac{\text{Price per unit of feed X}}{\text{Price per unit of feed Y}}$$

Thus if one extra unit of X, e.g. concentrates, just substitutes for 3 of Y, e.g. hay, and the price of Y is £40 per tonne and X is £120 per tonne, this is the optimal point. The principle, and the optimum

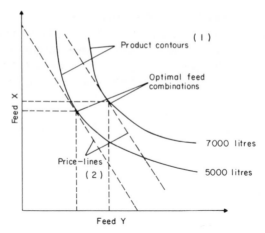

FIGURE 6.2. Factor : factor relationships. (1) Product contours (iso-quants) = combinations of the two feeds giving the same yield. (2) Price-lines = combinations of the two feeds available for the same total cost.

combination, is illustrated, for two feeds only, in Figure 6.2. For more complex mixtures, where many 'straight' feeds may be being considered, linear programming can be employed to find the optimal (least-cost) feed mix (Taylor 1965).

This principle assumes that both, or all, factors under consideration are freely available in whatever amounts are required. If this is not so, the optimum use of a particular factor is determined by the *law of equi-marginal returns*, which states that the optimal utilization of a scarce factor is obtained when its marginal return from all alternative possible uses is the same, i.e. when nothing can be gained from transferring some of it from one use to another. This is allied to the concept of *opportunity cost*, which is the value forgone by not using a particular resource in the most profitable alternative way. This is particularly relevant when the optimal use of forage is being considered.

6.1.3   *Difficulties in implementing the theory*

If life were simple, optimal levels could be quickly determined, from the physical input substitutions and input–output relationships and the cost of each feed and the price of the product. In practice, however, there are many problems. Some of these are listed below. Those relating to grazing and conserved forage are amongst the most difficult to resolve.

(i) *With regard to the optimal input/yield level:*

    (a)   Seasonality effects, i.e. variations in prices during the year and, for example, in growth rate or milk yield.

    (b)   Compensatory and longer-term effects: for example, in the case of dairy cows, changes in the weight of the animal during the lactation and dry period.

    (c)   The incidence of disease.

(ii) *With regard to the optimal combination of feeds:*

    (a)   Frequent, mainly unpredictable, variations in the prices of purchased feeds.

    (b)   The considerable problems of costing grazing and home-grown conserved bulk fodder.

    (c)   Limited available resources, particularly land, but also capital and seasonal labour, which require the application of opportunity costs instead of 'unit costs' and the former are far from easy to calculate.

    (d)   Uncertainty and variability concerning the marginal rates of substitution between alternative feeds, depending on their digestibility and intake characteristics.

(iii) *With regard both to the optimal yield/input level and the optimal combination of feeds:*

    (a)   Variations between breeds and individual animals within the herd or flock.

    (b)   Variations between years, owing primarily to the effect of variations in weather, on the timeliness of conservation and on the yields and quality of grazing and conserved fodder.

    (c)   Variations in the operator's skill from farm to farm and on any one farm with changes in personnel or their skill.

    (d)   Variations in managerial ability.

However, despite these difficulties concerning practical application, the basic economic principles provide a rational way of looking at problems and alternative approaches, although in practice there is considerable room for pragmatism and trial-and-error.

6.2   MAIN ECONOMIC FACTORS AFFECTING PROFITABILITY

6.2.1   *Milk production*

It is obviously impossible to draw a clear line between economic and husbandry factors, and differences in the quality of animal and grassland husbandry explain many of the variations between farms in the level of the economic factors discussed below.

Many reports consider and compare the relative importance of the various economic factors. Those produced by the University Agricultural Economics Departments (e.g. MAFF 1980a), the Milk Marketing Board (MMB 1979), and ICI (ICI 1978) appear regularly, some each year. The latest available MMB results for the top and bottom 25% of herds, together with the overall average, are shown in Table 6.1. Where data are derived from a random sample they may be subjected to detailed statistical analyses. Williams & Jones (1969), in one of the earliest rigorous statistical studies in the UK, refer to 'the overwhelming importance of stocking rate'. The other major factor positively correlated with profitability per cow, and often per hectare, is yield per cow. Obviously the cost of obtain-

TABLE 6.1. Comparison of top and bottom 25% (G.M. per ha). (FMS results, 1978–79: excluding Channel Island herds.) (After MMB 1979.)

	Top 25%	Bottom 25%	Overall average
Yield per cow (l)	5590	4863	5195
Concentrates per cow (kg)	1846	1939	1872
Concentrates per litre (kg)	0·33	0·40	0·36
Concentrate cost per tonne (£)	101	105	104
Stocking rate (LSU ha^{-1})	2·43	1·49	1·99
Nitrogen use ha^{-1} (kg)	289	175	214
Summer milk (%)	51·6	51·0	50·0
Dry cows (%)	16·5	16·7	15·6
Replacement rate (%)	24·5	21·5	20·2
	£ per cow		
Output:			
Milk sales	588	504	542
Calf sales	53	48	46
Less herd depreciation	28	48	29
Output per cow	613	504	559
Variable costs:			
Concentrates	187	204	194
Purchased bulk feed	12	13	10
Forage	40	42	39
Sundries	31	35	32
Total variable costs per cow	270	294	275
Margin over concentrates	401	300	348
Gross margin per cow	343	210	284
Gross margin per ha	832	312	565

ing a higher yield is vital; since the main variable is concentrate costs per cow, the margin of milk value over concentrate costs is more useful and relevant than simply yield. The milk : concentrate price ratio and the beef : concentrate price ratio are major factors affecting the profitability and optimal yield levels for these two enterprises.

All economic surveys show a strong correlation between both stocking rate and yield per cow, and both gross and net margin per hectare. However, the correlation with yield per cow weakens at the higher yield levels, owing mainly to heavy increases in concentrate costs. Certain fixed costs are likely to rise as stocking rate increases, but to a much lesser extent as yield rises. The relationship between yield and fixed costs is considered in 6.3.

Stressing the importance of stocking rate and yield per cow, together with concentrate use, does not of course imply that no other factors are important. For example, labour costs, net replacement cost (which combines the cost of replacements and the value of culls and calves), expenditure on buildings and fixed equipment, forage making and conservation costs, and fertilizer costs per hectare are also important. Figure 6.3 shows a detailed analysis that can be used to trace reasons for differences in profitability between herds.

6.2.2   Beef systems: rearing and fattening

The results from many systems of beef production and the reasons for differences in profitability (or at least in gross margins) are published annually by the Meat and Livestock Commission (e.g. MLC 1979). The vital economic factors, which vary according to the system, are summarized in Table 6.2. The number of asterisks (maximum four) indicates the relative importance of each factor, particularly as it affects *differences* in profitability per hectare between farms. Some factors may be important, but may vary little from farm to farm, or season to season. As with milk production, stocking rate is a major factor in all systems involving grazing and conserved forage.

Yield is less easily defined in beef than in milk production; often it is 'fixed', i.e. the sale of a fattened animal will usually be defined within certain weight limits, in which case the time to achieve the required weight, or daily live weight gain, is the measure of yield.

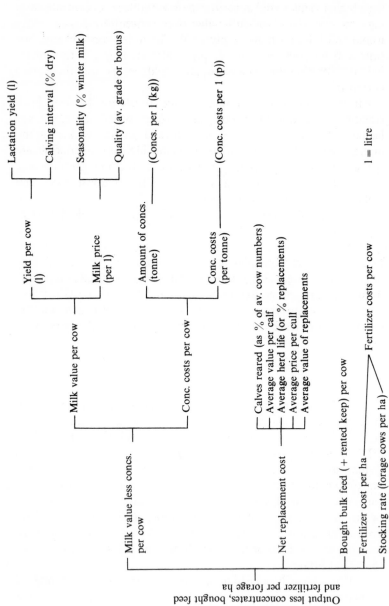

FIGURE 6.3. Outline analysis of profitability of milk production. (After Barnard & Nix 1979.)

TABLE 6.2. Main profit factors in beef production.

	Stocking rate	No. calves sold cow^{-1}	Purchase price of calf/store	Sale price of animal	Conc. feed (head^{-1})	LWG (d^{-1})
Single-suckling	****	*	—	***	**	**
Multiple-suckling	****	**	***	***	***	***
Bucket-rearing	—	—	***	***	**	**
Winter fattening	**	—	***	***	***	***
Summer fattening	****	—	***	***	*	***
Semi-intensive beef (18 m)	****	—	***	***	***	***
Intensive beef (12 m)	—	—	***	***	***	**

Where a continuous system of production is operating (e.g. a finishing cattle shed, which is kept in continual use), live weight gain per day will affect throughput. Although this tends to be of greater relative importance in a pig enterprise or in intensive cereal beef than in beef production from grass (Barnard & Nix 1979), it reinforces the importance of maintaining stocking rate on pasture.

In beef finishing systems, or in producing heavy stores for sale, a major profit determinant is the 'market margin' which depends on the price per kg at which the animal is bought and sold. It is illustrated in Table 6.3. In this example selling at 10p per kg less than

TABLE 6.3. Market margin (MM) and feeder's margin (FM) (£).

Sold:	500 kg at 80p = 400	Sold:	500 kg at 70p = 350
− Bought:	350 kg at 70p = 245	− Bought:	350 kg at 80p = 280
	155		70
MM =	350 kg at +10p = (+)35	MM =	350 kg at −10p = (−)35
FM =	150 kg at 80p = 120	FM =	150 kg at 70p = 105
Total margin	155	Total margin	70

the purchase price is worth £70 per head in market margin compared with the opposite. Although this may appear to be relevant only when store cattle are purchased, it also applies when they are reared on the same farm, since the farmer has the option of selling the cattle as stores instead of fattening them: the sale price that he could obtain is the opportunity cost.

6.2.3   Sheep

Whether lamb is produced in the lowlands, uplands or highlands, two factors account for some 75% of the difference between profit-

TABLE 6.4. Sheep production, lowland flocks selling lambs off grass, 1978. (After MLC 1979.)

	Average	Top third
Lambing percentage	140	158
Average price per lamb (£)	26·14	26·68
Stocking rate (ewes ha^{-1})		
Summer grazing	14·9	16·5
Overall grazing	11·9	13·6
Grass and forage	10·6	12·7
Kg of N per ha	115	139
Output	£ per ewe to ram	
Lamb sales	36·60	42·15
Wool	3·11	3·10
	39·71	45·25
Less flock replacements	5·71	4·80
Output per ewe	34·00	40·45
Variable costs		
Concentrate feed	4·90	4·84
Other purchased feed	0·35	0·30
Forage	4·50	4·21
Veterinary and medicine	1·40	1·29
Miscellaneous and transport	0·67	0·70
Total variable costs per ewe	11·82	11·32
Gross margin per ewe	22·18	29·13
Gross margin per hectare	235·70	369·20

ability in any one year: stocking rate (ewes per hectare all the year round) and lambing percentage (lambs reared per 100 ewes put to the ram). These two factors, together with the live weight gain per lamb, determine the total weight of lamb sold per hectare. The stocking rate obviously depends both on the quality of the land and on the skill of management. When different seasons are compared, lamb price per kg is another vital factor, especially in the hills. If the cost of replacement females is high ewe depreciation also becomes important.

As with beef, the Meat and Livestock Commission's commercial recording schemes provide the main source of data (MLC 1979). Table 6.4 gives the 1978 average and top third results for lowland flocks selling lambs off grass. The top third have a gross margin per hectare 57% above the overall average for the sample surveyed, which itself is almost certainly above the national average, partly as a result of a 20% higher stocking rate.

6.3   THE IMPORTANCE OF YIELD

Apart from the obvious fact that yield is one of the two major determinants, with price, of receipts, the main reason why yield is such an important determinant of profitability is that as yield increases fixed costs per head or per hectare are spread over a greater output, thus reducing fixed costs per unit of output. Fixed costs are a high proportion of total costs in most forms of production; they represent about two-thirds of costs in milk production. By 'fixed costs' in this context are meant all those costs which are necessarily incurred, and remain the same, once the herd or flock size has been determined, regardless of the yield. They include all, or at least most of, the herd or flock depreciation, interest on buildings, fixed and field equipment, depreciation, rent or mortgage charges, regular labour, and several smaller cost items. By contrast the 'variable costs' change with yield. The main variable costs for most systems are the cost of concentrate feed and fertilizer, but there may be increases also in herd or flock depreciation, labour costs, forage conservation costs and veterinary and medicine expenses associated with an endeavour to raise yields. Figure 6.4 illustrates this point. No profit is made until points X and profits increase till

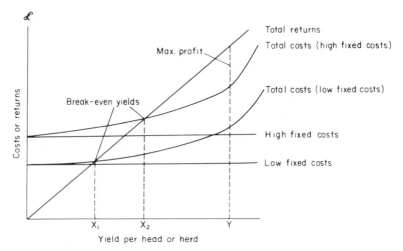

FIGURE 6.4. Relationship between yield, returns and costs. Variable costs = total costs − fixed costs.

point Y, beyond which the addition to variable costs (i.e. the marginal cost) exceeds the value of the additional output (i.e. the marginal revenue).

Figure 6.4 illustrates a further important point: that a higher level of fixed costs requires a greater output before a profit can be made. A higher level of fixed costs may in itself raise output given the same level of variable costs, but the important question is whether the added returns will cover the additional costs, e.g. of erecting a tower silo instead of a clamp silo. There appears to be no evidence in dairying or beef production that extra capital spent, for example, on buildings or mechanized feeding systems will raise output per animal (Coward 1971), although they may reduce labour costs. When economic pressures are severe, systems with lower fixed costs are better able to survive (see Chapter 7).

6.4   YIELD PER HEAD AND YIELD PER HECTARE

As stocking rate is increased, at a given level of grassland production per hectare, some reduction in yield per head must eventually be expected. It may be possible, up to a point, to maintain the yield per head by increased fertilizer use or supplementary feeding, but this means higher costs. Even if yield per head falls, or supplementary feeding costs are increased, the decline in yield or increased cost per animal will not necessarily be uneconomic, provided yield per hectare continues to increase. Increased output per hectare will further spread some fixed costs, but at the same time there will be an increase in other fixed costs per unit of production, and in variable costs. The effect on items of fixed cost such as buildings and other whole-farm effects will depend on whether the increased stocking rate is achieved through keeping an increased number of stock on the same area or the same number on a smaller area, or some combination in between; this is discussed further in Section 6.9.

Because of the additional costs incurred in raising yield per hectare, maximum yield per hectare is likely to be beyond the point of maximum profit per hectare. The relationships involved are illustrated in Figure 6.5. Furthermore, where capital is more limiting than land, it will pay to put more emphasis on profit per head than profit per hectare.

Evidence of declining yields per head as stocking rate is increased

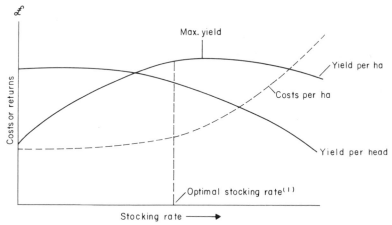

FIGURE 6.5. Yield per head, and yield and profit per hectare. Yield = returns.
(1) Total returns per ha less total costs per ha at maximum.

is not easy to find from farm survey data, since improved swards, higher fertilizer inputs and better management often accompany the higher density of stocking, and offset any reduction in yield per head. This supports the view that in many farm circumstances stocking rate can be increased with advantage.

There has been a considerable amount of experimental work on this subject, referred to in Chapter 4 and, for example, by Morley (1978).

6.5   TIMELINESS AND SEASONALITY

Where production is not continuous, as in milk production, there is often a choice of starting and finishing time, as with rearing beef cattle or finishing beef stores. Even where it is continuous, as with beef from the dairy herd, it is still usually possible to vary the numbers produced seasonally. Yield, prices and costs may all be affected by decisions made about seasonality of production. Prices of beef cattle are normally higher in the spring and summer than in the autumn and winter. Costs are always higher in the winter than in the summer. Thus it is necessary to balance and calculate the net effect of differences in yields, prices and real costs in making decisions concerning seasonality.

6.5.1 Milk production

In dairy farming, all recent surveys have shown that emphasis on winter milk production (i.e. predominantly autumn calving) paid better than summer production (i.e. mainly spring calving): the higher milk yield and the higher price more than outweighed the higher costs. This is illustrated in Table 6.5. (MMB 1979). Although

TABLE 6.5. Winter versus summer milk production.* (FMS costed herds, 1978–79.) (After MMB 1979.)

	Winter milk	Summer milk
% summer milk	42	65
Yield per cow (l)	5301	4553
Concentrates per cow (t)	1·92	1·42
Concentrates per litre (kg)	0·36	0·31
Stocking rate (LSU ha^{-1})	1·89	1·80
	£ per cow	
Milk sales	547	454
Concentrate costs	192	139
Margin of milk sales over concentrates	355	315
Gross margin per cow	289	256
Gross margin per hectare	546	462

* Winter milk: less than 46% production in the six summer months. Summer milk: more than 60% production in the six summer months.

TABLE 6.6. Autumn- versus spring-calving herds (block calving).* (LCP costed herds, 1976–77.) (After Amies 1978.)

	Autumn calving	Spring calving
% summer milk	40	67
Yield per cow (l)	5084	4684
Concentrates per cow (t)	2·01	1·45
Concentrates per litre (kg)	0·40	0·31
Stocking rate (LSU ha^{-1})	1·95	1·99
	£ per cow	
Milk sales	484	440
Concentrate costs	188	140
Margin of milk sales over concentrates	296	300
Gross margin per cow	216	245
Gross margin per hectare	422	487

* Autumn-calving: over 75% calving between August and December inclusive. Spring-calving: over 75% calving between January and April inclusive.

the differences between 'the top 25%' of each type of producer usually reveal the same relative advantage in favour of winter milk production, it is frequently argued that this is because the summer milk producers contain a higher proportion of poorly managed herds. Thus a recent report (Amies 1978) showed that if herds were classified according to calving time, instead of according to the proportion of milk sold in the six winter months, the spring-calving herds gave higher profits than the autumn-calving herds (Table 6.6). The importance of 'block calving' at the right time was far more important in the case of spring calving (Jan.–April) than with autumn calving (Aug.–Dec.).

6.5.2   Beef

With regard to beef, many examples occur, e.g. autumn- versus spring-born calves in semi-intensive (18-month) beef production, autumn/winter- versus spring-calving single-suckling herds. Table 6.7 contrasts winter and summer fattening of store cattle. Of major

TABLE 6.7. Results from winter versus summer finishing of beef stores. (After MLC 1981.)

	Winter finishing[1]	Summer finishing[2]
Days feeding/grazing	175	179
Weight at start (kg)	323	333
Weight at finish (kg)	452	468
Daily live weight gain (kg)	0.75	0.75
Purchase price per kg (p)	79.7	92.1
Sale price per kg (p)	90.4	79.1
Feed costs per head per day (p)	42.4	—
Stocking rate (no. ha^{-1})	—	4.1
Live weight gain ha^{-1} (kg)	—	560
	£ per head	
Sales	409	370
Cost of store	257	307
Concentrates	49	3
Other feed/fert., seed and other forage costs	25	13
Other variable costs	13	8
Gross margin per head	62	37

[1] Winter finishing of medium stores, 1981 (selling late winter and spring).
[2] Grass finishing of medium weight stores, 1980 (selling late summer and autumn).

importance are the market margin (see page 223), the level of concentrate feeding in winter finishing, which is largely dependent, given the target live weight gain per day, on the quality of the bulk fodder, the amount and quality of arable by-products available, if any, and the rate of live weight gain per day actually achieved. Of course more than one batch of cattle may be fattened, particularly in grass finishing. For example, two batches of early maturing crosses and heifers may be preferable to one late maturing batch to utilize fully all the grass grown during the summer, replacement cattle being introduced as those from the first batch are finished. The second batch will have a lower stocking rate and daily gains, and probably require supplementary feeding, in contrast to the first batch. Table 6.8 compares results from two batches of earlier maturing Hereford crosses with a single batch of Charolais crosses.

TABLE 6.8. Grass finishing of beef stores of contrasting types. (After MLC 1978.)

| | Hereford X | | Charolais X |
	First batch	Second batch	Single batch
Slaughter age (months)	17	18	19
Slaughter weight (kg)	430	430	520
Daily LWG on grass (kg)	0·8	0·7	0·8
Grazing period (d)	100	80	180
Stocking rate (cattle/ha^{-1})*	4·9	3·7	3·9
Concentrates head^{-1} (kg)	0	50	100
LWG ha^{-1} (kg)	390	205	560
		595	

* assuming 300 kg N ha^{-1}.

To take another example, with silage of a given quality alternative feeding strategies may be employed, depending on the quantity available. Increasing the daily allowance of concentrates reduces the amount of silage eaten and increases the rate of gain. Higher daily gains mean a faster finish and a lighter slaughter weight. When the quantity of silage available is limited, therefore, the combined economic effect of these different factors has to be calculated. It may be more profitable to feed more concentrates to finish all the animals earlier, at lighter weights, than to sell a proportion of the cattle as stores and give the others more silage and finish them at heavier weights.

6.5.3   Sheep, lowland fat lamb production

Early lambing results in a lower yield (lower lambing percentage and lower weight per lamb sold) and higher costs in feed and labour. On the other hand, price per kg of lamb and the stocking rate should both be higher. Just how much higher the lamb price per kg is in April–May compared with the late summer and autumn tends to be the crucial factor. On average there is little to choose between early and later lambing on a profit per hectare basis. Greater skill and more care is needed for successful early lambing. Hence most producers tend to opt for the easier life of mid-season or late-lambing (Table 6.9). In 1978 early lambing flocks in the

TABLE 6.9. Early versus later lambing flocks (1980 results). (After MLC 1981.)

	Early lambing[1]	Later lambing[2]
Lambing percentage	131	141
Price lamb^{-1} (£)	34·2	27·30
Stocking rate (ewes ha^{-1})	11·9	11·5
	£ per ewe to tup	
Lamb sales	44·85	38·49
Concentrate feed costs: ewe	5·64	5·20
lambs	5·60	1·05
Other variable costs	8·88	7·61
Gross margin per ewe	21·18	21·33
Gross margin per hectare	252	246·34

[1] Early lambing flocks, Dec. 1979 and Jan. 1980 (50 flocks).
[2] Lowland flocks selling lambs off grass, summer and autumn, 1980 (380 flocks).

MLC sample showed a lower gross margin per ewe but a higher gross margin per hectare, owing to a higher stocking rate. Comparative results in any one year depend largely on the severity of the winter and the price for early fat lamb at Easter time. It has also to be remembered, when comparing the averages, that the size of the average flock lambing early was only half that of those lambing later, and those farmers opting for early lambing are often particularly keen producers and more likely to be farming in kinder areas as regards climate and exposure.

6.6   Fixed and working capital

One of the major reasons why many farmers in arable areas eschew livestock production despite the likely advantages of alternate husbandry, on many, if not all soil types, is the high capital cost. The additional skills, labour and management needed are of course further reasons. Capital is required for the livestock themselves, the buildings (unless outwintering is possible or adequate old buildings are available for winter fattening of beef, single suckling or sheep production), and working capital is also needed. The relative importance of each of these depends on the system. Little working capital is necessary to run an established dairy herd, but that required for an intensively stocked 18-month beef enterprise is considerable. All these capital items, especially buildings, vary from farm to farm even for the same system. Table 6.10 gives some idea of capital costs per head and per hectare for selected systems.

TABLE 6.10. Capital costs in livestock production (approximate 1980 values) (£).

	System			
	Dairy cows	Single suckling (spring calving)	18-month beef	Lowland lamb
Animals (head^{-1})[1]	400	350	80	40
Buildings (head^{-1})[1]	600	—[2]	250	—[2]
Working (head^{-1})	20	100	200	20
Total (head^{-1})	1020	450	530	60
Total per hectare:				
Av. stocking rate	1825	725	1325	540
High stocking rate	2325	900	1750	720

[1] capital cost after grant.
[2] assuming outwintered.

6.7   The relative costs of grass and alternative feeds

All 'enterprise costing', which involves estimating the full cost of production of individual products, usually on a mixed farm, is fraught with difficulties. These include problems of allocating joint costs, including, for example, tractors and general overhead expenses, and allowing for supplementary (i.e. use of 'surplus' resources) and complementary (i.e. beneficial effects on other enterprises) factors and the opportunity cost principle. The evaluation of the product for grazing and conserved fodder raises still further problems, largely because of variations in quality within a single season and between seasons. The problems are so considerable and the value of the results so dubious, in fact, that most farm economists are loath to make the attempt.

One of the few published sources of relatively recent fodder costings is the National Investigation into the Economics of Milk Production 1976/77. The results are given in Table 6.11, which also updates these to 'rounded' 1980 levels.

TABLE 6.11. Average costs of production of grazing and other fodder crops. (After MAFF/MMB 1980.)

Type of food	1976/7 (£)	1980 (est.) (£)
Grazing (ha^{-1})	91	152
Hay (t^{-1})	19·0	31·5
Silage (t^{-1})	6·2	10·25
Kale (t^{-1})	7·2	12·0
Roots (t^{-1})	12·5	20·75

The hay : silage cost ratio (approximately 3 : 1 fresh weight) accords with the usual approximation of their relative energy values, with the protein ratio favouring silage. In practice, the balance swings further in favour of silage in the wetter parts of the country, or where above average levels of nitrogen are used. These conditions produce heavier crops of grass which are more difficult to make into good quality hay. Although good results are obtained from barn-dried hay, the increased cost of fuel (for carting and artificial drying) has shifted the balance towards traditional haymaking. On the individual farm, the labour available, the seasonal labour needs of other crops and the type and amount of storage available have also to be taken into account in deciding between hay and silage, kale and roots.

The importance of high quality forage may be illustrated from dairying as follows. On the common winter basis of feeding 0·4 kg per litre, the difference between a bulk fodder providing Maintenance only and that giving Maintenance + 5 litres, assuming concentrates average £130 a tonne in 1980, is £42 a year, assuming the cow is in milk over the whole of a 180-day winter. This amounts to £2750 for an 80 cow herd, assuming all-the-year round calving and an average 18% dry, and gives an extra profit, at average stocking rates, of £60 per hectare. This assumes no difference in the *amount* of bulk fodder fed (i.e. quality differences only) and no effect on yield per cow, although the higher quality might well improve yield.

However, the high quality fodder should not be obtained at too high a cost in terms of lower yield. The DOM yield *per hectare* is also important. For example, a high quality three-cut system of silage-making led to a lower DM yield per hectare and an increased silage DM intake per cow compared with a conventional two-cut system; the net result was a 35% increase in the forage area required per cow (Moisey & Leaver 1979). Similar conclusions from Grassland Research Institute and ADAS trials carried out between 1975 and 1977 were used to demonstrate the economic advantage of less frequent cutting systems (Brooke 1979), which also incur lower cutting costs.

Figures showing the equivalent values and comparative costs per unit of nutrient of different feeds are given in Table 6.12. Such data are commonly provided to 'prove' how much more economic it is to feed bulk feeds rather than concentrates, within the limits of appetite. But this ignores the opportunity cost of the land needed to produce extra bulk feeds on the farm.

TABLE 6.12. Typical cost of growing some feed crops (1975). (After MLC 1976.)

	Fresh yield (t ha^{-1})	DM yield (t ha^{-1})	Yield ME ha^{-1} (GJ)	Relative costs (£ GJ^{-1} ME)		Relative costs (£ t^{-1} DCP)	
				Variable costs	Cost of production	Variable costs	Cost of production
Grazed grass	37·1	7·4	87	1·0	1·0	1·0	1·0
Grass silage	33·0	7·4	67	1·50	5·8	2·3	8·0
Hay	6·5	5·5	47	1·59	2·8	6·1	9·5
Maize silage	44·0	9·7	105	1·54	4·24	4·2	10·2
Dried grass	12·6	11·3	120	3·73	11·54	4·4	12·2
Swedes	60·5	7·3	93	1·18	2·28	2·9	5·0
Turnips	58·0	5·2	58	1·34	2·60	5·8	6·2
Barley	4·3	3·7	51	2·27	5·0	6·7	13·0

Costs have been related to grazed grass. The original values for variable and total costs were £0·40 and £0·50 per GJ and £25 and £32 per tonne of digestible crude protein respectively in 1975.

6.8   GRASS, FERTILIZER AND CONCENTRATES

Every detailed study of dairying reveals that the 'bulk feed' herds that make the highest profits are those that get the highest yields despite their greater stress on bulk feeds, and that the 'high yielders' that fare best are those that achieve these yields with only a moderate use of concentrates per litre, in both cases combined with a good stocking rate. There is a continual range of 'systems', and an individual farm's circumstances largely determine its optimum 'system' (see Chapter 7). Although herds with a high dependence on concentrates would suffer most from a worsening of the milk price: concentrate cost ratio, this is true only if the price of concentrates rises more rapidly than the production costs of other feeds.

In several recent analyses of data from recorded farms, simple relationships have been established between economic performance and such factors as stocking rate, fertilizer use and concentrates fed. Linear relationships apply only to relatively small deviations from the means of the populations from which they were derived; curvilinear relationships must be expected when the inputs deviate widely from the mean. Moreover the samples are seldom randomly chosen and relationships shown are usually the result not only of direct effects of the inputs but also from correlated effects. Also, the type of model chosen for the relationship may influence the conclusions. However, with these qualifications, examples include:

(1)   An increase in stocking rate of 0·1 beef cattle per hectare increased gross margin (at 1975–77 prices) by £13·1 (18-month beef), £21·6 (24-month beef), £14·9 (autumn-calving suckler cows), £12·7 (spring-calving suckler cows) (MLC 1978).

(2)   Each extra 100 kg N per ha increased cows per ha by 0·29, milk per ha by 1507 kg and gross margin per ha by £77 (MMB 1976).

(3)   More detailed interrelationships of concentrates, fertilizer N and stocking rate have been shown, e.g. Turkington and Townson (1978). Their results were as follows:

$$M = 2400 + 1697\ C + 2{\cdot}446\ N$$
$$- 160{\cdot}9\ C^2 - 0{\cdot}8\ CN - 0{\cdot}00038\ N^2$$
$$(RSD \pm 470)$$
$$D = 0{\cdot}6655 + 0{\cdot}00066\ C - 0{\cdot}00059\ N - 0{\cdot}0123\ C^2$$
$$+ 0{\cdot}000032\ CN + 0{\cdot}00000014\ N^2$$
$$(RSD \pm 0{\cdot}086)$$

where M = litres per cow, C = concentrate tonnes per cow, N = nitrogen kg per ha, and D = hectares per cow.

Using such equations, ICI have calculated relationships between concentrates fed, nitrogen use, milk yields and stocking rate as shown in Table 6.13 (ICI 1979), which may be taken as guidelines for well-managed herds in British conditions.

TABLE 6.13. Relationship between yield, stocking rate, concentrates and nitrogen use. (After ICI 1979.)

| | | (Assuming average grass growing conditions) Nitrogen: Kg/ha | | |
		250	345	440
(A)	Concentrates ($t\ cow^{-1}$)		Cows per forage hectare	
	1·0	1·55	1·90	2·25
	1·6	1·90	2·25	2·65
	2·2	2·25	2·75	3·30
			(assuming average yield cow^{-1} of 5500 litres)	
(B)	Milk yield cow^{-1} (litres)		Concentrates required $t\ cow^{-1}$	
	4500	1·5	1·0	0·4
	5500	2·2	1·6	1·0
	6500	2·8	2·2	1·6
			(assuming stocking rate of 2·25 cows per forage ha)	

(4)   With beef cattle, Holmes (1974) showed that live weight gain per ha was closely associated with utilized ME per ha and could be predicted from the equation:

$$LWG\ ha^{-1} = 697 + 1·4\ N\ (kg\ ha^{-1}) - 0·00084\ N^2$$

(Equation 4, Holmes 1974)   RSD $\pm$ 191

These relationships can be used to describe the response curves referred to in Section 6.1.1, although their variability must be remembered.

6.9   WHOLE FARM ASPECTS

6.9.1   *Effects on the whole farm*

Decisions on the optimal choice of feeds of different types, stocking rates and purchases of winter fodder, normally as hay, should be based on the effect on whole-farm profitability. This depends on many factors. Increasing the gross margin per hectare from a particular grazing livestock enterprise does not necessarily result in an increase in total farm profitability (Craven 1975). If this were achieved through an increase in stocking rate, extra fixed costs (e.g. depreciation and interest on additional housing, a new milking parlour, extra labour, additional interest charges on the larger number of stock) might outweigh the increase in gross margin. If the higher gross margin is achieved by keeping the same number of stock on a smaller forage area, much depends on the cost of intensification through extra fertilizer and/or additional purchased feed and the use to which the land saved is put. The budgeted gross margin should be considered together with any increase in fixed costs resulting, for example, from increasing the area of cereals. There are also possible rotational effects: a reduced area of ley on a grass/cereals farm may reduce the area of winter wheat and will certainly mean a longer run of cereals, with possibly decreasing yields and/or higher fertilizer and spray costs. Only a careful partial budget can indicate the net effect on total farm profit of all these possible effects (Nix 1971).

6.9.2   Purchase of fodder

Buying in all, or most, of the winter fodder will almost certainly raise the gross margin per hectare from the dairy enterprise, but, again, it will not necessarily increase total farm profitability. In addition to the points made in the previous paragraph, further relevant factors include the price of purchased fodder and its quality compared with home-grown fodder, and the effect on seasonal labour and tractor requirements. Suppose the gross margin per cow, with fodder conserved on the farm, is £300 per cow and £545 per forage hectare, with 0·3 ha grazing and 0·25 ha for conservation per cow. If the conserved fodder can be bought in as two tonnes of hay per cow at £40 per tonne, the additional variable costs could be £60 per cow (£80 less £20 in variable costs saved on the 0·25 ha). The 'shadow' gross margin from the conserved area is £240 per ha (£60 ÷ 0·25), and the gross margin from the grazing area £800 per ha {(300 − 60) ÷ 0·3}. However, if the previously conserved area were then devoted to sheep, with a gross margin of £200 per ha, or cereals, with a gross margin less additional fixed costs at a similar level, farm profitability would be decreased. On the other hand, if the purchase of fodder allowed a larger herd to be maintained on a small farm the financial benefit could be substantial.

FURTHER READING

BARNARD C. S. & NIX J. S. (1979) Farm planning and control. (2e.) Part II. Chs 6–12. Cambridge University Press.

MAFF (Ministry of Agriculture, Fisheries and Food) (1980) Costs and efficiency in milk production, 1976–77. H.M.S.O,

MAFF (Ministry of Agriculture, Fisheries and Food) (1970's) Profitable farm enterprises. Series. H.M.S.O.

NIX J. S. (1980) Farm management pocketbook. (11e.) Farm Business Unit, Wye College, University of London.

NORMAN L. & COOTE R. B. (1971) *The farm business.* Chs 6 & 7. Longman, London.

Chapter 7

Application on the farm

7.1   RECORDING GRASSLAND PRODUCTION

A record of the overall productivity of grassland is valuable on a well run grassland farm and detailed records of individual fields may be required. The whole farm record can be calculated from the data normally assembled for the annual farm accounts. Formerly this was calculated as utilized starch equivalent (USE) (Baker *et al.* 1964). It is now expressed as utilized metabolizable energy (UME) (Forbes *et al.* 1977). A precise comparison of USE and UME is difficult but for normal conditions 2·1 GJ of UME per hectare approximately equals 1 cwt of USE per acre. Pasture productivity is generally expressed in terms of energy since energy intake normally limits production, and on temperate grassland protein supply is seldom the limiting factor.

UME may be calculated as follows. From the numbers of ruminant stock in each age group (based on valuation numbers at the beginning and end of the year, or preferably on monthly or quarterly records) and the livestock produce sold, the quantity of metabolizable energy required for the stock population for the year is calculated. From this is deducted the value in ME of all purchased feed. The remainder divided by the area of grass (and forage crops) gives the ME 'utilized' per hectare. It is a crude measure and has been criticized because it gives full credit to purchased feed, while all waste or inefficiency of feed use is debited to grass. However, if high values (more than 80 GJ per ha) are recorded, the productivity of grass is satisfactory. If the values are low, below 20 GJ per ha, the manager should determine whether low grass productivity, poor utilization in grazing or conservation, excessive use of purchased feeds, or a combination of these are responsible.

If an estimate of the production from individual fields is required, a detailed record of type of stock, grazing days, quantities of feed conserved from the field, and of supplementary feed provided, may be maintained and converted to UME.

More simply, field data, and indeed whole farm data may be converted to *Livestock unit grazing days* (LUGD) from factors such as those in Appendix Table 7.1. On this basis, a pasture from which 7500 kg dry matter was utilized would yield:

3235 grazing days with ewes

of 72 kg with 150% lambing = 550 LUGD

1108 grazing days with cattle 11–20 m old × 0·5 = 554 LUGD

730 grazing days with cattle 21–30 m old × 0·75 = 547 LUGD

550 grazing days with cows × 1·0 = 550 LUGD.

Unfortunately there are several sets of livestock unit factors which differ in detail, particularly in the values for sheep. Comparisons between fields or farms based on LUGD or indeed on UME are subject to some error and should be made with caution.

Even simpler measures can be valuable provided that their limitations are understood. Where grazing by the same group of animals takes place in rotation over a sequence of paddocks, a record of grazing days, i.e. no. of animals × no. of days, in each field will indicate any major difference in productivity between fields, but the possibility that this is the result of management decisions must not be forgotten. From records of milk yield or live weight gain, litres of milk per ha or kg live weight gain per ha can be calculated. These, however, ignore the maintenance requirements, or the level of productivity of the animals. For example, a spring-calving herd producing 10 500 kg milk per ha would utilize the same quantity of ME (80 GJ per ha) as an autumn-calving herd yielding 6500 kg milk per ha. Again if a finishing group of cattle weighing 400 kg were contrasted with calves of 200 kg at turnout, for a utilization of 56 GJ per ha, the live weight gain per ha of the finishing cattle might be 660 kg while that of the calves, because of their higher relative growth rate could be 1000 kg live weight gain per ha. A simple example of several measures of grassland production is given in Table 7.1.

Even if records of grass utilization per farm or per field are not required it is good practice to record where each group of livestock has grazed throughout the season so that frequency of grazing can be controlled, risks of parasitic infection avoided and 'clean fields'

TABLE 7.1 Calculation of utilized metabolizable energy

If one cow of 550 kg weight is maintained for one year on the produce of 0·4 ha grassland and 1 tonne of purchased concentrated feed to yield 5500 kg milk containing 38 g kg^{-1} butter fat and 87 g kg^{-1} solids not fat, gains 50 kg in the year and calves again in 12 months. Total requirement of ME:

Maintenance
365 days × (8·3 + 0·091 W) MJ   = 21·3 GJ

Milk production
5500 litres × 5·10 MJ   = 28·0 GJ

Live weight gain
    80 kg × 34 MJ   = 2·72 GJ
Less
live weight loss
in early lactation
    30 kg × 28 MJ   = 0·84 GJ

Net live weight change   1·88   = 1·9 GJ
Pregnancy allowance
    120 days × 12·5 MJ   = 1·5 GJ

Total requirement for the year   = 52·7 GJ
Less concentrates, 1000 kg at 12·5 MJ per kg DM   10·6 GJ
Metabolizable energy from grass   42·1 GJ
UME per ha   42·1 ÷ 0·4   105 GJ
Based on MAFF Bulletin No. 33, 1975

If the cow grazed for 175 days on 0·2 ha of grass the yield in LUGD would be: 175 × 1·0 ÷ 0·2 or 875 LUGD per ha.
If it produced 2500 kg milk in the grazing period it would yield 12 500 kg milk per ha of grazing, before allowing for concentrates fed. If concentrates were fed at the average rate of 0.10 kg per kg milk over the summer period 250 kg would be used. Conventionally, concentrates are allowed for at 0·4 kg per kg milk. On this basis
250 kg   = 625 kg milk
Milk per cow from grazing   = 2500 − 625 = 1875 kg
Adjusted milk per hectare from grazing = 1875/0·2 = 9375 kg
Alternatively, allowance may be made for concentrates in terms of the area to grow barley at, say, 4000 kg grain per ha. Then 250 kg = 250/4000 ha = 0·0625 ha
and adjusted milk per ha of feed = $\dfrac{2500}{0·2 + 0·0625}$ = 9524 kg

identified. These records may be made for each group of stock or for each pasture field.

7.2 TARGETS IN RELATION TO LAND POTENTIAL AND FERTILIZER USE

The optimal stocking rate for the farm depends both on the productivity of the grassland and forage area and on additional feed purchases. The justifiable quantity of purchased feed depends on costs

TABLE 7.2. The influence of summer rainfall and soil type on site quality for grassland production.

Moisture-holding capacity of soil	Summer rainfall mm		
	< 275	275–375	> 375
High	2	1	1
Medium	4	3	2
Low	5	4	3

Site quality 1 = very good; 2 = good; 3 = average; 4 = poor; 5 = very poor.

and prices, and on the overall size of the farm business. Some assessment of the potential grass productivity can be made from the physical characteristics of the farm, or its individual fields, the level of fertilizer use and the expected range of weather conditions. The most important factors are shown in Table 7.2. Potential production multiplied by the efficiency of utilization gives an indication of grazing or forage available. In more detail:

$$\text{Herbage allowance per animal (kg DM)} = \frac{\text{ME requirement}}{\text{MJ ME kg}^{-1}\text{ DM}} \times n \times \frac{100}{E}$$

when n is number of days and E is assumed efficiency of grazing (%). Guidelines to appropriate stocking rates of dairy cows, cattle and sheep are given in Table 7.3 and Appendices 7.2, 7.3 and 7.4.

7.3. PRACTICAL FEEDING

The practical feeding of stock is dealt with in MAFF (1975) and MAFF (1979e). Detailed calculations can be made based on the requirements and the expected appetite of the animals. It should be appreciated, however, that there are many assumptions inherent in all feeding systems and that assessment of performance by the stock in comparison with expectation is essential.

When stock are fed entirely on grazing or in the main on conserved products they are in fact receiving complete feeds (although care must be taken to ensure that there is no deficiency of protein minerals or vitamins). In these circumstances when the feed is readily available and offered *ad libitum* the overall energy concentration of the diet has a major influence on intake and animal performance.

It can be calculated that for the most productive stock, cows in early lactation, calves and lambs in the early stages of ruminant growth and finishing cattle, a concentration of about 12 MJ ME per kg DM is needed. Cows in mid-lactation, growing cattle and suckler cows need diets in the range 10–11 MJ per kg dry matter and the requirements of animals at low levels of performance are satisfied with diets in the range 8–9 MJ, provided protein and

TABLE 7.3. Target stocking rates in relation to quality of site and level of nitrogen fertilizer for 180-day grazing period.

Site* quality	Fertilizer N (kg ha^{-1})	DM yield (t ha^{-1})	Dairy cows	Suckler cows with calves	Cattle from 200 kg	Cattle from 350 kg	Ewes with lambs
			a.	b.	c.	d.	e.
1. Poor	150‡	6·7	2·7	2·2	5·0	3·4	10
	300	7·7	3·1	2·6	5·8	3·9	11
3. Average	150‡	8·9	3·6	3·0	6·7	4·5	14
	300	10·3	4·2	3·5	7·7	5·3	16
	450	11·5	4·7	—	8·6	5·9	
5. Excellent	150‡	11·1	4·5	3·7	8·3	5·7	17
	300	12·9	5·2	4·4	9·7	6·6	20
	450	14·4	5·8	—	10·8	7·4	—
Approx. daily DM intake kg d^{-1}			13·0	14·0	5·9	8·7	3·0
Herbage allowance** for 180 days (kg)			2463	2965	1327	1957	635

a. Average Friesian cow receiving 0·1 to 0·2 kg concentrate per kg milk 95% efficiency of grass utilization. Add 8% for autumn calvers, deduct 8% for spring calving herd.

b. Suckler cow, 480 kg calving February and raising calf to 250 kg, 85% efficiency of grass utilization.

c. Cattle 200 kg at turnout to gain 160 kg in 180 days, 80% efficiency of grass utilization.

d. Cattle 350 kg at turnout to gain 180 kg in 180 days, 80% efficiency of grazing.

e. Ewes of 70 kg with 1·5 lambs raised to 40 kg, 85% efficiency of grass utilization.

* Intermediate values for site grades 2 and 4 (see Table 7.2).

** This takes account of efficiency of grazing.

‡ A good grass clover sward can give yields similar to 150 kg N ha^{-1}.

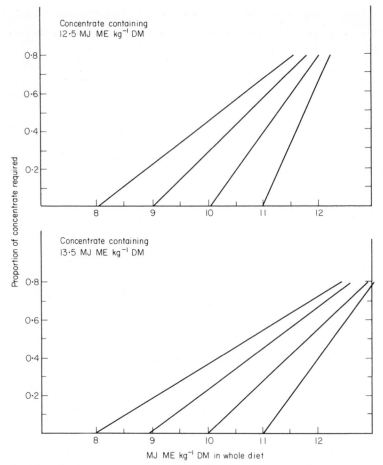

FIGURE 7.1. The proportion of concentrate in the dry matter of the whole diet to give the required ME concentration in the whole diet with forages containing 8–11 MJ ME kg⁻¹ DM.

mineral contents are adequate (MAFF 1975). Figure 7.1 shows the proportion of concentrates and forages of various qualities to provide a range of overall dietary concentrations and the approximate levels of supplementation for these various groups are indicated in Table 7.4. These are intended as guidelines rather than precise recommendations. They do show how the use of concentrated feeds can supplement the lower grade forages to supply an adequate diet. Nutritive values of the more common feeds are in Appendix Table 7.5.

TABLE 7.4. Daily allowance of concentrates (86% DM) to provide various proportions of total DM intake.

Class of stock	Total daily DM intake (kg)		Proportion of DM %						
			20	30	40	50	60	70	80
Sheep	2	2	0·45	0·7	0·9	1·2	1·4	1·6	1·9
Calves	4	4	0·9	1·4	1·9	2·3	2·8	3·2	3·7
Young	6–8	6	1·4	2·1	2·8	3·5	4·2	4·9	5·6
cattle		8	1·9	2·8	3·7	4·6	5·6	6·5	7·4
Finishing cattle	8–12	10	2·3	3·5	4·6	5·8	7·0	8·1	9·3
Low-yielding									
or suckler cows	10–14	12	2·8	4·2	5·6	7·0	8·4	9·8*	11·2*
Average		14	3·2	4·9	6·5	8·1	9·8	—	—
milk cows	12–16	16	3·7	5·6	7·4	9·3	11·2	—	—
High-yielding		18	4·2	6·3	8·4	10·5	12·5	—	—
milk cows	16–22	20	4·6	7·0	9·3	11·6	13·9	—	—
		22	5·1	7·7	10·2	12·8	15·3	—	—

* Not for cows.

7.4 FEED BUDGETING

It is important in the long and short term to estimate feed requirements in relation to stock numbers.

7.4.1 Assessing year round stocking rates

The stocking rates from Table 7.3 provide an overall estimate of the grazing stocking rate for the farm and of the quantity of forage available for winter use. In straightforward dairy herd pasture systems, relationships have been estimated between forage area, fertilizer use and concentrated feed and these are given in Chapter 6. In more varied grazing enterprises where dairy cows, dairy followers, dairy beef and sheep are all produced, the calculations are more complex. To simplify these it is normal to standardize the numbers of animals by conversion to Livestock Units (Section 7.1). On good land with good management and normal levels of concentrated feed use an overall target for the year is 2·5 Livestock Units per ha of forage. Higher figures generally demand very high pasture productivity, or appreciable quantities of purchased bulk feed or of concentrates.

7.4.2 Assessing short-term pasture supply

Feed budgeting also refers to the assessment of pasture supply in the short term. Particularly with continuous stocking it is important to know whether the feed supply is adequate, and with rotational paddock grazing some method of forecasting stock-carrying capacity is also helpful. A grass meter has been developed which measures the average height of a sward (Castle 1976). The meter consists of a metal disc or plate which slides on a calibrated rod. When the rod is placed vertically on the pasture the plate is pushed up by the grass and the height of the plate above ground level can be recorded. With experience this is more precise than visual inspection. However, the vegetative condition of the sward and whether or not it has been cut during the year for silage or hay will influence the estimates of height. Any pasture which has been grazed, particularly by cattle becomes uneven, so that an average of at least 30 readings is needed to give an accurate measure. Continuously stocked swards are likely to limit cattle performance if they are less than 5–6 cm in average height and rotational or strip grazed paddocks should be vacated before they fall below 7–8 cm in average height. Changes in pasture height over the season can be monitored with the grass meter. The meter gives a lower value than measuring with a rule.

7.5   THE ALLOCATION OF GRASSLAND BETWEEN DIFFERENT TYPES OF STOCK AND BETWEEN GRAZING AND CONSERVATION

Practical matters of access, drainage and crop rotation normally influence how individual fields of grassland are used. Parasite control and uniformity of distribution of fertility should be considered also.

The control of parasites. The control of parasitic worms is improved, although seldom complete, if young stock graze on newly sown grass, grass that has been conserved throughout the previous year or grass on which a different species has grazed in the previous year. The East of Scotland College of Agriculture (ESCA 1978) recommended a three field system based on these principles where a 3-year ley would be utilized in successive years by (1) sheep, (2) cattle, (3) conservation followed by lambs on the aftermath. Grazing of sheep and cattle in alternate years is preferable to repeated grazing by one type of stock. These systems require stock-proof fencing for sheep and cattle in each field and easy access to each field for conservation, sheep handling, etc. Parasite control is also improved by resting and conservation within the season as in the integrated grazing and conservation (1, 2, 3) system. Earlier claims that rotational pasture management with a 20–30 day cycle might of itself control parasites have not been realized but leader follower systems where the younger, more susceptible animals graze first on each cycle, reduce the risk of worm infestation (Leaver 1970).

Stabilization of fertility. Grazing recycles nutrients while cutting for conservation removes N, P and K from the system. Alternating grazing and conservation from year to year or within the year reduces the risks of depletion of soil fertility by conservation cuts, or the accumulation of excessive levels of nutrients from repeated grazing. Repeated night grazing on some areas by dairy cows may accumulate fertility because of the higher proportion of the 24 hours spent there. Slurry applications on grazing may also raise the K content of the soil to dangerous levels.

Practical aspects. Topography or amenity often dictate grassland use. Steep banks are best used by sheep, parkland with trees by grazing cattle or sheep. The use of the same area for both grazing and conservation may be restricted by the shape of the farm and ease of access to the dairy, the presence of main roads through the farm, or the reliability of the fences. Here, especially for dairy cows, a two-sward system may be preferred, where the grassland accessible to the dairy herd is grazed with but few conservation cuts, and the less accessible areas provide forage for conservation and receive most of the slurry and farmyard manure. Fertilizer use should be adjusted accordingly.

The movement of stock from field to field is time wasting and grazing should be planned for minimal stock movement. For dairy cows, whether rotational grazing or continuous stocking is practised, the access route to and from the dairy should be short and easily negotiated. With sheep and young cattle, appropriate size groups should be allotted to fields with the additional area for use later in the season nearby, as in the integrated (1, 2, 3) system.

7.6 MANAGEMENT CONTROL

The guidelines in the preceding sections should enable the formulation of reasonable targets for the season. It is vital that the management should use records to monitor performance. Major variable expenditures are feed stuffs and fertilizers. The concentrate requirements if any for each month of the grazing season should be estimated for cows from predicted milk yields and calvings. The need for supplementary feeding of concentrates for grazing beef cattle at grass should be assessed. The quantities of feed consumed month by month should then be checked against these estimates. Similarly the fertilizer requirements over the season can be planned and actual consumption checked. Target areas for hay and ensilage must also be indicated. Failure to conserve silage or hay of sufficient quantity or quality can increase costs. A mid-grazing season weighing enables cattle gains in the first and second half of the grazing season to be estimated. The gains in the second half of the season are a reflection of the success of the grassland management. MLC records consistently show that, on average, gains in the second half of the grazing season are about 80% of those achieved in the first half.

The utilization of grass is, in part, dependent on the weather. Increased use of supplementary feed in adverse conditions, and indeed reduced use of feed and fertilizer in favourable conditions should however be the result of a conscious reassessment by management. Regular inspection of the records and visual assessment of the pasture and of the stock are important.

7.7 SYSTEMS STUDIES IN GRASS UTILIZATION

Farmers realized long ago that grassland management, even more than other aspects of farming, is a complex activity, where factors affecting soil fertility, the growth of grass, and the nutrition of the animal, interact and culminate in the production of meat, milk or wool. With the development of a more quantitative approach to all aspects of agriculture and the availability of computers the possibility of examining the interrelationships involved and of predicting the outcome of a range of possible procedures, has arisen. Spedding

TABLE 7.5. Components of a sheep system.

1. Breed of ewe	11. Amount and form of conservation
2. Time of mating	12. Sheep movement between paddocks
3. Wool yield	13. Weaning
4. Herbage species	14. Supplementation
5. Fertilizer application, quantity and timing	15. Lamb disposal
6. Breed of ram	16. Ewe flushing
7. Pregnancy nutrition	17. Off-grazing
8. Stocking rate	18. Immunization policy
9. Grazing system	19. Parasite control
10. Lactation nutrition	20. Housing

(1975) and Eadie & Maxwell (1975) have fostered these ideas in relation to grassland. The development and validation of a sheep production system was described by Newton & Brockington (1975).

A first step in the systems approach is to establish the important components of the system and to indicate and quantify their relationships one with the other. The components listed by Newton & Brockington are shown in Table 7.5 and the interrelationships in Figure 7.2. An alternative method of describing the relationships is the circular diagram described by Spedding (1975, 1979). This procedure is valuable in itself in forcing the farmer to consider all important components. It may also draw attention to a lack of knowledge about some components of the system. If the relationships are not known, it may be necessary in the short term to make best guesses at them and in the longer term to initiate specific investigations to measure them. The information is then formulated in a mathematical model which allows the prediction of the probable outcome from various levels of input. It is, then important that the predictions are validated by comparison with independent data. Once the model is validated the possible effects on production of a wide range of inputs can be examined in physical terms and, with the appropriate price information, economic predictions can be made. The possible effects of weather, of changes in animal performance, feed or fertilizer level or in price can then be predicted. The components of the system which have a major influence on production and those price changes which would seriously influence profitability can be identified by the systems approach. It is not often justifiable for the individual farm but it is increasingly used for advisory services.

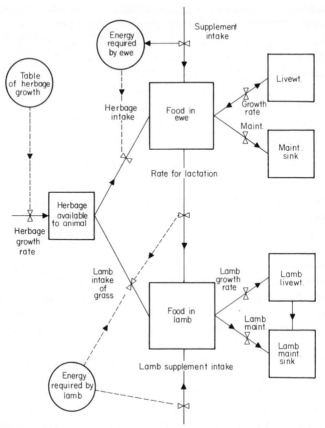

FIGURE 7.2. Some relationships between ewes and lambs at pasture and their feed supply. (From Newton & Brockington 1975).

7.8   RISK AND UNCERTAINTY IN GRASSLAND MANAGEMENT

It is difficult to predict precisely the level of production from grass. The main uncontrollable factor is weather and, as the GM20 experiment (Chapter 2) showed, much of the variation in grassland yield is related to the summer rainfall and water-holding capacity of the soil. Because of the variability of climate and the high cost of replacing a shortage of grass, farmers often stock their land below the level needed to utilize fully its production. An integrated grazing and conservation system at modest stocking rates reduces the risks from drought while still ensuring efficient utilization of the grass. Weather imposes other limitations. Drought may impair the establishment of a pasture, a late spring may delay the grass growth, successful haymaking depends on good weather and good silage also requires reasonably good weather.

To avoid under-stocking the farmer may develop 'buffers' to combat yield variation, by reserving some paddocks to be grazed or cut depending on the season, building up stocks of conserved feed, investing in irrigation equipment, providing purchased feed to augment the pasture, or growing specific forage crops in anticipation of shortages. Where sufficient information is available the systems method may help. For example on the basis of data accumulated over nine years Newton & Brockington (1975) showed that the probability of an unacceptably low financial margin could be calculated and indicated that under the conditions which they defined, while the average margin would be £83 per ha (over the period 1965–1973) with either 14 or 16 ewes per ha, the chance of one year providing a margin less than £25 per ha increased from 1 in 500 with 14 ewes per ha to 1 in 20 at 16 ewes per ha.

7.9   CASE STUDIES—MILK FROM GRASS

To illustrate the diversity of acceptable systems of grass utilization, some examples, based on actual farm records are shown in the following pages. They do not represent average performances but those achieved by the best farms. In all three examples of milk production the intensity of land use is high. However, account must be taken of the quantity of purchased feed (concentrates and bulks) within the system. Because of soil type, climate and conservation as hay in example 1, fertilizer use is lower and intensity is raised by feed purchase. The proportion of home produced forage is greater in the other two examples. Provided high milk yield per cow can be achieved in example 1, gross margins, although lower than the other examples, are satisfactory. Gross margins can, however, be misleading as an indicator of profit within or between systems since the fixed or overhead costs on farms vary widely. Each farm is different, some have employees, others family labour; some farms are rented; some owned outright; some have sophisticated machinery, others have the bare essentials: some have overdrafts, others have deposit accounts. It is therefore unwise to generalize about overhead costs. In particular, interest charges on borrowed capital can severely erode profitability and offset good technical performance.

7.9.1 *Example 1. Small dairy farm with traditional cowshed system*

Some 61% of dairy farms in the UK had herds of under 50 cows in 1978, most of them milked and housed in traditional cowsheds, with hay and concentrates forming the major part of the dairy ration. Both farm size and the escalating costs of modernizing buildings and purchasing silage machinery are constraints to expansion. Whilst overhead costs are likely to be relatively low compared with the highly capitalized farm, the pressures of inflation force producers to increase productivity to maintain profitability.

Objectives
(1) Ensure that the number of milking cows is maximized within the accommodation, milking facilities and labour available.
(2) If possible rent summer grazing or arrange contract heifer rearing so that the constraint of farm size is reduced.
(3) Maximize the production from grass by generous fertilizer application to the grazing area. Fertilizer application rates will be lower than optimum on the area conserved as hay.
(4) Increase the carrying capacity of the farm by judicious purchase of additional feedstuffs, e.g. concentrates, brewers grains, sugar beet pulp, hay.

Data
20 hectares of average permanent grass, 45 cows (25 heifers contract reared), family labour, housed and milked in cowshed, hay conservation.

Annual target performance
2·0 tonnes compound dairy cake per cow
1·5 tonnes brewers grains per cow   6500 litres per cow in herd
Stocking rate 2·25 cows per ha   250 kg N per ha
Utilized dry matter: 7·6 tonnes per ha (75% of total DM production).

Annual nutritional balance	*GJ per cow*
Cow maintenance (see Table 7.1)	21·3
6500 litres milk	33·1
Net liveweight change	3·4
Total requirement	57·8

Feed input	
2000 kg concentrates (1700 kg DM × 12·5 MJ per kg)	21·2
1·5 tonnes brewers grains	3·3
Hay and grazing from 0·44 hectares	33·3
(Utilized dry matter at average 10 MJ per kg)	
Total input	57·8

Utilized forage output per hectare (33·3 × 2·25) = 75 GJ

An important assumption is the average energy value of the grass dry matter. Whilst the hay crop is likely to be nearer 9·5 MJ per kg DM, the grazed grass quality ought to exceed 10·5 MJ per kg DM if good management is practised. A reduction in energy provided from grass will require a higher concentrate input.

Estimated financial results (Assuming March 1982 year end)

	£ per cow	
Milk	877	6500 litres at 13·5p per litre
Calf sales	60	42 live calves per year;
	937	34 sold at £80
		8 reared on contract
Less		
Herd replacement	31	10 culls sold at £350;
		rearing fees for 24 heifers
		at £17 per month, £4896.
		Average 30 months at calving.
Output	906	
Variable costs		
Concentrates	278	Average costs
		at £139 per tonne;
		2000 kg per cow
Brewers grains	31	1·5 tonnes per cow
		at £21 per tonne

	£ per cow	
Forage	78	250 kg N per ha; stocking rate 2·25 cows per ha
Miscellaneous costs	40	Vet, AI, straw, etc. (based on costed farms).
Total variable costs	427	

Margin over		
concentrates per cow	£599	Concentrates per litre 0·31 kg
Gross margin per cow	£479	
Gross margin per ha	£1077	

Overhead costs
Whilst the gross margin per ha may be lower than on a more self-sufficient farm, the low capital investment coupled with the family labour input should ensure that overhead costs are low and profit is at a satisfactory level.

Gross margin for whole farm	£21540	
Overhead costs:		
Casual relief labour	£1900	£95 per ha
Power and machinery	£4050	£202 per ha
Rent and rates	£2050	£102 per ha
Miscellaneous	£1950	£98 per ha
Total overheads	£9950	£497 per ha
Profit	£11590	
Profit per LSU	£257	
Profit per ha	£579	

The profit of £11 600 would be the return for the farmer's own labour, and management, tax liability and capital replacement. If he has overdraft facilities, interest payments will have to be paid as well as any repayment of capital. The overall result, however, illustrates the return which can be achieved on the small farm with good technical performance.

7.9.2   *Example 2. A medium-sized specialist dairy farm*

This is on good land with ideal climate for grass growth, modern housing and milking system, self-fed silage and one full-time employee.

Objectives
(1) Maximize production and utilization of grass.
(2) Supplement forage with limited amounts of concentrates.
(3) Simplify herd management by adopting block calving in Feb/March.
(4) Use machinery and technical innovation to minimize physical labour requirements.

Data
65 hectares; short term leys and permanent grass; 130 cows and 60 followers (32 LSU); heifers calving at 24 months of age; silage conservation.

Annual target performance
1·0 tonne concentrates per cow   5500 litres per cow in herd
Stocking rate: 2·49 LSU per ha   400 kg N per ha
Utilized grass dry matter yield: 10·5 tonnes per ha.

Annual nutritional balance	*GJ per cow*
Cow maintenance (see Table 7.1)	21·3
5500 litres milk	28·0
Net live weight change	3·4
Total requirement	52·7

Feed input

1000 kg concentrates (850 kg DM × 12·5 MJ per kg)	10·6
Silage and grazing from 0·40 ha	42·1
(utilized dry matter at average 10 MJ per kg)	
Total input	52·7
Utilized forage output per ha (42·1 × 2·49)	105 GJ

Yield of utilized dry matter per ha is 40% higher than example 1 due to a better site and climate, higher nitrogen use and a silage-based system. The average energy value of the utilized dry matter at 10 MJ per kg should be achievable in spite of the bigger enterprise and quantities involved.

Estimated financial results (Assuming March 1982 year end)

	£ per cow	Assumptions
Milk	742	5500 litres at 13·5p per litre
Calf sales	72	121 live calves per year; 32 kept for rearing at £70 each; 89 sold at £80
Less		
Herd replacement	39	30 culls sold at £350; 30 in-calf heifers transferred in at £520
Output	£775	
Variable costs		
Concentrates	139	1·0 tonne concentrate at £139 per tonne
Forage	90	400 kg N per ha; stocking rate 2·49 LSU per ha
Miscellaneous costs	40	
Total variable costs	269	
Margin over concentrates per cow	£603	Concentrates per litre 0·18 kg
Gross margin per cow	£506	
Gross margin per ha	£1260	

Overhead costs

Gross margin per ha exceeds the figure in example 1 but employed labour, higher machinery costs and higher rent for better land and buildings will result in higher overhead costs.

Dairy herd gross margin	£65780	
Heifer rearing gross margin	£7200	
(£240 per heifer reared per year)		
Total gross margin	£72 980	

Paid labour	£8950	£138 per ha
Power and machinery	£11000	£169 per ha
Rent and rates	£7000	£108 per ha
Miscellaneous	£4600	£71 per ha
Total overheads	£31550	£486 per ha
Profit	£41430	

Profit per LSU £256
Profit per ha £637

Whilst the total profit from example 2 is over three times that in example 1, profit per LSU is similar because young stock are carried, but profit per ha is higher due to more intensive use of the grassland. However, the financial commitment in terms of capital replacement and tax liability will be much greater in example 2 as will the effect of inflation on overhead costs.

7.9.3   *Example 3. Large arable-dairy farm on good land with low rainfall*

This utilizes short-term grass leys and arable by-products; modern housing and milking system; trough feeding. Two full-time herdsmen are employed and additional labour is available for relief and support work.

Objectives
(1)   Incorporate the forage area into an arable rotation to maximize both forage production and subsequent yields of arable crops.
(2)   Utilize home-produced arable by-products and cereals to minimize supplementary feed costs.
(3)   Monitor effectively with minimum farmer involvement by block calving in Sept/November.

Data
To provide an example of this system is more difficult as the available feed resources will vary each year. In addition, the dairy enterprise becomes a smaller contributor to farm profitability. Nor is it possible to allocate overhead costs to the dairy herd with accuracy. There is the opportunity for greater sophistication, e.g. complete diet feeding, automatic milk recording and concentrate feed provision.

As a guide rather than specific example therefore:
130 hectares of grass and forage crops: 20 ha maize
                                            10 ha kale
                                            70 ha 2–3 year leys
                                            30 ha permanent grass.
250 cows plus 70 LSU of followers calving at 24 months
Overall stocking rate 2·46 LSU per ha.
(Additional feed such as sugar beet tops, stockfeed potatoes can be included in the diet as available. However, their area is excluded from stocking rate calculations.)

Annual target performance
6000 litres milk per cow
1·5 tonnes concentrates (mainly home-grown cereals)
Stocking rate 2·46 LSU per ha   300 kg N per ha
Utilized grass dry matter yield: 8·5 tonnes per ha.

Annual nutritional balance	*GJ per cow*
Cow maintenance (see Table 7.1)	21·3
6000 litres milk	30·6
Net live weight change	3·4
Total requirement	55·3

Feed input	
1500 kg concentrates (1275 kg DM at 12 MJ per kg)	15·3
0·85 tonnes DM, maize silage (at 10·8 MJ per kg DM)	9·2
0·35 tonnes DM kale: zero grazed (at 11·0 MJ per kg DM)	3·8
0·29 ha of grass and silage (utilized dry matter at average 10 MJ per kg)	27·0
Total input	55·3
Utilized forage output per ha (40·0 × 2·46)	98 GJ

Yield levels from forage crops are variable and a system which relies heavily on high-risk crops such as maize must have alternative feed supplies should that crop fail. If additional by-products are available, their inclusion with a corresponding lowering of the concentrate portion of the diet becomes an alternative, up to the point where bulk of ration limits maximum dry matter intake. Rations need to be reviewed regularly to take advantage of availability of resources and prevailing prices.

Estimated financial results (Assuming March 1982 year end)

	£ per cow	*Assumptions*
Milk	810	6000 litres at 13·5p per litre
Calf sales	69	225 live calves per year; 65 retained at £70 each; 160 sold at £80 each
Less		
Herd replacement	41	60 culls sold at £350; 60 in-calf heifers transferred in at £520
	838	

Variable costs

Concentrates	187	1·5 tonnes at £125 per tonne home-grown and home-mixed
Forage	75	Lower than example 2 because of contract work
Miscellaneous	38	
Total variable costs	300	
Margin over concentrates	£623	Concentrates per litre 0·25 kg
Gross margin per cow	£538	
Gross margin per ha	£1323	

7.10 CASE-STUDIES—MEAT FROM GRASS

The three diverse examples all operate beef or sheep enterprises that make major contributions to farm profit. The common features despite contrasting situations, are high live weight production per hectare allied to gross margins within the top 5% recorded by MLC for each production system.

All three farms achieve high animal performance with high output per hectare, at lower than average levels of concentrate feeding. Despite higher forage costs per hectare forage costs per head are only slightly above average.

The components of success are:
(1) good animal performance;
(2) high stocking rates related to the quality of the location;
(3) above-average levels of fertilizer N applications;
(4) good quality conserved feeds reducing dependence on concentrates.

7.10.1 *Example 4. Upland suckled calf and lamb production*

Grass leys integrated with upland grazing and grazing rights on open-hill. Beef and sheep enterprises allow 'clean' grazing and give a better financial balance when combined.

Area: 195 ha, plus grazing rights on open hill
Main enterprises: beef cows, sheep, store cattle and cereals
Grass: 2-year ryegrass leys, 48 ha, permanent pasture 13·5 ha,
upland grazing (200–320 m above sea level) 57 ha,
hill, 28 ha + grazing rights on open hill.

Beef

Fifty Hereford x Friesian cows calving in October and November
loose-housed on straw in mid-December and fed silage *ad libitum*
behind a barrier. Mated with Charolais bull from late December.
Calves have access to a creep area with hay *ad libitum* and concentrates up to about 1 kg per head per day. Cows and calves are
turned out in late April and continuously stocked till August when
the calves are weaned, the biggest calves are sold and the rest graze
silage aftermaths and are sold in the autumn.

Sheep

Four hundred and fifty Welsh halfbred ewes; replacements bought
as yearlings and tupped with Suffolk rams, are housed from early
January until they lamb in March and fed on hay with a cereal mix
based on home-grown whole barley from early February. Ewes and
lambs graze together until July when lambs are weaned and the
ewes go to the hill. Some lambs are sold as stores at weaning, the
rest finish on silage aftermaths and are sold from August until
November.

Silage

All silage is made from 48 hectares of leys cut twice. The first cut
receives 100 kg N per ha. After the first cut, the accumulation of
slurry from the slatted area is spread on the silage ground with
55 kg N per ha. Aftermaths receive 55 kg N per ha and are grazed
by weaned suckled calves and lambs. The first cut silage is mostly
fed to cows, the second cut to store cattle, a number of which are
purchased each year depending upon feed supplies and prices. Approximately 100 tonnes of hay are made for the sheep from the
permanent pasture which is then grazed.

Production: Physical

	kg live weight produced per ha	LUGD per ha	LU per ha (grazing)	Overall stocking rate head per ha	Daily live weight gain per head at grass (kg)	Calves reared per cow
Suckler herd	601	780	3·8	1·8	0·95	0·98
MLC averages	437	630	3·1	1·5	0·80	0·92
					Silage (tonnes)	Lambs per ewe
Sheep flock	430	789	3·4	10·8	41·6	1·2
MLC averages	295	635	2·8	8·6	26·5	1·25

Inputs

kg N per ha	Total concentrates (kg)	
	per cow	per ewe
227	198	30
MLC averages		
98	283	33

Production: Financial (1981 prices)

	Beef herd			Sheep flock		
	per head £	per ha £	MLC ave per ha	per head £	per ha £	MLC ave per ha
Returns	277	499	394	55	590	495
Less						
Replacements + variable costs	88	158	160	13	144	148
Gross margin	189	341	234	42	446	347

7.10.2 Example 5. 18-month beef production on a mixed arable farm

A grass enterprise that competes with the return from cereals.
Area: 170 ha   Rainfall: 760 mm p.a.   Soil: medium loam
Main enterprises   Cereals and 18-month beef
Grass: 21 ha permanent pasture mainly grazed, 39 ha two and three year ryegrass leys, mainly conserved by two cuts of silage with aftermath grazing

18-month beef system
One hundred and eighty Friesian steers purchased as reared calves in November, housed in old converted buildings, reared on grass silage and about 4·5 kg of concentrates (6 parts barley: 1 part, 34%

CP proprietary supplement) per head, per day. Calves are turned out during April and rotationally grazed for the first part of the season on the permanent grass. Leys are set aside for silage. Two cuts of silage are made and the silage is double chopped. The first cut of silage is made in the third or fourth week of May. After the second cut of silage the cattle graze the aftermaths, with supplementary feed at grass prior to yarding in straw yards in late October. The cattle finish on grass silage and mineralized rolled barley, up to 3·5 kg per head per day (average over winter 2·5 kg per head per day) and are sold from March to late June. The high yields of good quality silage consistently achieved reduce concentrate requirements for finishing. The permanent pasture receives about 220 kg and the leys 400 kg fertilizer N per ha. Of this, 290 kg are applied for first and second cut silage and 110 kg for aftermath grazing.

Production: Physical

kg live weight produced per ha	LUGD per ha	LU per ha	Grazing stocking rate cattle per ha	Overall stocking rate cattle per ha	Daily live weight gain per head at grass kg	Silage t per ha
1137	666	3·8	7·6	3·8	0·85	33·4
MLC averages						
681	442	2·5	4·9	3·1	0·70	28·7

Inputs

kg N per ha	Total concentrates per head (kg)
301	980
MLC averages	
148	1038

Production: Financial (1981 prices)

	£ per head	£ per ha	MLC average £ per ha
Sales	461	1750	1399
Less			
Calf purchases	92	351	287
Variable costs	180	684	623
Gross margin	189	715	489

7.10.3   Example 6. Intensive lowland sheep

Dairying is located close to the buildings and sheep are used on the outlying areas. The sheep use a grass break that is essential for high cereal yields on this farm. Nevertheless sheep have to show a return, competitive with the arable crops. Sheep also facilitate the autumn management of the cow paddocks.

Area: 749 ha; average rainfall: 960 mm; Soil types: from light loam with chalk outcropping through to medium–heavy loam. Grass mainly in 2- and 3-year leys.

Enterprises: Cereals, oil seed rape, 1150 ewes, 240 dairy cows, 140 sows and 3000 finishing pigs.

Sheep enterprise

Dorset Down, Suffolk and Texel rams are mated with Mule ewes, lamb in March–early April and are stocked at 16 ewes and lambs per ha in the first year of a two-year ley. They also graze surplus autumn grass on cow paddocks. Lambs are finished mainly off grass or stubble turnips with minimum concentrate feeding.

The two and three year leys are grazed by sheep in the first year and conserved for silage in the second. Various mixtures of Italian and perennial ryegrass are used. The leys for sheep receive regular dressings of 60 kg N per ha up to a total of 300 kg N per ha on the 'Follow N' principle. The conservation area receives basic slag in the autumn and up to 300 kg N per ha. The first cuts are for silage, second cuts for silage and/or hay.

Production: Physical

kg live weight produced per ha	LUGD per ha	LU per ha	Overall stocking rate ewes per ha	Lambs reared per ewe	Silage t per ha
927	972	3·0	16·0	1·81	46·5
MLC averages					
417	745	2·3	11·9	1·40	30·3

Inputs

kg N per ha	Total concentrates per ewe & lamb (kg)
286	42
MLC averages	
115	51

Production: Financial (1981 prices)

	£ per head	£ per ha	MLC average £ per ha
Lamb sales + wool	63	1009	641
Less			
Replacements + variable costs	25	398	290
Gross margin	38	611	351

FURTHER READING

DENT J. B. & BLACKIE M. J. (1979) *Systems simulation in agriculture.* Applied Science Publishers, Ltd, London

NORMAN L. & COOTE R. B. (1971) *The Farm Business.* Longman, London

SPEDDING C. R. W. (1979) *An introduction to agricultural systems.* Applied Science Publishers Ltd, London

APPENDIX 7.1

Livestock unit values by type of stock

Type of stock	Specifications	Unit values
Dairy cows	Holstein, Friesian	1·0
	Ayrshire, Shorthorn	0·9
	Guernsey	0·8
	Jersey	0·75
Grazing cattle	Under 204 kg (0–11 months)	0·25
	204–340 kg (11–20 months)	0·5
	340–477 kg (21–30 months)	0·75
	Over 477 kg (over 30 months)	1·00
Suckler cows	Dry cow	1·0
	Spring-calving cow with calf	1·2
	Autumn-calving cow with calf	1·4
Weaned calves	Weaned calf, spring born	0·2
	Weaned calf, autumn born	0·4
Breeding ewes (*dry*)	18–36 kg	0·08
	36–55 kg	0·1
	55–68 kg	0·13
	68–77 kg	0·15
	77–91 kg	0·17
	Over 91 kg	0·2
Weaned lambs	Light lambs (27–36 kg)	0·08
	Heavy lambs (36–54 kg)	0·1
Breeding ewes (*lactating*)		Add 0·01 per ewe to the dry ewe standard for each 25% lambing %. 1 tonne of silage 　　　　= 20 LUGD 1 tonne of hay 　　　　= 70 LUGD

APPENDIX 7.2

Target overall stocking rates when one conservation cut is to be taken from half of the total area in May/June, conserving one quarter of the total production.

		Animals per hectare				
Site quality	Fertilizer N (kg ha^{-1})	Dairy cows	Suckler cows with calves	Cattle from 200 kg	Cattle from 350 kg	Ewes with lambs
1. Poor	150+	2·0	1·6	3·7	2·5	7·5
	300	2·3	1·9	4·3	2·9	8·2
3. Average	150+	2·7	2·2	5·0	3·4	10·5
	300	3·1	2·6	5·8	3·9	12·0
	450	3·5	—	6·4	4·4	—
5. Excellent	150+	3·4	2·8	6·2	4·2	13·0
	300	3·9	3·3	7·3	4·9	15·0
	450	4·3	—	8·1	5·5	—

APPENDIX 7.3

Target overall stocking rates when the whole area will be cut for conservation, two-thirds in May/June and one-third in July/August conserving 40–50% of the total production.*

		Animals per hectare				
Site quality	Fertilizer N (kg ha^{-1})	Dairy cows	Suckler cows with calves	Cattle from 200 kg	Cattle from 350 kg	Ewes with lambs
1. Poor	150+	1·5	1·2	2·7	1·9	5·5
	300	1·7	1·4	3·2	2·1	6·0
3. Average	150+	2·0	1·6	3·7	2·5	7·7
	300	2·3	1·9	4·2	2·9	8·8
	450	2·6	—	4·7	3·2	—
5. Excellent	150+	2·5	2·0	4·6	3·1	9·3
	300	2·9	2·4	5·3	3·6	11·0
	450	3·2	—	5·9	4·1	—

* These approximate to annual stocking rates since the conserved forage, plus concentrates for productive animals and straw for the less productive, would meet the remaining requirements.
† A good grass clover sward can give yields similar to 150 kg N ha^{-1}.

APPENDIX 7.4

Target stocking rates for separate periods over the grazing season. If the growing season is divided into three 60-day periods the data of Morrison *et al.* 1980 indicate that 45–52% of the total herbage dry matter is produced in mid April–mid June, 25–32% in mid June–mid-August and 20–25% in mid August–mid October. Variations in fertilizer practice may modify these proportions to a limited extent. For stock such as dairy cows and beef cattle whose appetite remains fairly uniform over the season, appropriate stocking rates for each period of the season can then be indicated.

					Animals per hectare					
		mid April to mid June			mid June to mid August			mid August to mid October		
Site quality	Fertilizer N kg ha⁻¹		Beef*			Beef*			Beef*	
		Dairy cows	230 kgW	390 kgW	Dairy cows	290 kgW	450 kgW	Dairy cows	350 kgW	500 kgW
Poor	150+	3·8	7·0	4.8	2·2	4·0	2·7	1·9	3·5	2·4
	300	4·3	8·1	5·5	2·5	4·6	3·1	2·1	4·0	2·7
Average	150+	5·0	9·4	6·3	2·9	5·4	3·6	2·5	4·7	3·1
	300	5·9	10·8	7·4	3·4	6·2	4·2	2·9	5·4	3·7
	450	6·6	12·0	8·3	3·8	6·9	4·7	3·3	6·0	4·1
Excellent	150+	6·3	11·0	8·0	3·6	6·6	4·6	3·1	5·8	4·0
	300	7·3	13·6	9·2	4·2	7·8	5·3	3·6	6·8	4·6
	450	8·1	15·1	10·4	4·6	8·6	5·9	4·0	7·5	5·2

* Approximate mid weights in each period for cattle of 200 kg and 350 kg weight at turnout

For suckler cows and ewes with lambs it is normal for weaning to take place between the second and third period. Accordingly for these animals stocking rates are shown for the dams with progeny in the first two periods and for the separated groups in the third period.

| | | | | Animals per hectare | | | | | |
| | | Period 1 | | Period 2 | | Period 3 | | | |
Site quality	Fertilizer N kg ha⁻¹	Suckler cows with calves	Ewes with lambs	Suckler cows with calves	Ewes with lambs	Suckler cows	Weaned calves†	Ewes	Weaned lambs†
Poor	150	3·1	14	1·8	8	2·4	2·5	15	12
	300	3·6	15	2·1	9	2·8	4·1	18	14
Average	150	4·2	20	2·4	11	3·2	4·7	21	16
	300	4·9	22	2·8	13	3·7	5·4	24	19
Excellent	150	5·2	24	3·0	14	4·0	5·8	26	21
	300	6·2	28	3·5	16	4·7	6·8	30	24

† Approximate, to be varied according to the needs of the stock

APPENDIX 7.5

Nutritive value of feeding stuffs

Feed	Dry matter content $(g\ kg^{-1})$	D-value $(\%)$	ME $(MJ\ kg^{-1})$	Crude protein $(g\ kg^{-1})$	DCP $(g\ kg^{-1})$
Pasture					
well-stocked					
Spring	200	74	12·0	160	110
Summer	200	69	11·2	240	207
Autumn	200	71	11·2	220	180
under-stocked	220	64	10·0	175	124
Silages					
Grass	200	68	11·4	170	116
Grass	220	63	10·5	160	102
Grass	240	58	9·5	150	97
Grass	260	52	8·2	120	85
Red clover					
1st cut	180	60	9·9	160	103
6 wk regrowth	180	60	10·1	180	120
Lucerne early	220	58	9·0	180	120
late	240	52	8·6	160	103
Maize	230	67	10·6	110	70
Barley (whole crop)	400	62	9·6	95	50
Sugar beet tops	230	50	7·9	104	65
pulp	120	62	9·7	83	42
Hays					
Grass	850	67	10·1	132	90
Grass	850	61	9·0	101	58
Grass	850	57	8·4	85	39
Grass	850	51	7·5	92	45
Grass	850	47	7·0	88	38
Red clover	850	61	9·6	184	128
	850	50	7·8	131	67
Lucerne	850	54	8·3	193	143
	850	51	7.7	171	116
Dried grass					
Grass (very leafy)	900	70	10·8	161	113
Grass (leafy)	900	68	10·6	187	136
Grass (flowering)	900	64	9·7	154	97
Lucerne (bud)	900	60	9·4	244	174
(in flower)	900	57	8·7	178	128
Straws					
Barley (spring)	860	49	7·3	38	9
(winter)	860	39	5·8	37	8
Oat	860	46	6·7	34	11
Wheat	860	39	5·6	34	10

Feed	Dry matter content (g kg^{-1})	D-value (%)	ME (MJ kg^{-1})	Crude protein (g kg^{-1})	DCP (g kg^{-1})
Cereal feeds					
Barley (grain)	860	86	13·7	108	82
(brewers grain fresh)	220	59	10·0	205	149
(ensiled)	280	59	10·0	204	149
(dried)	900	60	10·3	204	145
Oats (grain)	860	68	11·5	109	84
(bran)	900	55	8·8	89	44
Wheat (grain)	860	87	14·0	124	105
(bran)	880	61	10·1	170	126
(middlings)	880	72	11·9	176	129
Maize (grain)	860	87	14·2	98	78
(flaked)	900	92	15·0	110	106
(germ meal)	900	80	13·2	112	90
(gluten meal)	900	85	14·2	394	339
(starch feed)	900	83	14·1	251	211
Starch feeds					
Cassava pellets	900	80	12·6	31	20
Citrus pulp	930	87	14·1	63	51
Root crops					
Kale	140	70	11·0	114	150
Mangels	120	79	12·4	83	58
Swedes	120	82	12·8	108	91
Sugarbeet (root)	230	87	13·7	48	35
(tops)	160	62	9·9	125	88
(pulp pressed)	180	84	12·7	106	66
(pulp dried)	900	84	12·7	99	59
(pulp molassed)	900	79	12·2	106	61
Protein feeds					
Oil cakes					
Cottonseed (cake)	900	51	8·7	263	203
(decorticated)	900	70	12·3	457	393
Groundnut (decorticated)	900	76	12·9	504	449
(extracted)	900	75	11·7	552	491
Linseed meal (extracted)	900	74	11·9	404	348
Rape meal (extracted)	900	67	10·9	413	343
Soya bean (cake)	900	79	13·3	504	454
(meal)	900	79	12·3	503	453
Animal product					
Whole cows milk	128	93	20·2	266	250
Fishmeal, white	900	68	11·1	701	631
Meat and bone meal	900	57	9·7	597	465

Appendix

The common temperate grasses
and legumes

GRASSES

Latin name	Common name	Agricultural importance
Agropyron repens	Couch grass	weed
Agrostis canina	Brown bent	major
Agrostis tenuis	Fine bent	major
Alopecurus geniculatus	Floating foxtail	minor
Alopecurus pratensis	Meadow foxtail	minor
Alopecurus myosuroides	Black grass	weed
Anthoxanthum odoratum	Sweet vernal	minor
Arrhenatherum elatius	Tall or false oat grass	minor
Avena fatua	Spring or common wild oat	weed
Avena ludoviciana	Winter wild oat	weed
Brachypodium pinnatum	Tor grass	weed
Bromis inermis	Upright brome	weed
Bromis mollis	Soft brome	weed
Bromis sterilis	Sterile brome	weed
Cynosurus cristatus	Crested dogstail	minor
Dactylis glomerata	Cocksfoot	major
Deschampsia caespitosa	Tussock grass	weed
Deschampsia flexuosa	Wavy hair grass	minor
Festuca arundinacea	Tall fescue	major
Festuca ovina	Sheep's fescue	minor
Festuca pratensis	Meadow fescue	major
Festuca rubra	Red fescue	minor
Holcus lanatus	Yorkshire fog	minor
Holcus mollis	Creeping soft grass	weed
Hordeum murinum	Wall barley	weed
Lolium italicum = L. multiflorum	Italian ryegrass	major
L. italicum var Westerwoldicum	Westernwold's grass	minor
Lolium perenne	Perennial ryegrass	major
Molina caerulea	Purple moor grass	minor
Nardus stricta	Mat grass	minor
Phleum pratense	Timothy or Cats tail	major
Poa annua	Annual meadow grass	weed
Poa pratensis	Smooth meadow grass	minor
Poa trivialis	Rough meadow grass	minor
Sieglingia decumbens	Heath grass	minor
Trisetum flavescens	Golden oat grass	minor

LEGUMINOUS PLANTS

Latin name	Common name	Agricultural importance
Lotus corniculatus	Birdsfoot trefoil	minor
Onobrichis viciifolia	Sainfoin	minor
Medicago sativa	Lucerne	major
Trifolium hybridum	Alsike clover	minor
Trifolium pratense	Red clover	major
Trifolium repens	White clover	major

References

AERTS J. E., DE BRABANDER D. L., COTTYN B. G., BURSSE F. X., CARLIER L. A. & MOERMANS R. J. (1978) Some remarks on the analytical procedure of Van Soest for the prediction of forage digestibility. *Anim. Feed Sci. Technol.*, **3**, 309–22

AGRICULTURAL RESEARCH COUNCIL (ARC) (1965) *The nutrient requirements of farm livestock. 2. Ruminants.* Agricultural Research Council. HMSO, London

AITKEN F. C. & HANKIN R. G. (1970) *Vitamins in Feeds for Livestock.* Technical Communication No. 25 Commonwealth Bureau of Animal Nutrition. Commonwealth Agricultural Bureau, Farnham Royal

ALDRICH D. T. A. & DENT J. W. (1963) The interrelationships between heading date, yield, chemical composition and digestibility in varieties of perennial ryegrass, timothy, cocksfoot and meadow fescue. *J. nat. Inst. agric. Bot.* **9**, 261–81.

ALEXANDER C. L., MEYER R. M. & BARTLEY E. E. (1969) Rumen removal rates of some chemically defined fractions of ^{14}C labelled alfalfa. *J. Anim. Sci.*, **29**, 746–53

ALLEN H. P. (1979) Renewing pastures by direct drilling. In Charles A. H. & Haggar R. J. (eds), *Changes in Sward Composition and Productivity*, 217–222. Occasional Symposium No. 10. Hurley, British Grassland Society

AMIES S. J. (1978) The importance of block calving in relation to seasonality of production. *LCP Information Unit Report No. 15, MMB*, Milk Marketing Board, Thames Ditton

ANDERSON B. & LARSSEN B. (1961) Influence of local temperature changes in the preoptic area and vestial hypothalamus in the regulation of feed and water intake. *Acta physiol. scand.*, **52**, 75–89.

ANDREWS R. P., ESCUDER-VOLENTE J., CURRAN M. K. & HOLMES W. (1972) The influence of supplements of energy and protein on the intake and performance of cattle fed on cereal straws. *Anim. Prod.*, **15**, 165–76

ANSLOW R. C. (1967) Frequency of cutting and sward production. *J. agric. Sci., Camb.*, **68**, 377–84

ANSLOW R. C. & GREEN J. O. (1967) The seasonal growth of pasture grasses. *J. agric. Sci., Camb.*, **68**, 109–22

ARNOLD G. W. (1970) Regulation of food intake in grazing ruminants. In Phillipson A. T. (ed.), *Physiology of digestion in the ruminant*, 264–76. Oriel Press, Newcastle upon Tyne

ARNOLD G. W. & DUDZINSKI M. L. (1978) *Ethology of free-ranging domestic animals.* Elsevier North Holland Inc., Amsterdam

BAILE C. A. & FORBES J. M. (1974) Control of feed intake and regulation of energy balance in ruminants. *Physiology Rev.*, **160**, 214

BAKER H. K., BAKER R. D., DEAKINS R. M., GOULD J. L., HODGES J. & POWELL R. A. (1964) Grassland Recording. V. Recommendations for recording the utilized output on dairy farms. *J. Br. Grassld Soc.*, **19**, 160–8

BAKER R. D. (1978) *Beef cattle at grass. Intake and production* 2 : 1–2 : 7. Winter meeting, British Grassland Society

BAKER R. D. & BARKER J. M. (1978) Milk-fed calves. 4. The effect of herbage allowance and milk intake upon herbage intake and performance of grazing calves. *J. agric. Sci., Camb.*, **90**, 31–8

BAKER R. D., LE DU Y. L. P. & ALVAREZ F. (1979) The response of suckler cows and calves to a range of grazing severities. *Anim. Prod.*, **28**, 421–2

BALCH C. C. & CAMPLING R. C. (1969) Voluntary intake of food. In Lenkeit W., Brierem K. & Craseman E. (eds), *Handbuch der Tierernahrung*, Vol. 1. Verlag Paul Pavey, Hamburg and Berlin

BALCH C. C. & LINE C. (1957) Gut fill changes in cows. *J. Dairy Res.*, **24**, 11–19

BARNARD C. S. & NIX J. S. (1979) *Farm Planning and Control*, 2e. Cambridge University Press, Cambridge

BARTHOLOMEW P. W. & CHESTNUTT D. M. B. (1977) The effect of fertiliser nitrogen and defoliation intervals on dry matter production, seasonal response and chemical composition of perennial ryegrass. *J. agric. Sci., Camb.*, **88**, 711–21

BATH D. L., WEIR W. C. & TORRELL D. T. (1956) The use of oesophageal fistula for the determination of the consumption and digestibility of pasture forage by sheep. *J. Anim. Sci.*, **15**, 1166

BEEVER D. E., CAMMELL S. B. & WALLACE A. S. (1974) The digestion of fresh, frozen and dried perennial ryegrass. *Proc. Nutr. Soc.*, **33**, 73A–74A

BHATTACHARYA A. M. & WARNER R. G. (1967) Rumen pH as a factor controlling voluntary feed intake. *J. Anim. Sci.*, **26**, 913

BLAXTER K. L. & BOYNE A. W. (1978) The estimation of the nutritive value of feeds as energy sources for ruminants and the derivation of feeding systems. *J. agric. Sci., Camb.*, **90**, 47–68

BLAXTER K. L. & GRAHAM N. McC. (1956). The effect of the grinding and cubing process on the utilization of the energy of dried grass. *J. agric. Sci. Camb.* **47**, 207–17

BLAXTER K. L. WAINMAN F. W. & WILSON R. S. (1961) The regulation of food intake by sheep. *Anim. Prod.*, **3**, 51–61

BLAXTER K. L. & WILSON R. S. (1963) The assessment of a crop husbandry technique in terms of animal production. *Anim. Prod.*, **5**, 27–42

BLOOD D. C. & HENDERSON J. A. (1974) *Veterinary medicine*. Bailliere Tindall, London

BLOOD T. F. (1963) Effect of height of cutting on the subsequent regrowth of a sward. *Nat. agric. advis. Serv. Q. Rev.*, **14**, 139–43

BROOKE D. (1979) Silage: Quantity or Quality? *Fm Mgt*, **3**, 520–9

BROWN R. H. & BLASER R. E. (1968) Leaf area index in pasture growth. *Herb. Abstr.*, **38**, 1–9

BUENO L. (1975) Role de l'acide D-L lactique dans le controle de l'ingestion alimentaire chez le mouton. (Role of D-L lactic acid in the control of food intake in sheep *Annls Rech. vet.*, **6**, 325–36

BUTLER G. W. & JONES D. I. H. (1973) Mineral Biochemistry of Herbage. In Butler G. W. & Bailey R. W. (eds), *Chemistry and Biochemistry of Herbage*, Vol. 1, Ch. 19. Academic Press, London and New York

CAMPLING R. C. (1970) Physical regulation of voluntary feed intake. In Phillipson A. T. (ed.), *Physiology of Digestion and Metabolism in the Ruminant*. Oriel Press, Newcastle upon Tyne

CAMPLING R. C. & MURDOCH J. C. (1966) The effect of concentrates on the voluntary intake of roughages by cows. *J. Dairy Res.*, **33**, 1–11

CARR A. J. H. (1967) Plant Pathology. *Report Welsh Plant Breeding Station, 1966*, 117–19

CARTER W. R. B. (1960) A review of nutrient losses and efficiency of conserving herbage on silage, barn-dried hay and field-cured hay. *J. Br. Grassld Soc.*, **15**, 220–30

CASHMORE W. H. & DENHAM H. J. (1938) The drying of hay in the swath and window. *J. Minst. Agric.*, **45**, 211–20

CASTLE M. E. (1976) A simple disc instrument for estimating herbage yield. *J. Br. Grassld Soc.*, **31**, 37–40

CASTLE M. E. & WATKINS P. (1979) *Modern Milk Production.* Faber and Faber, London

CASTLE M. E. & WATSON J. N. (1975) A comparison between barley and dried grass as supplements to silage of high digestibility. *J. Br. Grassld Soc.*, **30**, 217–22

CHESTNUTT D. M. B., MURDOCH J. C., HARRINGTON F. J. & BINNIE R. C. (1977) The effect of cutting frequency and applied nitrogen on production and digestibility of perennial ryegrass. *J. Br. Grassld Soc.* **32**, 177–83

CLEMENT C. R. & HOPPER M. J. (1968) The supply of potassium to high yielding cut grass. *Nat. agric. advis. Serv., Q. Rev.* **79**, 101–9

CLEMENT C. R. & WILLIAMS T. E. (1964) Leys and soil organic matter. I. The accumulation of organic carbon in soil under different leys. *J. agric. Sci., Camb.*, **63**, 377–83

CLEMENT C. R. & WILLIAMS T. E. (1967) Leys and soil organic matter. II. The accumulation of nitrogen in soils under different leys. *J. agric. Sci., Camb.*, **69**, 133–8

CLEMENTS R. O. (1980) Grassland pests—an unseen enemy. *Outl. Agric.* (in press)

COLLINS D. P. (1979) *The use of animal manures on pasture.* Mimeo Publication, An Foras Taluntais

COLLINS D. P., DRENNAN M. J. & FLYNN A. V. (1977) Potential of Irish grassland for beef production. *Proceedings of International Meeting on Animal Production from Temperate Grassland*, Dublin. 12–19

COMERFORD P. (1979) The effects of chop length and laceration of grass silage on weight gain of beef animals. *Proceedings of European Grassland Federation Meeting*, Brighton

CONNEL J. & HOUSEMAN R. J. (1976). The utilization by ruminants of the pressed green crops from fractionation machinery. (Ed. R. J. Wilkins). *British Grassland Society/British Society of Animal Production Occasional Symposium No. 9*, 57–64

CONRAD H. R., PRATT A. D. & HIBBS J. W. (1964) Regulation of feed intake in dairy cows. I. Change in importance of physical and physiological factors with increasing digestibility. *J. Dairy Sci.*, **47**, 54–62

CONWAY A. (1962) *An Foras Taluntais Research Report*, Animal Production Division, 15–16

CONWAY A. (1963) Effect of grazing management on beef production. II. Comparison of three stocking rates under two systems of grazing. *Ir. J. agric. Res.*, **2**, 243–58

COOPER J. P. (1952) Studies on the growth and development in Lolium. III. Influence of season and latitude on ear emergence. *J. Ecol.*, **40**, 532–79

COOPER J. P. (1960) The use of controlled life-cycles in the forage grasses and legumes. *Herb. Abstr.*, **30**, 71–9

COOPER J. P. (1966) The significance of genetic variation in light interception and conversion for forage-plant breeding. *Proceedings of the Tenth International Grassland Congress Helsinki, Finland*, 715–20

COOPER J. P. (1969) Potential forage production. *Grassland Forage Breeding, Occasional Symposium No. 5*, British Grassland Society, 5–13

COOPER J. P. (1970) Potential production and energy conversion in temperate and tropical grasses. *Herb. Abstr.*, **40**, 1–15

COOPER J. P. (1973) Genetic variation in herbage constituents. In Butler G. W. & Bailey R. W. (eds), *Chemistry and Biochemistry of Herbage.* Academic Press, London and New York

COOPER J. P. & TAINTON N. M. (1968) Light and temperature requirements for the growth of tropical and temperate grasses. *Herb. Abstr.*, **38**, 167–76

CORBETT J. L., LANGLANDS J. P. & BOYNE A. W. (1961) An estimate of the energy expended for maintenance by strip grazed dairy cows. *Proceedings of the 8th International Congress of Animal Production, Hamburg, Schlussbericht* 245

CORRALL A. J., LAVENDER R. H. & TERRY, CORA P. (1979) Grass species and varieties, seasonal pattern of production and relationships between yield, quality and date of first harvest. *Technical Report No. 26*, Grassland Research Institute, Hurley

COWARD N. (1971) Finance for dairy farm buildings. *J. Univ. Newcastle agric. Soc.*, **24**, 4–10

COWLING D. W., LEIGH J. H. & LOCKYER D. R. (1962) *Experiments in Progress No. 14*, Grassland Research Institute, Hurley, 18

CRAVEN J. A. (1975) *The cash crisis as it affects a sample of LCP dairy farms.* LCP Information Unit Report No. 2, MMB

CULPIN C. (1962) Developments in methods of barn hay drying. *J. Br. Grassld Soc.*, **17**, 150–6

CUNNINGHAM J. M. M. & RUSSEL A. J. F. (1979) The technical development of sheep production from hill land in Great Britain. *Live Stk Prod. Sci.*, **6**, 379–85

CURRAN M. K. & HOLMES W. (1970) Prediction of the voluntary intake of food by dairy cows. *Anim. Prod.*, **12**, 213–24

CURRAN M. K., WIMBLE R. & HOLMES W. (1970) Prediction of voluntary intake of food by dairy cows. I. Stall-fed cows in late pregnancy and early lactation. *Anim. Prod.*, **12**, 195–212

DAVIES W. (1928) The factor of competition between one species and another in seeds mixtures. *Bulletin H8 Welsh Plant Breeding Station, Aberystwyth*, 82–149

DAVIES W. (1941) The grassland map of England and Wales. *Agriculture, London*, **48**, 112–21

DAVIES W. E., ap GRIFFITHS G. & ELLINGTON A. (1966). The assessment of herbage legume varieties. II. *In vitro* digestibility, water-soluble carbohydrate, crude protein and mineral content of primary growth of clover and lucerne. *J. agric. Sci., Camb.*, **66**, 351

DEINUM B. (1966) Influence of some climatological factors on the chemical composition and feeding value of herbage. *Proceedings of 10th International Grassland Congress*, Helsinki. 415–18

DEMARQUILLY C. & DULPHY J. P. (1977) Effect of ensiling on feed intake and animal performance. *Proceedings 1st International Meeting of Animal Production from Temperate Grassland.* edit. B. Gilsenon, Dublin, 53–61

DIBB C. & HAGGAR R. J. (1979) Evidence of sward changes on yield. In Charles A. H. & Haggar R. J. (eds), *Changes in Sward Composition and Productivity*, 11–20. Occasional Symposium No. 10, British Grassland Society, Hurley

DONALD C. M. (1958) The interaction of competition for light and nutrients. *Aust. J. agric. Res.*, **9**, 421–35

DONALD C. M. (1963) Competition among crop and pasture plants. *Adv. Agron.* **15**, 1–118

DONALD C. M. & BLACK J. N. (1958) The significance of leaf area in pasture growth. *Herb. Abstr.*, **28**, 1–6

EADIE J. & MAXWELL T. J. (1975) Systems research in hill sheep farming. In Dalton G. E. (ed.) *Study of agricultural systems.* 395–413. Applied Science Publishers, London

EDMOND D. B. (1970) Effects of treading on pastures using different animals and soils. *Proceedings 11th International Grassland Congress, Surfers Paradise, Australia*, 604–11

EDWARDS C. A. & HEATH G. W. (1964) *The Principles of Agricultural Entomology.* Chapman and Hall Ltd, London

EGAN A. R. (1965) Nutritional status and intake regulation in sheep. III. The relationship between improvement of nitrogen status and increase in voluntary intake of low protein roughages by sheep. *Aust. J. agric. Res.*, **16**, 463–72

EKERN A., BLAXTER K. L. & SAWERS D. (1965) The effect of artificial drying on the energy value of grass. *Br. J. Nutr.*, **19**, 417–34

ESCA (East of Scotland College of Agriculture) (1978) *Planning a clean grazing system.* Speedy A. W. Technical Note 187A, Edinburgh School of Agriculture

ESCUDER J. C., ANDREWS R. P. & HOLMES W. (1971) The effect of nitrogen, stocking rate and frequency of grazing by beef cattle on the output of pasture. *J. Br. Grassld Soc.*, **26**, 79–84.

FENTON E. W. (1931) The influence of sectional grazing and manuring on the flora of grassland. *J. Ecol.*, **19**, 75–97

FENTON E. W. (1934) Grassland retrogression in Devonshire permanent pastures. *J. Ecol.*, **22**, 279–88

FORBES J. M. (1978) Integration of metabolic and physical control into a model of feeding behaviour in ruminants. *J. Physiol., London*, **281**, 37P–38P

FORBES J. M., EL SHAHAT A. A., JONES R., DUNCAN J. G. S. & BOAZ T. G. (1979) The effect of day length on the growth of lambs. I. Comparisons of sex, level of feeding, shearing and breed of sire. *Anim. Prod.*, **29**, 33–42

FORBES T. J., DIBB C., GREEN J. O. & FENLON K. A. (1977) *Permanent grassland. 1. The permanent pasture project objectives and methods.* GRI-ADAS Joint Permanent Pasture Group, Hurley

FRYER J. D. & MAKEPEACE R. J. (eds) (1978) *Weed control handbook, Vol. II Recommendations.* 8e. Blackwell Scientific Publications Oxford

GAIR R. & ROBERTS E. T. (1969) Pest and disease control in grass and fodder crops. In Martin H. (ed.) *Insecticide and Fungicide Handbook.* 3e. Blackwell Scientific Publications, Oxford

GARWOOD E. A. (1969) Seasonal tiller populations of grass and grass/clover swards with and without irrigation. *J. Br. Grassld Soc.*, **24**, 333–44

GARWOOD E. A. & SHELDRICK R. D. (1978) Dry matter production by tall fescue under dry conditions. *J. Br. Grassld Soc.*, **33**, 67–8

GARWOOD E. A. & TYSON K. C. (1973) The response of S.24 perennial ryegrass swards to irrigation. 1. Effects of partial irrigation on DM yield and on the utilization of applied nitrogen. *J. Br. Grassld Soc.*, **28**, 223–33

GARWOOD E. A. & WILLIAMS T. E. (1967a) Soil water use and growth of a grass sward. *J. agric. Sci., Camb.*, **68**, 281–92

GARWOOD E. A. & WILLIAMS T. E. (1967b) Growth, water use and nutrient uptake from the subsoil by grass swards. *J. agric. Sci., Camb.*, **69**, 125–30

GIBB M. J. & TREACHER T. T. (1976) The effect of herbage allowance on herbage intake and performance of lambs grazing perennial ryegrass and red clover swards. *J. agric. Sci., Camb.*, **86**, 355–65

GIBB M. J. & TREACHER T. T. (1978) The effect of herbage allowance on herbage intake and performance of ewes and their twin lambs grazing perennial ryegrass. *J. agric. Sci., Camb.*, **90**, 139–147

GILL M. (1979) The principles and practice of feeding ruminants on complete diets. *Grass Forage Sci.*, **34**, 155–61

GORDON C. H., KANE E. A., DERBYSHIRE J. C., JACOBSON W. C., MELIN C. G. & McCALMONT J. R. (1959). Nutrient losses, quality and feeding values of wilted and direct-cut orchard grass stored in bunker and tower silos. *J. Dairy Sci.* **42**, 1703–11

GORDON C. H., HOLDREN R. D. & DERBYSHIRE J. C. (1969) Field losses in harvesting wilted forage. *Agron. J.*, **61**, 924–7

GORDON F. J. (1973) The effect of high nitrogen levels and stocking rates on milk output from pasture. *J. Br. Grassld Soc.*, **28**, 193–201

GORDON F. J. (1974a) The use of nitrogen fertilizer on grassland for milk production. In *The role of nitrogen in grassland productivity. Proceedings* No. 142. 14–27 The Fertilizer Society, London

GORDON F. J. (1974b) A comparison of spring and autumn produced dried grass for milk production. *J. Br. Grassld Soc.*, **29**, 113–16

GORDON F. J. (1975) The effect of including dried grass in the supplement given to lactating cows at pasture. *J. Br. Grassld Soc.*, **30**, 79–83

GORDON F. J. (1979) The effect of interval between harvests and wilting of herbage for silage on milk production. *Proceedings European Grassland Federation Meeting*, Brighton

GORDON F. J. & MCMURRAY C. H. (1979) The optimum level of protein in the supplement for dairy cows with access to grass silage. *Anim. Prod.*, **29**, 283–91

GORDON F. J. & MURDOCH J. C. (1978) An evaluation of a high-quality grass silage for milk production. *J. Br. Grassld Soc.*, **33**, 5–11

GRAHAM N. MCC. (1964) Energy costs of feeding activities and energy expenditure of grazing sheep. *Aust. J. Agric. Res.*, **15**, 969–73

GRANT, SHEILA A., BARTHRAM G. T., LAMB W. I. C. & MILNE J. A. (1978) Effect of season and level of grazing on the utilization of heather by sheep. 1. Responses of the sward. *J. Br. Grassld Soc.*, **33**, 289–300

GRASSLAND RESEARCH INSTITUTE (1961) *Research techniques in use at the GRI, Hurley. Bulletin 45*, Commonwealth Bureau of Pastures and Field Crops, Commonwealth Agricultural Bureau, Farnham Royal

GREEN J. O. (1955) Management of a lucerne-cocksfoot ley for green-crop drying. *Memoir No. 1. Lucerne Investigations 1944–53, Grassland Research Institute, Hurley*, 31–46

GREEN J. O. (1974) Preliminary report on a sample survey of grassland in England and Wales 1970/72. *Internal Report No. 310*, Grassland Research Institute, Hurley

GREEN J. O. & WILLIAMS T. E. (1975) *National grassland and forage resources.* Paper read at Winter Meeting, British Grassland Society, December

GREENHALGH J. F. D. (1975) Factors limiting animal production from grazed pasture. *J. Br. Grassld Soc.*, **30**, 153–60

AP GRIFFITHS G. (1963) Effect of flowering on water soluble carbohydrate content. *Report of Welsh Plant Breeding Station*, 1962. 87.

HAGGAR R. J. & SQUIRES N. R. W. (1979) The scientific manipulation of sward constituents in grassland by herbicides and one pass seeding. In Charles A. H. & Haggar R. J. (eds), *Changes in Sward Composition and Productivity*, 223–234. Occasional Symposium No. 10. Hurley, British Grassland Society

HANCOCK J. (1950) Grazing habits of dairy cows in New Zealand. *Emp. J. exp. Agric.*, **18**, 249–63

HARRINGTON F. J. & BINNIE R. C. (1971) The effect of height and frequency of cutting on grass production. *44th Annual Report of Agricultural Research Institute, Northern Ireland*, 17–24

HARROD T. R. (1979) Soil suitability for grassland. In Jarvis M. G. & Mackney D. (eds), *Soil Survey Applications* No. 13, Harpenden

'T HART M. L. (1956) Some problems of intensive grassland farming in The Netherlands. *Proceedings 7th International Grassland Congress, Palmerston North, New Zealand*, 70–9

HEALY W. B. (1973) Nutritional aspects of soil ingestion by grazing animals. In Butler G. W. & Bailey R. W. (eds), *Chemistry and Biochemistry of Herbage*, Vol. 1, Chap. 13, 567–88. Academic Press, London

HEARD A. J. (1965) The effect of the nitrogen content of residues from leys on amounts of available soil nitrogen and on yields of wheat. *J. agric. Sci., Camb.,* **64,** 329–34

HENDERSON A. R. & McDONALD P. (1975). The effect of delayed sealing on fermentation and losses during ensilage. *J. Sci. of Fd Agric.,* **26,** 653–67

HENDERSON I. F. & CLEMENTS R. O. (1977) Grass growth in different parts of England in relation to invertebrate numbers and pesticide treatment. *J. Br. Grassld Soc.,* **32,** 89–98

HENDERSON I. F. & CLEMENTS R. O. (1979) Differential susceptibility to pest damage in agricultural grasses. *J. agric. Sci.,* **73,** 465–72

HFRO (Hill Farming Research Organisation) (1979) Soils and vegetation of the hills and their limitations. In *Science and Hill Farming, HFRO, 1954–1979.* Hill Farming Research Organisation, Edinburgh

HODGSON J. (1975) The influence of grazing pressure and stocking rate on herbage intake and animal performance. In Hodgson J. & Jackson D. K. (eds), *Pasture utilization by the grazing animal.* Occasional Symposium No. 8, British Grassland Society, Hurley

HOLMES W. (1968) The use of nitrogen in the management of pasture for cattle. *Herb. Abstr.,* **38,** 265–77

HOLMES W. (1974) The role of nitrogen fertilizer in the production of beef from grass. In The role of nitrogen in grassland productivity, 57–69. *Proceedings No. 142 The Fertilizer Society,* London

HOLMES W. (1976) Aspects of the use of energy and of concentrate feeds in grazing management. In Hodgson J. & Jackson D. H. (eds), *Pasture Utilization by the Grazing Animal.* Occasional Symposium No. 8, British Grassland Society

HOLMES W. (1980) Secondary production from land. In Blaxter K. L., *Food Chains and Human Nutrition,* (Appendix 2, p. 129). Applied Science Publishers Ltd, London

HOLMES W. & ALLANSON G. (1967) Grassland systems. *J. Br. Grassld Soc.,* **22,** 77–84

HOLMES W., CAMPLING R. C. & JOSHI N. D. (1972) A comparison between a rigid rotational grazing system for dairy cows and a system in which grazing alternated with cutting. *Anim. Prod.,* **14,** 283–94

HOLMES W. & CURRAN M. K. (1967) Feed intake of grazing cattle. V. A further study of the influence of pasture restriction combined with supplementary feeding on production per animal and per acre. *Anim. Prod.,* **9,** 313–24

HOLMES W. & JONES J. G. W. (1965) The feed intake of milk cows. II. The effect of roughage quality during late pregnancy and lactation. *Anim. Prod.,* **7,** 39–51

HOLT D. A. & HILST A. R. (1969) Daily variation in carbohydrate content of selected forage crops. *Agron. J.,* **61,** 239–42

HONIG H. (1979) Mechanical and respiration losses during pre-wilting of grass. *Proceedings of European Grassland Federation Meeting,* Brighton

HONIG H. & WOOLFORD M. K. (1979) Changes in silage on exposure to air. *Proceedings of European Grassland Federation Meeting,* Brighton

HOPKINS A. (1979) Botanical composition of grasslands in England and Wales. *J. R. agric. Soc.,* **140,** 140–50

HOPKINS A. & GREEN J. O. (1979) The effect of soil fertility and drainage on sward changes. In Charles A. H. & Haggar R. J. (eds) *Changes in Sward Composition and Productivity,* British Grassland Society Occasional Symposium No. 10, 115–29

HORTON G. M. J. & HOLMES W. (1974) The effect of nitrogen, stocking rate and grazing method on the output of pasture grazed by beef cattle. *J. Br. Grassld Soc.,* **29,** 93–9

HUNGATE R. E. (1966) *The rumen and its microbes.* Academic Press, New York and London

ICI (1978) *The route to profitable dairy farming.* Imperial Chemical Industries Chemical Division, London

ICI (1979) Grass in dairy cow nutrition. *Proceedings of seminar. Imperial Chemical Industries,* London

INRA (1978) *Alimentation des Ruminants.* Ed. INRA Publications (Route de St. Cyr), 7800 Versailles

JACKSON M. V. & WILLIAMS T. E. (1979) Response of grass swards to fertilizer N under cutting or grazing. *J. agric. Sci., Camb.,* **92**, 549–62

JACKSON N., O'NEILL S. J. B. & DAWSON R. R. (1974) The composition and quality of grass silages made in Northern Ireland (1967–72). *Rec. agric. Res., Northern Ireland,* **22**, 45–54

JEPSON W. F. & HEARD A. J. (1959) The fruit fly and allied stem-boring Diptera in winter wheat and host grasses. *Ann. appl. Biol.,* **47**, 114–30

JEWISS O. R. (1966) Morphological and physiological aspects of growth of grasses during the vegetative phase. In Milthorpe F. L. & Ivins J. D. (eds) *The Growth of Cereals and Grasses,* 39–54. Butterworth, London

JONES A. S. (1976) The principles of greencrop fractionation. *British Grassland Society: British Society of Animal Production Occasional Symposium No. 9,* 1–7

JONES F. G. W. & JONES M. G. (1964) *Pests of Field Crops.* Edward Arnold Ltd, London

JONES MARTIN G. (1933a) Grassland management and its influence on the sward. I. Factors influencing the growth of pasture plants. *Emp. J. exp. Agric.,* **1**, 43–57

JONES MARTIN G. (1933b) Grassland management and its influence on the sward. II. The management of a clover sward and its effects. *Emp. J. exp. Agric.,* **1**, 122–8

JONES MARTIN G. (1933c) Grassland management and its influence on the sward. III. The management of a grassy sward and its effects. *Emp. J. exp. Agric.,* **1**, 223–34

JONES MARTIN G. (1933d) Grassland management and its influence on the sward. IV. The management of poor pastures. V. Edaphic and biotic influences on pastures. *Emp. J. exp. Agric.,* **1**, 361–7

JONES R. J. & SANDLAND R. L. (1974) The relation between animal gain and stocking rate. Derivation of the relation from the results of grazing trials. *J. agric. Sci., Camb.,* **83**, 335–42

JONES T. (1955a) Management of lucerne in the critical autumn period. *Memoir No. 1. Lucerne Investigations 1944–53,* Grassland Research Institute, Hurley, 53–7

JONES T. (1955b) Management of established lucerne-cocksfoot leys in late autumn, winter and early spring. *Memoir No. 1, Lucerne Investigations 1944–53,* Grassland Research Institute, Hurley, 58–62

JOURNET M. & DEMARQUILLY C. (1979) Grazing. In Broster W. H. & Swan H. (eds), *Feeding strategy for the high yielding cow,* 295–321. Granada Publishing Co, St. Albans

JOURNET M., POUTONS M. & CALOMITI S. (1965) Appetit de la vache lactière. I. Variations individuelles des quantités d'aliments ingerées. (Appetite of the dairy cow. I. Individual variation in the feed consumed.) *Annals Zootech.,* **14**, 5–37

KAUFMANN W. (1969) Feed consumption, regulation and signification for an index of feeding value. In Crop Conservation and Grassland, *Proceedings 3rd General Meeting of the European Grassland Federation,* Braunsweg, 259–66

KILKENNY J. B., HOLMES W., BAKER R. D., WALSH A. & SHAW P. G. (1978) Grazing Management. *Beef Production Handbook, No. 4,* Meat and Livestock Commission

KLINNER W. E. & HALE O. D. (1979) Engineering developments in the field treatment of green crops. *Proceedings of European Grassland Federation Meeting,* Brighton

KLINNER W. E. & SHEPPERSON G. (1975) The state of haymaking technology. *J. Br. Grassld Soc.*, **30**, 259–66

LAMBERT D. A. (1963) The influence of density and nitrogen in seed production stands of S.37 cocksfoot (*Dactylis glomerata* L.). *J. agric. Sci., Camb.*, **61**, 361–73

LANCASTER R. J. (1968) Quality and storage losses of silages made in bunkers, stacks and by vacuum compression. *N. Z. Jl agric. Res.*, **11**, 63–70

LANCASTER R. J. & MCNAUGHTON M. (1961) Effects of initial consolidation on silage. *N. Z. Jl agric. Res.*, **4**, 504–15

LANGER R. H. M. (1963) Tillering in herbage grasses. *Herb. Abstr.*, **33**, 141–8

LANGLANDS J. P., CORBETT J. L., MCDONALD I. & REID G. W. (1963) Estimates of the energy required for maintenance by adult sheep. *Anim. Prod.*, **5**, 11–16

LANGSTON C. W. IRVIN H., GORDON C. H., BOUMA C., WISEMAN H. G., MELIN C. G., MOORE L. A. & MCCALMONT J. R. (1958) Microbiology and chemistry of grass silage. *US Department of Agriculture, Technical Bulletin*, No. 1187

LAREDO M. A. & MINSON D. J. (1973) The voluntary intake, digestibility and retention time by sheep of leaf and stem fractions of five grasses. *Aust. J. agric. Res.*, **24**, 875–88

LE DU Y. L. P. & BAKER R. D. (1977) Influence of grazing intensity on milk production under rotational and continuous grazing managements. *Proceedings of the International Meeting on Animal Production from Temperate Grassland*, Dublin

LEAVER J. D. (1970) A comparison of grazing systems for dairy herd replacements. *J. agric. Sci., Camb.*, **75**, 265–72

LEAVER J. D. (1973) Rearing of dairy cattle. 4. Effects of concentrate supplementation on the liveweight gain and feed intake of calves offered roughages *ad libitum*. *Anim. Prod.*, **17**, 43–52

LEAVER J. D. (1976) Utilisation of grassland by dairy cows. In .Swan H. & Broster W. H. (eds), *Principles of cattle production*, 307–27. Butterworth, London

LEAVER J. D., CAMPLING R. C. & HOLMES W. (1968) Use of supplementary feeds for grazing dairy cattle. *Dairy Sci. Abstr.*, **30**, 355–61

LESTER E. & LARGE E. C. (1958) Surveys of clover rot with incidental observations on eelworm in clover: England and Wales, 1953–55. *Pl. Path.*, **7**, 115–24

LOW A. J. & ARMITAGE E. R. (1959) Irrigation of grassland. *J. agric. Sci., Camb.*, **52**, 256–62

MACLEOD J. (1975) Systems of grazing management for lowland sheep. In Hodgson J. & Jackson D. K. (eds), *Pasture utilization by the grazing animal*, 129–34. Occasional Symposium No. 8, British Grassland Society, Hurley

MACLUSKY D. S. (1959) Drinking habits of grazing cows. *Agriculture, London*, **66**, 383–6

MAFF (Ministry of Agriculture, Fisheries and Food) (1954a) *The Calculation of Irrigation Needs. Technical Bulletin No. 4.* HMSO, London

MAFF (Ministry of Agriculture, Fisheries and Food) (1954b) *Irrigation. Bulletin No. 138.* HMSO, London

MAFF (Ministry of Agriculture, Fisheries and Food) (1963). *Quick haymaking. Bulletin No. 188.* HMSO, London

MAFF (Ministry of Agriculture, Fisheries and Food) (1968) *Grass and Clover Crops for Seed. Bulletin 204*, HMSO, London

MAFF (Ministry of Agriculture, Fisheries and Food) (1969) *Fixed equipment on the farm. No. 6. Permanent farm fences.* HMSO, London

MAFF (Ministry of Agriculture, Fisheries and Foods) (1970) *Fixed equipment on the farm. No. 11. Farm and estate hedges.* HMSO, London

MAFF (Ministry of Agriculture, Fisheries and Food) (1975) *Energy Allowances and Feeding Systems for Ruminants.* MAFF Technical Bulletin No. 33, HMSO London

MAFF (Ministry of Agriculture, Fisheries and Food) (1976) *Electric fencing. Technical Bulletin No. 147.* HMSO, London

MAFF (Ministry of Agriculture, Fisheries and Food) (1977a) *Sampling of Farm Crops, Feedingstuffs, Milk and Water for analysis.* ADAS Advisory paper No. 20

MAFF (Ministry of Agriculture, Fisheries and Food) (1977b) *Silage. Bulletin No. 37.* HMSO, London

MAFF (Ministry of Agriculture, Fisheries and Food) (1978a) *Second year report on complete diet feeding of dairy cows.* HMSO, London

MAFF (Ministry of Agriculture, Fisheries and Food) (1978b) *Minimum requirements for the structural design of bunker silos for forage.* ADAS, Leeds. Farm Buildings Group

MAFF (Ministry of Agriculture, Fisheries and Food) (1979a) *The drying of grass seed. GFS 22. Grassland practice No. 6.* HMSO, London

MAFF (Ministry of Agriculture, Fisheries and Food) (1979b). *Harvesting grass seed. Booklet 2048, Grassland Practice No. 8,* HMSO, London

MAFF (Ministry of Agriculture, Fisheries and Food) (1979c) *Grassland Practice No. 1. Seeds mixtures 1979/80. Booklet 2041,* Agricultural Development and Advisory Service

MAFF (Ministry of Agriculture, Fisheries and Food) (1979d) Grass as a feed. *Grassland Practice No. 7. Booklet 2047.* HMSO, London

MAFF (Ministry of Agriculture, Fisheries and Food) (1979e) *Nutrient allowances and composition of feedingstuffs for ruminants.* LGR 21. HMSO, London

MAFF (Ministry of Agriculture, Fisheries and Food) (1980a) *Costs and efficiency in milk production 1976–1977.* HMSO, London

MAFF (Ministry of Agriculture, Fisheries and Food) (1981). *Output and Utilization of Farm Produce in the UK 1974–1980.* HMSO, London

MAFF/MMB (1980) *Milk production in England and Wales, 1977/78. Costs of milk production in England and Wales, 1976/77.* HMSO, London

MANBY T. C. D. & SHEPPERSON G. (1975) Increasing the efficiency of grass conservation. *Agricultural Engineer,* **30,** 77–85

MANNETJE L. 'T (1978) Measurement of grassland vegetation and animal production. *Commonwealth Bureau of Pastures and Field Crops, Bulletin No. 52.* Commonwealth Agricultural Bureau, Farnham Royal

MARSH R. (1975) Systems of grazing management for beef cattle. In Hodgson J. & Jackson D. K. (eds) *Pasture utilization by the grazing animal,* 119–128. Occasional Symposium No. 8, British Grassland Society, Hurley

MARSH R. (1976) Effect of rotary-drum-drier exit temperature and length of pre-drying storage time on digestibility of dried grass cobs. *J. Br. Grassld Soc.* **31,** 53–58

MARSH R. (1978) The effects of mechanical treatment of forages on fermentation in the silo and on the feeding value of the silages. *N. Z. Jl exp. Agric.,* **6,** 271–8

MARSH R. (1979) The effects of wilting on fermentation in the silo and on the nutritive value of silage. *J. Br. Grassld Soc.,* **34,** 1–9

MARSH R. & CAMPLING R. C. (1970) Fouling of pastures by dung. *Herb. Abstr.,* **40,** 123–30

MARSH R., CAMPLING R. C. & HOLMES W. (1971) A further study of a rigid grazing management system for dairy cows. *Anim. Prod.,* **13,** 441–8

MARSH R. & MURDOCH J. C. (1975) Effect of some green-crop-drying processes on the digestibility and voluntary intake of herbage by sheep. *J. Br. Grassld Soc.,* **30,** 9–15

MARTIN F. H. & BAILE C. A. (1972) Feed intake in goats and sheep following acetate or propionate injections into rumen, ruminal pouches and abomasum as affected by local anaesthetics. *J. Dairy Sci.,* **55,** 606–13

McCARRICK R. B. (1966) Effect of method of grass conservation and herbage maturity on performance and body composition of beef cattle. *Proceedings of 10th International Grassland Congress*, Helsinki, 575–80

McDONALD P., EDWARDS R. A. & GREENHALGH J. F. D. (1973) *Animal Nutrition*, (2e). Longman, London

McDONALD P., EDWARDS R. A. & GREENHALGH J. F. D., *Animal Nutrition*, (2e). Longman, London

McDONALD P., HENDERSON A. R. & McGREGOR A. W. (1968) Chemical changes and losses during the ensilage of wilted grass. *J. Sci. Fd. Agric.*, **19**, 125–32

McDONALD P. & WHITTENBURY R. (1967) Losses during ensilage. *British Grassland Society Occasional Symposium No. 3*. 76–84

McDOUGALL I. & JACKSON N. (1977) Chemical composition and nutritional value of hay made in Northern Ireland during the period 1966–75. *Rec. agric. Res., Northern Ireland*, **25**, 63–9

McFEELY P. C., BROWNE D. & CARTY O. (1975) Effect of grazing interval and stocking rate on milk production and pasture yield. *Ir. J. agric. Res.*, **14**, 309–19

McILMOYLE W. A. (1978) Silage for beef production. *51st Annual Report of Agricultural Research Institute*. Northern Ireland, 20–4

McILMOYLE W. A. & MURDOCH J. C. (1977a) The effect of dried grass and cereal-based concentrate on the voluntary intake of unwilted grass silage. *Anim. Prod.*, **24**, 227–35

McILMOYLE W. A. & MURDOCH J. C. (1977b) The effect of concentrate, barley and dried grass on the voluntary intake of different silages. *Anim. Prod.*, **24**, 393–400

McMEEKAN C. P. & WALSHE M. J. (1963) The inter-relationships of grazing method and stocking rate on the efficiency of pasture utilization by dairy cattle. *J. agric. Sci., Camb.*, **61**, 147–66

MICHAIL S. H. & CARR A. J. H. (1966) Effect of seed treatment on establishment of grass seedlings. *Pl. Path.*, **15**, 60–4

MICHEL J. F. (1976) The epidemiology and control of some nematode infections in grazing animals. *Adv. Parasit.*, **14**, 355–97

MICHEL J. F. & OLLERENSHAW C. B. (1963) Helminth diseases of grazing animals. In Worden A. N., Sellers K. C. & Tribe D. E. (eds), *Animal Health, Production and Pasture*, 445–57. Longman, London

MILLER I. L. (1973) Evaluation of feeds as sources of nitrogen and amino acids. *Proc. Nutr. Soc.*, **32**, 79

MILLER L. G., CLANTON D. C., NELSON L. F. & HOEHUE O. E. (1967) Nutritive value of hay baled at various moisture contents. *J. Anim. Sci.*, **26**, 1369–73

MILNE J. A., MAXWELL T. J. & SOUTER W. (1979) Effect of level of concentrate feeding and amount of herbage on the intake and performance of ewes with twin lambs at pasture in early lactation. *Proc. Br. Soc. Anim. Prod.*, **28**, 452, Abstr. 91

MILTON W. E. J. & DAVIES R. O. (1947) The yield, botanical and chemical composition of natural hill herbage under manuring, controlled grazing and hay conditions. *J. Ecol.*, **35**, 65–95

MINSON D. J. (1963) The effect of pelleting and wafering on the feeding value of roughage. *J. Br. Grassld Soc.*, **18**, 39–44

MINSON D. J. & COWPER J. L. (1974) An integrating wattmeter for measuring the energy used to grind pasture samples. *J. Br. Grassld Soc.*, **29**, 133–6

MINSON D. J., RAYMOND W. F. & HARRIS C. E. (1960) Studies in the digestibility of herbage. VIII. The digestibility of S37 Cocksfoot, S23 Ryegrass and S24 Ryegrass. *J. Br. Grassld Soc.*, **15**, 174–80

MLC (Meat and Livestock Commission) (1976), *Cattle Facts*, Table 11.1.4, p. 102. Meat and Livestock Commission, Milton Keynes

MLC (Meat and Livestock Commission) (1978) *Grazing Management*. Beef Production Handbook No. 4. Meat and Livestock Commission, Milton Keynes

MLC (Meat and Livestock Commission) (1979) *Meat Production—margins and performance on farms, 1978*. Livestock Improvement Services, Meat and Livestock Commission, Milton Keynes

MMB (1976). *Report of the Breeding and Production Organisation. No. 26 1975–76*. p. 35. Milk Marketing Board, Thames Ditton

MMB (Milk Marketing Board) (1979) An analysis of FMS costed farms. *Report No. 22*. Farm Management Services, Milk Marketing Board, Thames Ditton

MOIR R. J. (1968) Ruminant Digestion and Evolution. In Code C.F. (ed.), *Handbook of Physiology*, Vol. 5, 2673–94. Waverley Press, Baltimore

MOISEY F. R. & LEAVER J. D. (1979) A comparison of a three-cut with a two-cut silage system for dairy cattle. *Anim. Prod.*, **28**, 422 (Abstr.)

MONTEIRO L. S. (1972) The control of appetite in lactating cows. *Anim. Prod.*, **14**, 263–82

MONTEITH J. L. (1977) Climate and the efficiency of crop production in Britain. *Phil. Trans. R. Soc.*, **B 281**, 277–94

MOORE L. A., THOMAS J. W. & SYKES J. F. (1960) The acceptability of grass/legume silage by dairy cattle. *Proceedings of 8th International Grassland Congress*, Reading, 701–4

MOORE W. C. (1959) *British parasitic fungi*. Cambridge University Press, Cambridge

MORLEY F. H. W. (1978) Animal production studies of grassland. In Mannetje L.t' (ed.), *The Measurement of grassland vegetation and animal production. Bulletin 52*, Commonwealth Agricultural Bureau, Farnham Royal

MORRISON J. & IDLE A. A. (1972) À pilot survey of grassland in S.E. England. *Technical Report No. 10*, Grassland Research Institute, Hurley

MORRISON J., JACKSON M. V. & SPARROW P. E. (1980) The response of perennial ryegrass to fertilizer nitrogen in relation to climate and soil. *Technical Report No. 27*, Grassland Research Institute, Hurley

MUDD C. H. & MEADOWCROFT S. C. (1964) Comparison between the improvement of pastures by the use of fertilizers and by reseeding. *Expl Husb.*, **10**, 66–84

MUNRO I. A. (1958) Irrigation of grassland. The influence of irrigation and nitrogen treatments on yield and utilization of a riverside meadow. *J. Br. Grassld Soc.*, **13**, 213–21

MURDOCH J. C. (1965) The effect of length of silage on its voluntary intake by cattle. *J. Br. Grassld Soc.*, **20**, 54–8

MURDOCH J. C., BALCH D. A., HOLDSWORTH M. C. & WOOD M. (1955) The effect of chopping, lacerating and wilting of herbage on the chemical composition of silage. *J. Br. Grassld Soc.*, **10**, 181–8

MURDOCH J. C. & BARE D. I. (1960) The effect of mechanical treatment on the rate of drying and loss of nutrients in hay. *J. Br. Grassld Soc.*, **15**, 94–9

MURDOCH J. C. & BARE D. I. (1963) The effect of conditioning on the rate of drying and loss of nutrients in hay. *J. Br. Grassld Soc.*, **18**, 334–8

NASH M. J. (1959) Partial wilting of grass crop for silage. *J. Br. Grassld Soc.*, **14**, 65–73

NASH M. J. & EASSON D. L. (1972) Farmer's lung—an agricultural assessment of recent findings. *Scott. Agric.*, **51**, 1–7

NASH M. J. & EASSON D. J. (1977) Preservation of moist hay with propionic acid. *J. Stored Products Res.*, **13**, 65–75

NASH M. J. & EASSON D. L. (1978) Preservation of moist hay in miniature bales treated with propionic acid. *J. Stored Products Res.*, **14**, 25–33

NEDO (1974) *Grass and Grass Products*. National Economic Development Office, London

NEENAN M., CONWAY M. & MURPHY W. E. (1959) The output of Irish pastures. *J. Br. Grassld Soc.*, **14**, 78–87

NEWTON J. E. & BROCKINGTON N. R. (1975) A logical approach to the study of grazing systems. In Hodgson J. & Jackson D. K. (eds), *Pasture Utilization by the grazing animal*, 29–38. Occasional Symposium No. 8, British Grassland Society Hurley

NIAB (NATIONAL INSTITUTE OF AGRICULTURAL BOTANY) (1978) *Classified list of herbage varieties, England and Wales 1978/79*, Cambridge

NIAB (NATIONAL INSTITUTE OF AGRICULTURAL BOTANY) (1979a). *Recommended varieties of grasses, 1979/80. Farmers Leaflet No. 16*, Cambridge

NIAB (NATIONAL INSTITUTE OF AGRICULTURAL BOTANY) (1979b). *Recommended varieties of herbage legumes, 1979/80. Farmers Leaflet No. 4*, Cambridge

NIX J. S. (1971) Dairying—pursuing profits. *Farm Business*, X, No. 1. 17–24

NOLAN T. & CONNOLLY J. (1977) Mixed stocking by sheep and steers—A Review. *Herb. Abstr.*, **47**, 367–74

NOWAKOWSKI T. Z. (1962) Effects of nitrogen fertilisers on total nitrogen, soluble nitrogen and soluble carbohydrate contents of grass. *J. agric. Sci., Camb.*, **59**, 387–92

ØRSKOV E. R. & FRASER C. (1975) The effect of processing of barley based supplements on rumen pH, rate of digestion and voluntary intake in sheep. *Br. J. Nutr.*, **34**, 493–500

ØRSKOV E. R. & MCDONALD I. (1979) The estimation of protein degradability in the rumen from incubation measurements weighted according to rate of passage. *J. agric. Sci., Camb.*, **92**, 499–504

OSBOURN D. F. (1967) The intake of conserved forages. In *Fodder Conservation* 20–8. Occasional Symposium No. 3, British Grassland Society

OSBOURN D. F. (1978) Principles governing the use of chemical methods for assessing the nutritive value of forages—a review. *Anim. Fd Sci. Technol.*, **3**, 265–75

OSBOURN D. F., TERRY R. A., CAMMELL S. B. & OUTEN G. E. (1969) Some effects of feeding supplements of maize meal and sodium bicarbonate upon the digestion of forage cellulase by sheep. *Proc. Nutr. Soc.*, **29**, 12A

OSBOURN D. F., TERRY R. A. & CAMMELL S. B. (1976a) Relationships between the physical and chemical characteristics of feeds and their voluntary intake by ruminants. *Annual Report 1975, Grassland Research Institute*, 80–1

OSBOURN D. F., TERRY R. A., OUTEN G. E. & CAMMELL S. B. (1976b) The significance of a determination of cell walls as the rational basis for the nutritive evaluation of forages. *Proceedings of the 12th International Grassland Congress*, Moscow, 1974, **3**, 374–80

OSBOURN D. F., THOMSON D. J. & TERRY R. A. (1966) The relationship between voluntary intake and digestibility of forage crops by sheep. *Proceedings 10th International Grassland Congress*, Helsinki, 363–67

PATEL A. S. & COOPER J. P. (1961) The influence of changes in light energy in leaf and tiller development in ryegrass, timothy and meadow fescue. *J. Br. Grassld Soc.*, **16**, 299–308

PATERSON R. & CRICHTON C. (1960) Grass staggers in large scale dairying on grass. *J. Br. Grassld Soc.*, **15**, 100–5

PATTO P. M., CLEMENT C. R. & FORBES T. J. (1978) Permanent pasture studies. 2. Grassland poaching in England and Wales. *GRI/ADAS Joint Permanent Pasture Group, Hurley*

PAYNE J. M. (1977) *Metabolic diseases in farm animals*. Heinemann, London

PENMAN H. L. (1962) Woburn Irrigation, 1951–59. 2. Results for grass. *J. agric. Sci., Camb.*, **58**, 349–64

PETERSEN R. G., LUCAS H. L. & WOODHOUSE W. W. (1956) The distribution of excreta by freely grazing cattle and its effect on pasture fertility. 2. Effect of returned excreta on the residual concentration of some fertilizer elements. *Agron. J.*, **48**, 444–9

PHILIPSEN P. J. J. (1971) Heat treatment of the standing crop. *Pwr Fmg*, **47**, 22–4

PIKE I. H. (1972) Nutritional evaluation of silage made from grass treated with a formalin/sulphuric acid mixture. *J. Br. Grassld Soc.*, **27**, 195 (abstr.)

PLAYNE M. J. & MCDONALD P. (1966) The buffering constituents of herbage and of silage. *J. Sci. Fd Agric.*, **17**, 264–8

RAYMOND W. F. (1969) The nutritive value of forage crops. *Adv. Agron.*, **21**, 1–108

REID D. (1966) Studies on cutting management of grass clover swards. 4. The effects of close and lax cutting on the yield of herbage from swards cut at different frequencies. *J. agric. Sci., Camb.*, **66**, 101–6

REID D. & CASTLE M. E. (1965) The response of grass-clover and pure grass leys to irrigation and fertilizer nitrogen treatment. I. Irrigation effects. *J. agric. Sci., Camb.*, **64**, 185–94

RHODES I. (1969) The yield, canopy structure and light interception of two ryegrass varieties in mixed cultures and monoculture. *J. Br. Grassld Soc.*, **24**, 123–7

ROBERTS R. A. & HUNT I. V. (1936) The effect of shoot cutting on the growth of root and shoot of perennial ryegrass (*Lolium perenne* L.) and of timothy (*Phleum pratense* L.). *Welsh J. Agric.*, **12**, 158–74

ROOK J. A. F. (1981) *Silage for Milk Production.* NIRD-HRI Technical Bulletin No. 2. Hannah Research Institute, Ayr. (In preparation)

ROY J. H. B., BALCH C. C., MILLER E. L., ØRSKOV E. R. & SMITH R. H. (1977) Calculation of the N-requirement for ruminants from nitrogen metabolism studies. *Proceedings of the 2nd International Symposium on Protein Metabolism and Nutrition*, Lelystad, Netherlands, 126–9

RYLE G. J. A. (1964) A comparison of leaf and tiller growth in seven perennial grasses as influenced by nitrogen and temperature. *J. Br. Grassld Soc.*, **19**, 281–90

RYLE G. J. A. (1967) Effects of shading on inflorescence size and development in temperate perennial grasses. *Ann. appl. Biol.*, **59**, 297–308

RYLE G. J. A. & LANGER R. H. M. (1963) Studies on the physiology of flowering in timothy (*Phleum pratense* L.). I. Influence of day length and temperature on initiation and differentiation of the inflorescence. *Ann. Bot.* (N.S.), **27**, 213–31

SAMPSON K. & WESTERN J. H. (1954) *Diseases of British Grasses and Legumes.* Cambridge University Press, Cambridge

THE SCOTTISH AGRICULTURAL COLLEGES (1979) Classification of grass and clover varieties for Scotland 1979/80. *Publication no. 48*

SEARS P. D. (1950) Soil fertility and pasture growth. *J. Br. Grassld Soc.*, **5**, 267–80

SHAW P. G., BROCKMAN J. S. & WOLTON K. M. (1966) The effect of cutting and grazing on the response of grass/white clover swards to fertilizer nitrogen. *Proceedings Tenth International Grassland Congress, Helsinki*, 240–4

SHEPPERSON G. (1960) Effect of time of cutting and method of making on the feed value of hay. *Proceedings of 8th International Grassland Congress*, Reading, 704–8

SHEPPERSON G. & GRUNDEY J. K. (1962) Recent developments in quick haymaking techniques. *J. Br. Grassld Soc.*, **17**, 141–9

SIDDONS R. C., EVANS R. T. & BEEVER D. E. (1979) The effect of formaldehyde treatment before ensiling on the digestion of wilted grass silage by sheep. *Br. J. Nutr.*, **42**, 535–45

SMITH, DALE (1972) Total non structural carbohydrate concentrations in the herbage of several legumes and grasses at first flower. *Agron. J.*, **64**, 705–6

SOULSBY E. J. L. (1965) *Textbook of Veterinary Clinical Parasitology. Vol 1. Helminths.* Blackwell Scientific Publications, Oxford

SPEDDING C. R. W. (1975) *The Biology of Agricultural Systems.* Academic Press, London

SPEDDING C. R. W. (1979) *An introduction to agricultural systems.* Applied Science Publishers, London

SPEDDING C. R. W. & DIEKMAHNS E. C. (eds) (1972) *Grasses and Legumes in British Agriculture,* Bulletin 49, Commonwealth Bureau of Pastures & Field Crops, Commonwealth Agricultural Bureaux, Farnham Royal

STAPLEDON R. G. & DAVIES W. (1942) *Ley Farming.* Penguin Books, Harmondsworth, Middlesex

STAPLEDON R. G., DAVIES W., WILLIAMS T. E., HUGHES G. P. & DAVIS A. G. (1945) *Map, Vegetation: grassland of England and Wales.* Director-General, Ordnance Survey

STILES W. (1961) Irrigation of a ryegrass/white clover ley. *Exps Prog. Grassld Res. Inst., Hurley,* **13**, 65

STILES W. (1965) Ten years of irrigation experiments. *Annual Report 1965,* Grassland Research Institute, Hurley, 57–66

STILES W. & WILLIAMS T. E. (1965) The response of a ryegrass/white clover sward to various irrigation regimes. *J. agric. Sci., Camb.,* **65**, 351–64

STOBBS T. H. (1970) Automatic measurement of grazing time by dairy cows on tropical grass and legume pastures. *Trop. Grasslds,* **4**, 237–44

STOBBS T. H. (1973a) The effect of plant structure on the intake of tropical pastures. 1. Variation in the bite size of grazing cattle. *Aust. J. agric. Res.,* **24**, 809–19

STOBBS T. H. (1973b) The effect of plant structure on intake of tropical pastures. 2. Differences in sward structure, nutritive value and bite size of animals grazing. *Aust. J. agric. Res.,* **24**, 821–9

TAYLER J. C. (1970) Dried forages and beef production. *J. Br. Grassld Soc.,* **25**, 180–90

TAYLER J. C. & ASTON K. (1973) Dried grass *v* barley as a concentrate for milk production. *J. Ass. green Crop Driers,* **6**, 3–8

TAYLER J. C. & DERIAZ R. E. (1963) The use of rumen fistulated sheep in the direct determination of the nutritive value of ingested herbage in grazing experiments. *J. Br. Grassld Soc.,* **18**, 29–38

TAYLER J. C. & RUDMAN J. E. (1965) Height and method of cutting in grazing in relation to herbage consumption and liveweight gain. *Proceedings of 9th International Grassland Congress,* Sao Paulo, 1639–44

TAYLER J. C. & WILKINSON J. M. (1972) The influence of level of concentrate feeding on the voluntary intake of grass and on liveweight gain by cattle. *Animl. Prod.,* **14**, 85–96

TAYLOR N. W. (1965) The use of linear programming in least-cost feed compounding. *Publication No. 20., Agric. Econ. Research Unit, Lincoln College, N.Z.*

TERRY R. A., OSBOURN D. F., CAMMELS S. B. & FENLON J. S. (1973) *In vitro* digestibility and the estimation of energy in herbage. *Proceedings of the 5th General Meeting of the European Grassland Federation, Vaxtodling,* **28**, 19–25

TERRY R. A., TILLEY J. M. A. & OUTEN G. E. (1969) The effect of pH on cellulose digestion under *in vitro* conditions. *J. Sci. Fd Agric.,* **20**, 317–20

TETLOW R. M., WILKINSON J. M., CAMMELL S. B. & SPOONER M. C. (1978) Physical and chemical treatment of low quality grass to improve nutritive value. *Annual Report of Grassland Research Institute,* Hurley, 46–7

THOMSON D. J., BEEVER D. E., HARRISON D. G., HILL I. W. & OSBOURN D. F. (1971) The digestion of dried sainfoin and lucerne by sheep. *Proc. Nutr. Soc.,* **30**, 14A

THORNTON R. F. & MINSON D. J. (1973) The relationship between apparent retention time in the rumen, voluntary intake and apparent digestibility of legume and grass diets in sheep. *Aust. J. agric. Res.,* **24**, 889–98

TILLEY J. M. A. & TERRY R. A. (1963) A two stage technique for *in vitro* digestion of forage crops. *J. Br. Grassld Soc.*, **18**, 104–11

TRIBE A. J. & HERRIOTT J. B. D. (1969) Fungicidal treatment for herbage seed. *Expl Work Edinb. Sch. Agric.*, *1968*, 61

TROELSEN J. E. & CAMPBELL J. B. (1968) Voluntary consumption of forage by sheep and its relationship to size and shape of particles in the digestive tract. *Anim. Prod.*, **10**, 289–98

TROELSON J. E., MYHR P. I., LODGE R. W. & KILCHER M. (1968) Sensory evaluation of the feeding value of hay. *Can. J. Anim. Sci.*, **48**, 373–81

TURKINGTON D. J. & TOWNSON W. S. (1978) Statistical analysis of ICI 'dairymaid' results. *Grass and Forage Science*, **33**, 69–70

ULYATT M. J. (1971) Studies on the causes of differences in pasture quality between perennial ryegrass, short rotation ryegrass and white clover. *N. Z. Jl agric. Res.*, **14**, 352–67

UNDERWOOD E. J. (1966) *The mineral nutrition of livestock*. Commonwealth Agricultural Bureau, Farnham Royal

UNDERWOOD E. J. (1971) *Trace Elements in Human and Animal Nutrition*. Academic Press, New York

VADIVELOO J. & HOLMES W. (1979a) The effects of forage digestibility and concentrate supplementation on the nutritive value of the diet and performance of finishing cattle. *Anim. Prod.*, **29**, 121–30

VADIVELOO J. & HOLMES W. (1979b) The prediction of the voluntary feed intake of dairy cows. *J. agric. Sci., Camb.*, **93**, 553–62

VAN ES A. J. H. (1974). Energy intake and requirement of cows during the whole year. *Live Stk Prod. Sci.*, **1**, 21–32

VAN SOEST P. J. (1967) Development of a comprehensive system of feed analyses and its application to forages. *J. Anim. Sci.*, **26**, 119–28

VAN SOEST P. J. & MOORE L. A. (1966) New chemical methods for analysis of forages for the purpose of predicting nutritive value. *Proceedings 9th International Grassland Congress*, Sao Paulo, Brazil, **1**, 783–9

VAN SOEST P. J. & WINE R. H. (1967a) Acid detergent fibre determinations of lignin, cellulose and insoluble ash (silica) and their application to the estimation of digestibility in the summative equation. US Dept of Agriculture, Agricultural Research Service, Beltsville, Maryland pp. 8

VAN SOEST P. J. & WINE R. H. (1967b) Use of detergents in the analysis of fibrous feeds. IV. Determination of plant cell wall constituents *J. Ass. off. analyt. Chem.*, **50**, 50–6

VOISIN A. (1959) *Grass Productivity*. Crosby Lockwood, London

WAITE R. (1963) Grazing behaviour. In Worden A. N., Sellers K. C. & Tribe D. E. (eds), *Animal Health, Production and Pasture*. Longman, London

WAITE R. (1970) The structural carbohydrates and the *in vitro* digestibility of ryegrass and cocksfoot at two levels of nitrogenous fertilizer. *J. agric. Sci., Camb.*, **74**, 457–62

WALTERS R. J. K. (1976) The field assessment of digestibility of grass for conservation. *A.D.A.S. Q. Rev.*, **23**, 323–8

WALTERS R. J. K. & EVANS E. M. (1979) Evaluation of a sward sampling technique for estimating herbage intake by grazing sheep. *Grass Forage Sci.*, **34**, 37–44

WANYOIKE M. M. (1979) Beef production, studies on feed intake and on the use of a feed additive. Ph.D. thesis, University of London

WATSON S. J. & NASH M. J. (1960) *Conservation of grass and forage crops*. Oliver and Boyd, Edinburgh

WELSH PLANT BREEDING STATION (1978) *Principles of Herbage Seed Production*. 2e. Welsh Plant Breeding Station, Aberystwyth

WHEELER J. L. (1958) The effect of sheep excreta and nitrogen fertilizer on the botanical composition and production of a ley. *J. Br. Grassld Soc.*, **13**, 196–202

WHITEHEAD D. C. (1966) *Nutrient Minerals in Grassland Herbage.* Review Series 1/1966. Commonwealth Bureau of Pastures and Field Crops, Farnham Royal

WHITEHEAD D. C. (1970) *The Role of Nitrogen in Grassland Productivity. Bulletin 48.* Commonwealth Bureau of Pastures and Field Crops. Commonwealth Agricultural Bureau, Farnham Royal

WIERINGA G. W. (1960) Some factors affecting silage fermentation. *Proceedings of 8th International Grassland Congress*, Reading. 497–502

WILKINS R. J., WILSON R. J. & COOK J. E. (1974) Restriction of fermentation during ensilage: the nutritive value of silages made with the addition of formaldehyde. *Proceedings of 12th International Grassland Congress*, Moscow. 674–90

WILLIAMS R. E. & JONES M. T. (1969) Economic relationships in milk production. *J. agric. Econ.*, **20**, 81–109

WILMAN D., OJUEDERIE B. M. & ASARE E. O. (1976) Nitrogen and Italian ryegrass. 3. Growth up to 14 weeks: yields, preparations, digestibilities and nitrogen contents of crop fractions and tiller populations. *J. Br. Grassld Soc.*, **31**, 73–80

WIT C. T. de & BERGH J. P. VAN DEN (1965) Competition between herbage plants. *Neth. J. agric. Sci.*, **13**, 212–21

WOLDENDORP J. W., DILZ K. & KOLENBRANDER G. J. (1965) The fate of fertilizer nitrogen on permanent grassland soils. *Proceedings of the First General Meeting of the European Grassland Federation, Wageningen, 1965*, 53–68

WOLTON K. M. (1960) Some factors affecting herbage magnesium levels. *Proceedings of 8th International Grassland Congress, Reading, 1960* 544–48

WOLTON K. M. (1979) Dung and urine as agents of change. In Charles A. H. & Haggar R. J. (eds), *Changes in sward composition and productivity.* Occasional Symposium No. 10., Hurley, British Grassland Society

WOODS A. J., BRADLEY JONES J. & MANTLE P. G. (1966). An outbreak of gangrenous ergotism in cattle. *Vet. Rec.*, **78**, 742–9

WPBS (1978) *Principles of herbage seed production.* (2e). Welsh Plant Breeding Station, Aberystwyth

WRIGHT N. C. (1940) Britain's supplies of feeding stuffs. *Emp. J. exp. Agric.*, **8**, 231–48

YIAKOUMETTIS I. & HOLMES W. (1972) The effect of nitrogen and stocking rate on the output of pasture grazed by beef cattle. *J. Br. Grassld Soc.*, **27**, 183–91

Index

51005